Routledge Revivals

A Critical Edition of Richard Brathwait's Whimzies

A Critical Edition of Richard Brathwait's Whimzies

Edited by
Allen H. Lanner

First published in 1991 by Garland Publishing, Inc.

This edition first published in 2019 by Routledge
2 Park Square, Milton Park, Abingdon, Oxon, OX14 4RN
and by Routledge
52 Vanderbilt Avenue, New York, NY 10017, USA

Routledge is an imprint of the Taylor & Francis Group, an informa business

© 1991 by Allen H. Lanner

All rights reserved. No part of this book may be reprinted or reproduced or utilised in any form or by any electronic, mechanical, or other means, now known or hereafter invented, including photocopying and recording, or in any information storage or retrieval system, without permission in writing from the publishers.

Publisher's Note
The publisher has gone to great lengths to ensure the quality of this reprint but points out that some imperfections in the original copies may be apparent.

Disclaimer
The publisher has made every effort to trace copyright holders and welcomes correspondence from those they have been unable to contact.

A Library of Congress record exists under ISBN:

ISBN 13: 978-0-367-25479-7 (hbk)
ISBN 13: 978-0-367-25485-8 (pbk)
ISBN 13: 978-0-429-28800-5 (ebk)

The Renaissance Imagination

Important Literary and Theatrical Texts
from the Late Middle Ages through
the Seventeenth Century

Stephen Orgel, Editor

A Garland Series

A Critical Edition of Richard Brathwait's *Whimzies*

EDITED BY
ALLEN H. LANNER

GARLAND PUBLISHING, INC.
New York & London
1991

Copyright © 1991 by Allen H. Lanner
All Rights Reserved

Library of Congress Cataloging-in-Publication Data

Brathwait, Richard, 1588?–1673.
[Whimzies]
A critical edition of Richard Brathwait's Whimzies/
[edited by] Allen H. Lanner.
p. cm.—(The Renaissance imagination)
Originally published under title: Whimzies, or, A new cast of characters.
Originally presented as the author's thesis (Ph. D.—New York University), 1966.
Includes bibliographical references.
ISBN 0-8153-0463-3 (alk. paper)
1. Character sketches. 2. Characters and characteristics in literature.
I. Lanner, Allen H. II. Title. III. Series.
PR2214.B3W47   1991
822'.4—dc20   91-15584

Printed on acid-free, 250-year-life paper
Manufactured in the United States of America

For Joyce

Preface

The publication of an edition of Theophrastan characters twenty-five years after its original appearance as a university dissertation will most likely not herald a new resurgence of character-writing. *The New Yorker*'s "Talk of the Town" column will probably not resonate with poignant characters of "A Divorcee" or "A Homeless Man." Once referred to as a quaint literary "bypath," the character, because of its generic strangeness and its representation of a distant historical reality, will probably never shed its current antiquarian status or be anything but a passing footnote for most readers of scholarly texts.

But it may indeed be the character's marginal identity as a literary genre—something it was even in its heyday—that suggests its interest and usefulness for the modern reader. Like other manifestations of "the Renaissance imagination," the character was a highly stylized formal convention. Its practitioners confidently justified their efforts by referring to the character's origins—not as an avatar of Theophrastus' descriptions of human character types that deviated from the Aristotelian ideal of moderation. It is rather the character's ties to the emblematic tradition, with its emphasis on the link between the visual and verbal, that accounts for its vivid rhetorical energy, its often cogent analysis of social and ethical types, its constant need to assign praise or blame.

The "interpretive community" of the seventeenth century that formed the audience for reading characters had absorbed this emblematic tradition in both high and popular cultural forms. Whether through crude engravings or elaborate court masques, the "impress" of an abstract ethical principle or generalization could be made concrete through verbal representation. In the character form this depended on the liberal use of relatively few rhetorical devices of diction and syntax. For Brathwait, it was largely the pun, expanded and replicated, that made up the bulk of his character depictions.

In recent years a renewed interest in literary history, dubbed the New Historicism, has brought about a fresh approach to little-known literary and historical texts. Scholars like Stephen Greenblatt have demonstrated what we can learn from the interaction of "major" and "minor" texts from various historical periods. In a recent essay Greenblatt draws our attention to the opposing terms of "constraint and mobility," the "ensemble of beliefs and practices" that "function as a pervasive technology of control, a set of limits within which social behavior must be contained, a repertoire of models to which individuals must conform" (225).[1] As Greenblatt points out, in Western tradition this has largely been expressed through the literature of satire and panegyric, which provides the most effective container for the socially corrective praise and blame heaped on the representatives of a culture. However, because these literary expressions date so quickly, the cultural assumptions that fed them are also lost. As will become immediately apparent to any readers of Brathwait's *Whimzies*, a massive infusion of cultural reconstruction is necessary in order to re-enter his world.

Brathwait's characters rise from the lower depths, but never very far. Intrinsic to their characters is a constraint that derives from a broader, all-inclusive conception of English society as a social organism that resists any tendency to shatter its precarious but healthy balance of ethical and moral qualities. The majority of the characters in *Whimzies* live by their wits, using the knowledge of their trade to gull, cozen, or just generally dishonor the rest of society. Their poverty and pathetic deaths seem to reveal the limited mobility of each occupational type as it knocks against the implicit moral and social solidity of received tradition.

However, characters like the hospital-man, the laundress, and the metal-man retain a sad dignity in spite of the writer's troping assault on them. Brathwait seems to undermine his own verbal barrage by giving them a kind of emblematic virtue, the virtue of survival in a society that has stacked everything against them. In effect, Brathwait deconstructs his own moral outrage by making their transgressions against society seem the only realistic course of action for the underclass to take. They may die at the end, failures and outcasts, yet the social organism that spawned them persists in its beliefs and traditions. However, Brathwait's interest in the endangered observance of hospitality reveals in part his awareness of just how fragile the social organism is. At the same time, though, his fascination with these vocational eccentrics directs our attention to the absent powers of the church, state, and gentry that make use of their services and yet deny them any significant moral or social standing.

Brathwait's purpose and discursive method can seem arbitrary and excessively associative. The alphabetical framework appears to give all the subjects an equal significance—or insignificance—rendering them equally culpable in their failure to live up to the historical ideals of the occupational type they represent. But taken as a whole the collection swarms with seventeenth-century London's underworld vitality, displaying a kind of proto-Baudelairean crowd of lowlifes and misfits. The same crowd that makes its way through Jonsonian comedy is seen here through Brathwait's appeal to a less refined, less hermetic audience. This frees the author to express a genuine, sympathetic interest in the social types that most Jacobean and Caroline stage comedies dismissed with haughty contempt. Whatever were his artistic limitations, Brathwait can still delight readers as well as involve them in the complexities of a text that is thoroughly embedded in the life and discourse of its time.

ALLEN LANNER

1. Stephen Greenblatt, "Culture," in *Critical Terms for Literary Study*. Ed. Frank Lentricchia and Thomas McLaughlin. Chicago, Illinois: University of Chicago Press, 1990.

CONTENTS

FOREWORD xiii

GENERAL INTRODUCTION

    I.   The Character as a Literary Genre 1

   II. Joseph Hall's *Characters of Vertues and Vices* (1608) . 27

  III. The Overburian Characters 34

   IV. The Earlier Character-Writers: Breton, Stephens, . . 42
       and Mynshul

    V. John Earle's *Micro-cosmographie* (1628) 50

   VI. Brathwait and the Character-Writers of the Early . . 60
       1630's

  VII. The Character of Argument 77

 VIII. The Last Phase 104

RICHARD BRATHWAIT'S *WHIMZIES: OR, A NEW CAST OF CHARACTERS* (1631)

     Introduction to the Text 144

     Text of *Whimzies: Or, A New Cast of Characters* (1631) . 148

     Annotation to the Text 262

     List of Textual Changes 390

LIST OF WORKS CONSULTED 392

Foreword

The character was one of the dominant prose forms of the seventeenth century, appearing sporadically as particular events or literary fashions called it forth. Hundreds were printed, as collections, separate pamphlets, or scattered pieces among other literary types. Just as it seemed to have run its natural course, a crucial period arose, and the character was pressed into service as a polemical force. Throughout the age it was a medium both of literary expression and political argumentation. Reflecting as it does the strong feelings and beliefs of many men of the time, the character deserves more study than it has received.

One full-length work on the earlier period of the genre has appeared, Benjamin Boyce's The Theophrastan Character in England to 1642 (Cambridge, Massachusetts, 1947). Faced with a tremendous amount of material to synthesize, the author could hardly do more than attempt a broad survey of the form. As the pioneer study in its subject--although greatly indebted to the earlier work of Professor Greenough and others--much of it was concerned with tracing the character in its various guises and discussing in detail works unfamiliar to many readers of the period. In another book, The Polemic Character 1640-1661 (Lincoln, Nebraska, 1955), Professor Boyce continued his examination, in this case of works even less familiar because of their intense and complex involvement in the political and religious ideology of the Revolution. Again he was faced with the difficult task of making meaningful a vast sea of diverse materials, many of which had little claim to being called characters, but were nevertheless important for the overall historical perspective of this period.

There is little else to aid the reader who wishes to explore the broad range of the character type in the seventeenth century. The only other sources of criticism on the genre are in broad literary surveys and anthologies of the period, scattered articles in scholarly journals, or in introductions to character anthologies that are now out of print and inaccessible. There is an obvious need for a fuller critical treatment of the character than is presently available.

For the reader who wishes to investigate the genre there is a more basic problem. Access to the complete texts of seventeenth-century characters is difficult without resort to microfilm. Most collections have been out of print for many years, or they appear in editions that are extremely difficult to obtain. There are no editions in print of Healey's English translation of Theophrastus, and of Overbury, Cleveland, and Butler--most of the major character writers of interest. For the lesser-known authors of character books and for the anonymous pamphlet characters there is even less opportunity for direct contact with the works themselves.

The purpose of this dissertation is to provide a partial solution for both the problems outlined above. First, it discusses the important aspects of the character genre as it developed during the century, giving the important character writers fuller critical treatment than they have usually received. Secondly, it provides the edited text of characters by an author who found the form particularly suitable to his literary talents--Richard Brathwait. This combined approach to the character will show the reader how a literary type can be transformed as it responds to the social and political exigencies of an era; and it will provide him with the works of one of the character's ablest practitioners.

The works of Richard Brathwait have been almost totally neglected, and for obvious--if not defensible--reasons. Brathwait's career was a long one, extending over more than half of the century. His energies were diffused over a variety of literary forms--essays, characters, courtesy books, verse satires, exotic fiction, popular religious works, history, and biography. An author of such energy--and popularity--could not fail to influence the works of other authors. Although he was discursive in his literary habits and much of his work is vitiated by carelessness and haste--his artistic credo, imitating his subject the painter's, was "No day without a line," and copia is not a principle likely to receive critical approval in this age--there is much that is intrinsically interesting. Brathwait's character book, Whimzies: Or, A New Cast of Characters (1631), is certainly one of the best of the period. It is a racy excursion into seventeenth-century life and times that can still afford pleasure to the modern reader. Since its first publication in 1631 it has appeared only once--in an edition by James O. Halliwell (1859) that freely altered spelling and punctuation to suit nineteenth-century taste, and without annotation to aid the reader for whom many commonplace references of the time are now incomprehensible.

The plan of this dissertation comprises a general introduction to the character as a literary genre of the seventeenth century and an annotated edition of the characters of Richard Brathwait. The introduction will define the character, briefly relate it to its classical and native English forerunners, and discuss critically the important examples of character literature as they developed throughout the period.

The introduction does not purport to be an exhaustive study of all the characters produced in the age--that would hardly be possible in a work of this scope. The emphasis is on viewing the characters as literature, rather than as specimens for historical classification. Consequently, fuller critical attention has been given to authors whose works are virtually unknown--Brathwait, John Cleveland, and Richard Flecknoe; and to authors whose characters are praised, but rarely discussed--John Earle and Samuel Butler. The appearance of recent works indicates an increasing interest in the satire of the seventeenth century. The publication of two volumes of <u>Poems</u> <u>on</u> <u>Affairs</u> <u>of</u> <u>State</u>: <u>Augustan</u> <u>Satirical</u> <u>Verse</u>, <u>1660-1714</u> (New Haven, 1963, 1964) and the study by Ruth Nevo,

The Dial of Virtue: A Study of Poems on Affairs of State in the 17th Century (Princeton, 1963) should stimulate further inquiry into the satire of the age. The character, as an example of a satirical genre, deserves more attention. This study intends to show that the character has more than just passing historical interest--that it forms an important and vigorous chapter in the development of modern prose style.

    The sole authority for the text of Brathwait's *Whimzies* is the edition of 1631, hence the usual bibliographical problems of establishing an accurate text representing the intentions of the author have been removed. This text is an old-spelling edition based on a collation of two copies of the 1631 edition. The main emphasis has been placed on fitting Brathwait's work in its social, political, and religious contexts. *Whimzies* abounds in allusions to contemporary fashions and events, and in obsolete or unusual words that require explication if the work is to be understood and appreciated. The text of the characters is preceded by a brief introduction explaining the principles followed in the edition. Following the annotation is a list of all changes made from the copy-text.

I. The Character as a Literary Genre

i

The practitioners of the seventeenth-century character had a fairly clear idea of the nature and method of the genre they were engaged in. Joseph Hall, author of the first character book, <u>Characters of Vertues and Vices</u> (1608), was too preoccupied with the ethical purpose of his work to talk about the uniqueness of this book--as he did in his verse satires, where he claimed to be the first English satirist. But in the ninth impression of the book of characters produced by Sir Thomas Overbury and his friends--Dekker and Webster--there is a definition of "What a Character Is":

> Those Elements which we learne first, leaving a strong seale in our memories.
> Character is also taken for an Egyptian Hierogliphicke, for an impresse, or short Embleme; in little comprehending much.
> To square out a Character by our English levell, it is a picture (reall or personall) quaintlie drawne in various collours, all of them heightned by one shadowing.
> It is a quicke and soft touch of many strings, all shutting up in one musicall close: It is wits descant on any plaine song.

In true Renaissance fashion, the definition is itself a virtuoso piece, expressing the brevity and <u>sprezzatura</u> desirable in a character. The emphasis is on the free, yet highly selective, flow of ideas, all of which should relate to the subject. The definition, however, is emblematic in itself and does not contribute much to an illumination of the genre. Brevity and selectivity are important, but its formal and stylistic features remain unexplained. Richard Flecknoe, who worked over his characters constantly, revising them several times, gave a particularly interesting version of their method in Enigmaticall Characters (1658): "It gives you the hint of discourse, but discourses not; and is that in mass and ingot, you may coyn and wyer-draw to infinite; tis more Senica than Cicero, and speaks rather the language of Oracles than Orators: every line a sentence, and every two a period. It . . . tis all matter, and to the matter, and has nothing of superfluity, nothing of circumlocution. . . . Tis a Portraiture, not onely oth' Body, but the soul and minde . . ." (sigs. Hl^v-2^r). This is an oracular history of the change that English prose underwent in the seventeenth century, as well as a penetrating definition of the character. The character, according to Flecknoe, is analytic in method, giving the results of applied logic rather than the entire process of cognition. The style is Senecan, therefore pithy and dynamic. The result is the laying bare of human motives, as well as the lineaments of external appearance.

 Another observation on the character, this by Ralph Johnson in his Scholar's Guide from the Accidence to the University (1665), offers rules for constructing it as a stylistic exercise--an indication of how character-writing continued to stimulate the creation of satirical wit:

> 1. Chuse a Subject, viz, such a sort of men as will admit of variety of observation, such be, drunkards, usurers, lyars, taylors, excise-men, travellers, pedlars, merchants, tapsters, lawyers, an upstart gentleman, a young Justice, a Constable, an Alderman, and the like.
> 2. Express their natures, qualities, conditions, practices, tools, desires, aims, or ends, by witty Allegories, or Allusions, to things or terms in nature, or Art, of like nature and resemblance, still striving for wit and pleasantness, together with tart nipping jerks about their vices and miscarriages.
> 3. Conclude with some witty and neat passage, leaving them to the effect of their follies or studies. (p. 15)

The character, then, is a brief, witty, analytic description of a generic type. Almost anything is admissible in it except, perhaps, what Brathwait referred to as "opinionate singularitie." This was the excessive use of "strong lines," which indicated affectation and shallowness of thought. "<u>Characterisme</u>," Brathwait said, "holds good concurrence, and runnes with the smoothest current in this age; so it bee not wrapp'd up in too much ambiguitie." Wye Saltonstall, however, realized that "it is not in the nature of a Character to be as smooth as a bull-rush."

The soul of a character is its wit. Profound insight into human motives was something that only an Earle could accomplish. It was enough for the character to strip its subject of pretentions and affectations in a witty, entertaining fashion. This might include the use of dramatic description, direct comment by the author <u>in propria persona</u>, surrealistic invective, or pastoral idealism--if the subject were worthy of praise. Brevity as a stylistic ideal was rarely observed, occasionally jettisoned completely. It was especially considered inadequate for political and religious polemics.

The character, it will be seen, is more easily enjoyed if one does not attempt to fit each character book or separate character into a preconceived stylistic mould. The term "Theophrastan" has little validity as a descriptive word. Neither the stylistic techniques nor the raison d'être of the seventeenth-century character is related in any meaningful way to the sparse rhetorical exercises of the 4th century B.C. Greek author whose actual name was Tyrtamus. The genuine Theophrastan character was never practiced in England. Its unremitting pattern of definition and illustration was an interesting pedagogical method, but a literary cul de sac. No one would be pedantic or foolish enough to call Elizabethan tragedy "Senecan" or Jonson's comedies "Plautine" or "Terentian." Even Hall, who professed to follow Theophrastus, ignored the practice of Aristotle's protegé and employed his name for its ethical and classical association.

In this survey of the genre the term "character" will be used to describe a work that held up for witty scrutiny a generic member of contemporary society in a formal, detached manner. The intent might be serious or comic. As W. G. Crane states, "The character may hardly be defined more narrowly than as a concise representation by means of vivid and concrete yet prominently distinctive details, selected to make a generic picture."[1] A narrower, more discriminating definition of its

---

[1] Wit and Rhetoric in the Renaissance: The Formal Basis of Elizabethan Prose Style (New York, 1937), p. 154.

form was given by Gwendolen Murphy: "In one of the most usual forms the beginning is a definition, frequently conceited, the middle is an accumulation of characteristic traits, each phrase usually beginning with "he," the effect being that of a string of adjectives rather than of a reasoned narrative, and the progress is thus not logical but grammatical: the ending tends to be an epigrammatic summary expressed either simply or in a sounding conceit."[2]

The character was a form which, as F. P. Wilson said, "the century could not do without."[3] The sudden popularity of this genre is indicative of the growing dissatisfaction many must have felt towards the inability of existing forms of prose to deal imaginatively with the contemporary social scene. What today would naturally be rendered in the novel had few similar vehicles in the early seventeenth century. The popular fiction of the time found its material, generally, in the chivalric or pastoral modes. There were many popular works, such as Dekker's plague pamphlets, that dealt with real issues and lives, but the character was able to abstract from contemporary life the composite qualities of a social type and unite them into a witty analysis. When, in 1673, Richard Flecknoe stated "I study more to contract, than to dilate . . . ," he not only aptly summarized his own practice, but he intuitively

---

[2] A Cabinet of Characters (London, 1925), p.viii.
[3] Seventeenth-Century Prose (Univ. of California, 1960), p.13.

placed the genre in its appropriate position in the thought of the age. By its very nature the character could never become a major literary form. But it offers an insight into the vast changes that swept across the century with such intensity. If, as C. S. Lewis suggested in his literary history of an earlier period, Sidney's _Arcadia_ is a touchstone with which to test the depth of one's sympathy with the sixteenth century,[4] then the character is perhaps in a similar position with regard to the seventeenth.

ii

The character did not rise phoenix-like from the ashes of sixteenth-century culture. Neither was it suddenly reborn in the form of Isaac Casaubon's Latin translation of Theophrastus' _Characters_ in 1592. The seventeenth century found the character congenial to its temperament, held it closer to the light, and gave it the stamp of a distinctive, detached form. If the essence of the character genre is its reduction of disparate sensory data to a nonexistent abstract whole called a type, then it is linked to man's ability to transform his experiences into symbols--the very quality that makes him man.[5] The tendency to create types in literature is a constant, varying in method from age to age, but remaining

---

[4] _English Literature in the Sixteenth Century, excluding Drama_ (Oxford, 1954), p. 339.

[5] See Susanne K. Langer, _Philosophy in a New Key_ (New York, 1948).

a necessary quality in all art. Chaucer's pilgrims are both real and typical. It is a futile expenditure of critical effort to attempt to determine the extent of each quality in the prologue to the Canterbury Tales by searching for actual counterparts among Chaucer's acquaintances. The actual and typical are not mutually exclusive categories. Spenser's Faerie Queene has been unraveled as a roman à clef and mined for its archetypal equivalents. Any search, therefore, for a unique source of the character is certain to be a fruitless one. There are bound to be many partial analogues to it, both in classical and English literature; they can indicate a continuity of approach, but not a final explanation--if one is really needed--for the creation of the character.

In his brilliantly synoptic work, European Literature and the Latin Middle Ages (New York, 1953), Ernst Robert Curtius demonstrated how pervasive was the continuity of Latin literature throughout the Middle Ages and beyond. The important vehicle of this continuity was the knowledge of rhetorical techniques passed on through various redactions in Greek and Latin. Rhetoric dominated every aspect of public life in Periclean Greece. The aesthetically-motivated Gorgian rhetoric was given permanent value by Aristotle, who carefully subverted the strictures of Plato against emotive appeals in his Rhetoric and Poetics. With the decline of representative government in Greece, rhetoric became largely a matter of pedagogical training. Although Aristotle ceased to be read in the original, the textbooks that were based on his works became the dominant source of language training in schools even into the eighteenth century. This system of education profoundly influenced the creation of literature in all European vernacular languages for centuries.

The most important function of the rhetorical textbooks was to insure success in the principal form of rhetoric--panegyrical or epideictic oratory. Facility in this formal praise and blame was secured by the devising of preparatory exercises, or Progymnasmata. The three great exemplars of this method were the Greeks Hermogenes, Theon, and Aphthonius. The Latin works of Quintilian and Priscian were carefully based on their Greek predecessors. Thus a direct line of rhetorical transmission was formed from late antiquity to the English school curriculum of the sixteenth and seventeenth centuries. Erasmus's astoundingly popular formulary textbook, De Duplici Copia Verborum ac Rerum (1515), so influential in English education, was a compendium of those textbook techniques he knew so thoroughly.

Of obvious importance for the seventeenth-century character is that included in these storehouses of rhetorical knowledge were exercises and illustrations for the construction of characters. As W. G. Crane noted, there were among the many texts more than twenty different terms for basically the same type of activity. The Rhetorica ad Herennium (c.85 B.C.), the oldest Latin rhetorical text--it was long attributed to Cicero--illustrated the term notatio with a character sketch that was almost exactly like the later English product. Another type

of delineation often employed was that termed <u>descriptio
personae</u> by Cicero. The <u>locus classicus</u> for the influence
of the <u>descriptio</u> is found in Thomas Wilson's <u>The Arte of
Rhetorique</u> (1553):

> We describe the maners of men, when we set
> them forth in their kinde what they are. As in
> speaking against a covetous man, thus. There is no
> such pinch peney on live as this good fellowe is.
> He will not lose the paring of his nailes. His
> haire is never rounded for sparing of money, one
> pair of shone serveth him a twelve moneth, he is
> shod with nailes like a Horse. He hath bene knowne
> by his coate this thirtie Winter. He spent once a
> groate at good ale, being forced through companie,
> and taken short at his worde, whereupon he hath
> taken such conceipt since that time, that it hath
> almost cost him his life.[6]

There is little development needed in order to make this a
representative example of the character as it was later
practiced. Many more of these descriptions of men's nature
were no doubt created after the appearance of the first
comprehensive English formulary rhetoric, Richard Rainolde's
<u>The Foundation of Rhetorike</u>, in 1563. Here the student could
find illustrations for all the different oratorical techniques
used in working up a discourse. Rainolde's work was itself
based on a Latin translation of the <u>Progymnasmata</u> of
Aphthonius.[7] Such descriptive techniques as <u>characterismus</u>,
<u>prosopopoeia</u>, <u>ethopoeia</u>, and <u>topographia</u> encouraged men to
seek out the typical qualities in their experience and environment. The entire experience of the Middle Ages, in fact, was

---

[6] Ed. George Herbert Mair (Oxford, 1909), p.187.

[7] Formulary rhetorics are discussed by Wilbur S. Howell,
<u>Logic and Rhetoric in England</u>, 1500-1700 (Princeton, 1956),
pp.138-146.

oriented towards the construction of a "just representation of general nature," the characteristic of Shakespeare so admired by Samuel Johnson. Quintilian, in his <u>Institutio Oratoria</u>, recommended the plays of Terence for their illustrations of types discussed by Aristotle in his <u>Rhetoric</u>.[8] The stock character types of Terentian drama that became so important a part of Elizabethan comedy--the parasite, braggart, legacy-hunter, old man, and tricky slave--thus have their significance for the character as well. The pervasive influence of stylized <u>topoi</u> as discussed by Curtius shows the importance of typical modes in Western culture.

The effect of traditional rhetoric was powerful and lasting. In spite of the shift in fashion from Ciceronian to Ramistic and Systematic techniques, there still appeared in 1659 a stylistic rhetoric such as John Prideaux's <u>Sacred Eloquence: Or, the Art of Rhetorik, As it is Layd down in Scripture</u>.[9] The author had a peculiar like for dividing his subject into heptades, or groups of seven. Among the seven major parts of his text were instructions for the making of "Characters." Prideaux's suggestions included enumerating the qualities of a good bishop, the seven traits of old age, and the seven steps in the genealogy of sin. As a Neo-Ciceronian he cited for his authorities the major rhetorical works of tradition--Cicero, Quintilian, and the <u>Rhetorica ad Herennium</u>.

[8] Curtius, p.437.

[9] Howell, p.334.

Prideaux wrote his rhetoric after the period of the character's transformation into an instrument of political propaganda.

Important as the rhetorical tradition is, it is only part of the intellectual setting of the character. The ultimate explanation for the character's subject matter can probably be found in the idea that men have a limited capability for understanding the role of historical process in human culture. This was, Erich Auerbach said, the dominant intellectual quality in men until the appearance of Historism at the end of the seventeenth century. The narrow world view of Western culture, according to Auerbach, "does not see forces, it sees vices and virtues, successes and mistakes. Its formulation of problems is not concerned with historical developments either intellectual or material, but with ethical judgments."[10] The character was concerned with this approach to experience; as such, its subject matter is selected, generally, with the intent to illustrate a particular virtue or vice. In this respect the character is one link in a vast chain of homiletic works extending back to the Old Testament. In these works the tendency to abstract typical qualities was a natural result of the didactic impulse. The Old Testament Book of Proverbs, for example, gives the description of a virtuous woman. In the New Testament, I Corinthians xiii, there is an abstract description of the quality of charity: "Charity suffereth long, and is kind; charity envieth not; charity vaunteth not itself, is

---

[10] *Mimesis: The Representation of Reality in Western Literature*, trans. Willard Trask (Garden City, New York, 1957), p.33.

not puffed up, . . . Rejoiceth not in iniquity, but rejoiceth in the truth." In medieval homiletic literature this technique was often expanded into allegory, as in _Piers Plowman_. On a more homely level are the types of Chaucer's _Prologue_ and the _Ancren Riwle_. In medieval sermons the use of concrete illustrations of types brought the abstractions of vice and virtue into personal contact with the members of the congregation.[11] Another aspect of medieval life, the classification of society according to strict hierarchical degrees, or estates, contributed to the tendency to view human beings as types.

In the years just preceding the appearance of the character form other literary forces were at work that had direct bearing upon it. The rogue pamphlets of Harman and Awdeley meticulously classified the practitioners of coney-catching and purse-cutting, making available a fascinating underworld of subjects for the character. The fictionalized sociology of Greene, Nashe, Dekker, and Lodge also focused its attention on the same scene from which the character drew its material. More closely related in form are the verse satires and epigrams of the last decade of the sixteenth century. The insertion of character sketches was a common practice in the formal verse satires of Juvenal and Persius.[12] This practice was continued in the works of the Elizabethan satirists. The characters were often given classical names, but they are clearly examples of

[11] G. R. Owst, _Literature and Pulpit in Medieval England_ (Cambridge, 1933), pp. 87ff.

[12] See Mary Claire Randolph, "The Structual Design of Formal Verse Satire," _Philological Quarterly_, XXI (1942), 368-384.

contemporary reprehensible social types. Donne's "Satyre III" is probably the best example of the genre. In order to express different religious attitudes, Donne characterized them in the figures of Mirreus, Crantz, Graius, Graccus, and Phrygius:

> Mirreus
> Thinking her unhous'd here, and fled from us,
> Seekes her at Rome; there, because hee doth know
> That shee was there a thousand yeares agoe,
> He loves her ragges so, as wee here obey
> The statecloth where the Prince sate yesterday,
> Crantz to such brave Loves will not be inthrall'd,
> But loves her onely, who at Geneva is call'd
> Religion, plaine, simple sullen, yong,
> Contemptuous, yet unhansome;[13]

The selection of relevant characteristics in the short space allotted for each character is an essential of the detached character as well. A close approximation to the character form is found in John Marston's The Scourge of Villainy (1599). As a coach comes near, the satirist describes its female occupant:

> Her mask, her vizard, her loose-hanging gown
> For her loose-lying body, her bright, spangled crown,
> Her long slit sleeve, stiff busk, puff verdingall
> Is all that makes her thus angelical.
> Alas, her soul struts round about her neck;
> Her seat of sense is her rebato set;
> Her intellectual is a feigned niceness.
> Nothing but clothes and simpering preciseness.[14]

Closer to the detached form of the character is the epigram. In tone it resembles the verse satire, but its

---

[13] The Poems of John Donne, ed. Herbert J. C. Grierson (Oxford, 1912), I, 156.

[14] The Poems of John Marston, ed. Arnold Davenport (Liverpool, 1961), pp. 145-146.

circumscribed form allows for greater concentration of wit. Jonson's epigrams vary greatly in their subject matter, but the satirical one "On Lieutenant Shift" is a brilliant combination of typical description, narrative, and _tour de force_ of rhyme:

> Shift, here, in towne, not meanest among squires,
> That haunt Pikt-hatch, Mersh-Lambeth, and White-fryers,
> Keepes himselfe, with halfe a man, and defrayes
> The charge of that state, with this charme, god payes.
> By that one spell he lives, eates, drinkes, arrayes
> Himselfe: his whole revennue is, god payes.
> . . . .
> He steales to ordinaries; there he playes
> At dice his borrow'd money: which, god payes.[15]

This is close in tone to the satirical characters with which he prefaced _Every Man Out of His Humour_ (1599) and to those which he wrote as virtuoso set pieces for _Cynthia's Revels_ (1600). It remained for Joseph Hall to finally recognize that the character, when standing by itself or in a collection of similar pieces, made an effective appeal to the spirit as well as to the wit. There is little in the character that cannot be found in the several traditions that all coalesced at the end of the sixteenth and beginning of the seventeenth centuries. It drew its sustenance from classical, medieval, and contemporary sources and formed from them a distinctive genre.

---

[15] _The Complete Poetry of Ben Jonson_, ed. William B. Hunter, Jr. (New York, 1963), pp. 7-8.

iii

Basically the character was a static form. Within limits, however, it experienced enough change during the century to require a brief account of its variety. The first two character books, Hall's <u>Characters of Vertues and Vices</u> (1608) and Overbury's additions to his poem <u>A Wife</u> (1614), illustrate together the general attitude of the character-writers toward their subjects and the stylistic approach they considered appropriate. Hall's concern was with men's minds; thus his style is a reflective one, suited to his meditative purpose. The Overburian characters cast their net widely, attempting to render in witty metaphor an inclusive number of social types. The Overburian tone is similar to that of Middleton in his London comedies; Hall's work reflects the Stoic sententiousness of Chapman's tragedies.

The next group of character writers--Nicholas Breton, John Stephens, and Geffray Mynshul--labored under a confusion of the character with the Baconian essay. Their works, appearing in the years 1615-1618, generally included the word essay on the title page. Sometimes they distinguished between the style appropriate to each form--the reasoned order of the essay as opposed to the usually metaphoric spontaneity of the character--but quite often they merged the two. In their choice of subject matter they followed the example of Overbury.

The figure of John Earle, whose Micro-cosmographie appeared anonymously in 1628, stands apart from these names and from his successors. He was not an innovator, but he gave to the character genre a depth of insight it was not to possess again. The character-writers of the years 1629-1632-- R. M., Sir Francis Lenton, Donald Lupton, Wye Saltonstall, and Richard Brathwait--were strongly attracted to the social types of the mechanic laboring class and other easy targets for satirical comment. Only Brathwait had enough whimsical informality to make his work genuinely entertaining. The anonymous author of A Strange Metamorphosis of Man Transformed into a Wildernesse (1634) had the original impulse to characterize natural objects, giving them a charming delicacy in addition to human qualities. Lupton opened up the character to all of London and the country, offering a genial Baedeker to the reader who encountered his descriptions of London Bridge and Smithfield. Further experimentation might have been forthcoming, but the crisis of conscience between Roundhead and Cavalier intervened and turned the character into a medium for sharp criticism. Thomas Fuller, cultivating his conservative principles of quiet devotion, used the character as a slender stock to which he could graft the methods of biography, courtesy literature, the essay, and the literature of casuistry. But The Holy State and the Profane State (1642) has very few of the usual identifying marks of the character.

Benjamin Boyce aptly explained the resurgence of the character after the pronounced lull of the 'thirties: "The struggles of Puritan against Anglican, of middle-class Parliament-man against Royalist Cavalier were so profoundly rooted in English life and had developed along with so many divergences in religious observance, in daily manners, even in dress and habits of speech, that the descriptive Character after a ten-year quiescence took new life, about 1642, as the national crisis was reached."[16] The period of Professor Boyce's concern, 1640-1661, had far-reaching implications for all forms of English literature. It was the probable gestation period of Milton's Paradise Lost, but it was also a time that forced the author almost to abandon much of his literary work for the creation of prose tracts. The new character of argument is a decidedly important--and interesting--part of this environment. A few collections of characters still appeared--those of North, Wortley, and Ford, for example--but the rapid staccato of the separate pamphlet character, as it bounded from the press in response to political events or rival propaganda, was the new tempo of the genre.

The argumentative character offered what the older type lacked--the element of surprise. This new quality is found in the dazzling use of catachresis by John Cleveland and in the riotous comic persona of The Reformado (1643). The virtuosity of these and several other characters is sustained in the brilliant work of Samuel Butler. His characters,

[16] The Polemic Character 1640-1661 (Lincoln, Nebraska, 1955), p.12.

written in the late 'sixties but not published until 1759, have a sharp, yet firmly-controlled, satiric edge rarely achieved by the character writer.

The next generation of character-writers also reflects the form and pressure of the age. They directed their gaze at the coffee house and town gallant as well as at the political and religious subjects of the previous decades. Halifax turned the character into a serious discussion of the nature of political behavior. In place of the older metaphoric style he substituted one better suited to its subject--a terse and epigrammatic style that could skillfully be accommodated to the aphorism. Other character-writers responded to the inherent dangers of the Popish Plot. As a literary form, however, the character was largely replaced by the more specialized media of a diverse society--political verse satire, daily journalism, and the reflective essay.

Another literary form--the portrait character--arose in the latter part of the century. The heightened panegyrical stateliness of the formal portrait as it was practiced in France was very attractive to an England bent upon becoming the world's greatest power. But this form--masterfully practiced by Lord Clarendon--is not the character that was known during most of the century and will not receive attention in this discussion. Stylized biography is not the art of charactery.

The character could no longer exist when its metaphoric approach was considered inappropriate for a refined prose style. Henry Gally, in "A Critical Essay on Characteristic-Writings" that he attached to a translation of Theophrastus' <u>Moral Characters</u> in 1725, reflected the change in attitude toward the character style of the past: "Every Thing must be even, smooth, easy, and unaffected; without any of those Points and Turns, which conveys to the Mind nothing but a low and false Wit, in which our Moderns so much abound, and in which they seem to place their greatest Beauties."[17] Once the older character was considered "false Wit," nothing remained for it but to be subsumed by the Addisonian periodical essay with its newer "true wit." As a separate literary form the character had run its course.

iv

The character could not become such a popular genre without emitting influential lines of force in the direction of other genres. It might, of course, be set directly into different literary forms. Thomas Adams, the great London preacher, continued the tradition of medieval pulpit oratory by employing <u>exempla</u> in his sermons. Drawn as he was to simple, homely, concrete images, he found the character well-suited to his purposes. In <u>Mystical Bedlam, Or the World of Mad-Men</u> (1615), Adams attempted to adapt his method

---

[17] Augustan Reprint Society, Publication Number 33 (Los Angeles, 1952), p. 42.

to the quote from II Timothy that adorns the title page: "Their Madnesse shall be manifest to all men." He accomplished this by the use of vivid, descriptive characters of twenty representative madmen--the epicure, hypocrite, usurer, drunkard, and busybody, to name a few. In another work, Diseases of the Soule: A Discourse Divine, Morall, and Physicall (1616), he applied the style of the character to religious and psychological analysis--but always in a lively, emotive vein. In the section that examined the "Signes and Symptomes" of spiritual sickness, Adams described the brain-sick novelist (innovator), the envious man, the covetous man, the proud man, and the vainglorious man--many of the subjects treated by Hall and Overbury, and later by Earle. Although he borrowed from the first two authors named, he filtered ideas and images he found attractive through his own lively, distinctive style.[18]

Adams has an important place in the history of English prose style. In The Senecan Amble, George Williamson discussed him as a transitional figure in the shift of style from Euphuistic to Senecan.[19] The importance of the character in this change should be noted, for Adams was most Senecan when he assumed the genre's techniques. His sermons, as Williamson notes, were always developing into characters.

---

[18] Benjamin Boyce gives examples of Adams's borrowings in The Theophrastan Character in England to 1642 (Cambridge, Massachusetts, 1947), pp. 201-206.

[19] (London, 1951), pp. 241-242.

Other literary forms found the character a convenient way to infuse point and wit. William Habington inserted characters of a mistress, a wife, and a friend into the second edition of his play <u>Castara</u> (1635). Brathwait's habitual propensity for using the form resulted in its presence in his courtesy book <u>The English Gentleman</u> (1631)-- which supplied Fuller with material for <u>The Holy State and the Profane State</u>. Another indication of the character's magnetic attraction is its appearance among the gallimaufry of other literary elements in Richard Head's <u>The English Rogue: Described in the Life of Meriton Latroon, A Witty Extravagant</u> (1665). Detached from the context of the book's picaresque adventures are characters of a bottle of canary and a "hector or trapan." Head, however, did not only rely upon his own powers of invention. In the narrative of the story, between the two characters, is a stolen passage from Geffray Mynshul's character of a prison, taken from Mynshul's character book of 1618.[20]

Conspicuously absent from this discussion of the character genre has been the presence of the major artistic figures of the century. True, Donne and Webster contributed to the Overburian collection, and Marvell drew a biting "Character of Holland" in verse. Dryden no doubt profited from the character form when he set about creating the portraits of

[20] (New York, 1928), pp.67-68. The characters are on pp.60-61 and 70-72. Richard Head is the author of Part I of the story, which includes the characters. Francis Kirkman wrote Part II.

Achitophel and Zimri in his brilliant poem. But probably none of the great authors of the age used the character to the extent that it was an informing element in their work. This does not mean that no interesting currents of character technique flow through their work. John Milton and George Herbert often incorporated promising aspects of other genres into their works; there is evidence that the character was one of them.

Although Milton did not write any detached characters, the treatment of melancholy in "L'Allegro" and "Il Penseroso" possibly reflects the influence of the character. Lawrence Babb pointed out a parallel in the Overburian character of "A Melancholy Man" to "L'Allegro."[21] Both works use the traditional Galenic view of melancholy as a gloomy and unhealthy state of mind. Wye Saltonstall's character of "A Melancholy Man," written approximately the same time as Milton's two poems, expresses the theory of the more desirable Aristotelian melancholy illustrated in "Il Penseroso." A person with this type of melancholy affects a blunt simplicity and seeks out the essential meaning of things. The young poet might have focused his subject through the fashionable lens of the character--and the emblem and academic prolusion as well.

The witty epitaphs on Hobson, the Cambridge carrier of Milton's academic years, have the humor and epigrammatic point of the character. The two poems definitely attributed to Milton

---

[21] "The Background of 'Il Penseroso'," Studies in Philology, XXXVII (1940), 257-273.

make their satirical points in a series of discontinuous punning comments on Hobson's profession, much in the character manner. In <u>Areopagitica</u>, there is a concise characterization of a superficially religious man ironically cast in the imagery of commerce. One student of Milton has used this sketch as evidence for asserting that the poet must have read Theophrastus in the original Greek and that he instinctively grasped the essence of the character form.[22] The character element in a passage that was removed from Milton's <u>History of Britain</u> (1670), but later published separately, should not be ignored. Most important here are the feelings of bitter disappointment that he expressed toward the Long Parliament's failure to achieve its potential greatness. The abstract qualities of a well-ordered body of legislators are implied, while the faults of the defunct body are pointed out in Milton's accustomed magisterial manner. The usual wit of the character would surely have been grossly inappropriate in this piece. Although entitled <u>Mr John Miltons Character of the Long Parliament and Assembly of Divines In MDCXLI</u> when published in 1681, it is doubtful that the public viewed it as a genuine character. It is closer to the political analysis of Halifax's <u>Character of a Trimmer</u>.

The prose of George Herbert's <u>A Priest to the Temple</u> is close in time to the character's witty metaphoric style, but in its purpose and achievement could hardly be more removed.

---

[22] Irene Samuels, "A Theophrastan Character in Milton," <u>Notes and Queries</u>, V, No. 12 (December, 1958), 528-530.

Herbert's character of a parson is actually directed against
the witty preaching that could result in the character. He
sought a deliberate plainness in his prose--which is closer
to that of Tillotson than of Donne or Adams. In another way,
however, Herbert had a closer connection to the character.
Part of the spiritual activity at Nicholas Ferrar's Little
Gidding retreat was the group discussion. Its purpose was
to stimulate a meditative warmth, but it was also a form of
entertainment; the following is an example of what diversions
took place:

> He formed the family into a sort of collegiate
> institution of which one was considered as the founder,
> another guardian, a third as moderator, and himself as
> visitor of this little academy. The seven virgin
> sisters formed the junior part of this society, were
> called the Sisters, and assumed the names of 1st, The
> Chief, 2nd, The Patient, 3rd, The Cheerful, 4th, The
> Affectionate, 5th, The Submiss, 6th, The Obedient,
> 7th, The Moderate. These all had their respective
> characters to sustain, and exercises to perform suited
> to those characters.[23]

Herbert's intimate relationship with the Ferrar family and
his need to dramatize his religious experiences in his poetry
give credibility to the idea that he was perhaps acquainted
with this self-charactering intellectual exercise. The
metaphoric wit of the character could easily have been combined with this tendency to dramatize abstract ethical qualities. The result would have been a recognizable verse
character.

---

[23] P. Peckard, *Memorials of the Life of Mr. Nicholas Ferrar* (Cambridge, 1790). Quoted by A. L. Maycock, "Little Gidding Discovery," *Times Literary Supplement* (January 27, 1966), 72.

In his poem "Prayer (I)," for example, the succession of metaphors gives the whole sonnet the approach of the character:

> Prayer the Churches banquet, Angels age,
>   Gods breath in man returning to his birth,
>   The soul in paraphrase, heart in pilgrimage,
> The Christian plummet sounding heav'n and earth;
> Engine against th' Almightie, sinners towre,
>   Reversed thunder, Christ-side-piercing spear,
>   The six-daies world transposing in an houre,
> A kind of tune, which all things heare and fear;
> Softnesse, and peace, and joy, and love, and blisse,
>   Exalted Manna, gladnesse of the best,
>   Heaven in ordinarie, man well drest,
> The milkie way, the bird of Paradise,
>   Church-bels beyónd the starres heard, the souls bloud,
>   The land of spices; something understood.[24]

Only add "It is . . ." at the head of each line and this would make a moving yet witty contribution to the character genre. The same is true of the poem "Dotage," which begins:

> False glozing pleasures, casks of happinesse,
> Foolish night-fires, womens and childrens wishes,
> Chases in Arras, guilded emptinesse,
> Shadows well mounted, dreams in a career. . . .[25]

This does not mean that Herbert was consciously using the method of the character to achieve poetic effect. It does say, however, that the technique of the character form is linked in a fundamental way to what is distinctive in seventeenth-century sensibility. Wylie Sypher, in fact, uses Herbert's "Prayer" to illustrate what he considers a defining characteristic of Mannerist style. He views the poem's metaphoric playfulness as an example of "the constantly shifted

---

[24] *The Works of George Herbert*, ed. F. E. Hutchinson (Oxford, 1945), p.51.

[25] *Works*, p.167.

level of statement from extreme concreteness to abstraction" that one also finds in Milton's *Lycidas* and in Sir Thomas Browne's prose.[26]

This technique was constantly being employed by the character-writer; it was a result of his failure to make any positive distinction between the form of the character and of the essay. The twentieth-century reader, his critical faculty formed by a tradition of realistic and naturalistic fiction, expects to see maintained a distinction between the vividly concrete and the ethically-motivated general statement. The author of characters, of course, did not live in such divided and distinguished worlds. Even in the midst of Cleveland's intense catalog of epithets, the reader senses the regret expressed by the author for the loss of those conservative, hierarchical principles that once held sway over men. The character-writer was always affirming more than just his power of wit.

---

[26] *Four Stages of Renaissance Style* (Garden City, New York, 1955), p.176.

II. Joseph Hall's Characters of Vertues and Vices

When Joseph Hall wrote Characters of Vertues and Vices (1608), he professed that he patterned his anatomy of moral and ethical types after the characters of Theophrastus, "that ancient Master of Morality."[1] Hall's work, however, bears little real resemblance to its supposed model. Theophrastus' utter objectivity, with his unvaried pattern of definition and illustration, was inadequate and austere. Hall adapted the classical form to English needs by grafting it to the richer homiletic tradition of English Protestantism. Thus, Hall provided a delineation of virtues to counter the vices, since Theophrastus probably did not compose any.

Perhaps Hall sought a more direct outlet for his ethical program than the harvest of rods he brandished in Virgidemiarum,

---

[1] From the proem to The First Booke. Characterismes of Vertues. The full sentence reads: "I have here done it as I could, following that ancient Master of Morality, who thought this the fittest taske for the ninety and ninth yeare of his age, and the profitablest monument that he could leave for a farewell to his Grecians." The persona of advanced age added by a later redactor is matched by Hall's satirist's promise to leave virtue and vice "stript naked to the open view." All quotations are from the edition of Rudolf Kirk, Heaven Upon Earth and Characters of Vertues and Vices (New Brunswick, 1948), referred to hereafter as Characters.

the verse satires of 1597 and 1598 that were collected and almost burned in 1599. The characters, in fact, exhibit the planned toning-down of ethical qualities that Hall had previously treated with the vituperative harshness characteristic of the Renaissance definition of satire. In addition, by 1608 Hall was deeply involved in the Continental tradition of the meditation which had already resulted in The Arte of Divine Meditation in 1606.[2] The characters reflect this warming influence on the typically austere Christian Stoicism of "our English Seneca."

What makes Hall's work distinctively memorable is the living tone of voice, sometimes barely audible in the Vertues, but heard most often in his treatment of the Vices. As in Donne's sermons, the reader is always aware of the presence of a personality whose exact nature is difficult to ascertain. In the Vertues there are eleven characters, nine buttressed by the Stoic wise man at the beginning, and the happy man-- the beatus vir--at the end.[3] The edition of 1608 ended with the character "Of the good Magistrate," in the tradition of the manual for princes with its emphasis on the Christian humanistic qualities of the leader as the "faithfull Deputy of his Maker."[4] Between the twin Stoic poles of wisdom and

---

[2] Louis Martz discusses Hall's relation to the Ignatian meditation in "Mauburnus, Hall, and Crashaw: the 'Scale of Meditation'," The Poetry of Meditation (New Haven, 1962), pp. 331-352.

[3] Two characters, "Of the Penitent" and "He is an Happy man," were added to the nine characters of the first edition in 1614. Hall probably added his work to give greater symmetry to the structure of the whole.

[4] Characters, p. 160.

happiness lie the necessary qualities for living a moral life and attaining the elusive goal of spiritual tranquillity. This harmony is embodied in the thought and feeling of each of the characters in the <u>Vertues</u>. Implied in each sentence is a reconciliation between the inner nature of the subject and the restless temptations of the world that are constantly pressing upon him: "His power is limited by his will, and he holds it the noblest revenge, that he might hurt, and doth not."[5] He can be more ashamed of honour, than grieved with contempt; because he thinkes that causelesse, this deserved."[6] "That divine part goes ever uprightly and freely, not stooping under the burden of a willing sinne, not fettered with the grieves of unjust scruples."[7] The effect is that of a voice possessing imaginative certainty moving steadfastly and unhesitatingly through a sequence of moral combats.

The voice in the <u>Vices</u> is a more elusive one to examine, since the writer who would strip and despoil the ornaments of vice faces a problem. Hall implies the nature of the problem in the proem to the <u>Vices</u>: "Perhaps in some of these (which thing I doe at once feare, and hate) my stile shall seem to some lesse grave, more Satyricall: if you find me not without cause jealous, let it please you to impute it to the

[5] <u>Characters</u>, p.154.
[6] <u>Characters</u>, p.152.
[7] <u>Characters</u>, p.166.

nature of those Vices, which will not be otherwise handled."[8] This is the *apologia* of the classical satirist explaining his separation of styles and justifying his "lesse grave, more Satyricall" manner.[9] The satirist must expose vice with a vivid clarity, but must temper his style so that it does not appear that he himself has fallen victim to these vices. Maintaining a consistent tone throughout the Vices is, as in formal verse satire, an impossibility. Hall changes from the ironically condescending, to the objectively dramatic, to the tone of grieved outrage, all without any apparent devices of transition.

In the "Character of the hypocrite," Hall sketches a vivid and pointed vignette of his subject in action: "Walking early up into the Citty, he turnes into the great Church, and salutes one of the pillars on one knee, worshipping that God which at home he cares not for; while his eye is fixed on some window, on some passenger, and his heart knowes not whether his lips goe."[10] This continues, as Hall describes him in several other poses: taking out his notebook to jot down a note to remember from the sermon being delivered, when in reality he is just checking on a forgotten errand; loudly

---

[8] Characters, p.180.

[9] For a brief discussion of the use of the *apologia* in verse satire, see Robert C. Elliott, The Power of Satire: Magic, Ritual, Art (Princeton, 1960), pp.113-115.

[10] Characters, p.171.

turning the pages of his Bible to catch an omitted quotation; and noisily asking for the name of the preacher by whose sermon he pretends to be enraptured. The result is a dramatically-evolved portrait that almost makes the delineation of vice an attractive quality--an artistic problem that Milton faced when creating the figure of Satan.

Never far removed from the presentation of dramatic action in Hall's work is the tendency to deal directly with the pressing religious problems of the day: "At first like another Ecobolius [a Sophist who changed his religion with the succession of emperors] he loved simple truth; thence diverting his eyes, he fell in love with idolatrie . . . and now of late he is leapt from Rome to Munster, and is growne to giddie Anabaptisme. . . ."[11] And a favorite device in Hall--as important for the sermon as for the character--is the metaphoric peroration: "In briefe, he is the strangers Saint, the neighbours disease, the blot of goodnesse; a rotten sticke in a darke night, a Poppie in a corne field, an ill tempered candle, with a great snuffe, that in going out smells ill; and an Angell abroad, a Devill at home; and worse when an Angell, than when a Devill."[12] Hall used these devices--dramatic description, direct comment on contemporary issues, and patterned language--as part of his attack on spiritual error.

[11] Characters, p.180.
[12] Characters, pp.172-173.

The structure of the characters indicates Hall's well-known interest in the anti-Ciceronian movement and in the art of the Continental meditation. There are throughout the *Characters* *of* *Vertues* *and* *Vices* many examples of what Morris W. Croll termed the curt style, or *stile* *coupé*: the brief members of the sentences; the asymmetrical length of these members; the hovering, imaginative order of thoughts that are amplified associatively rather than logically; and the omission of the ordinary devices of syntactic connection.[13] These techniques give the characters the effect of spontaneity, of the mind's working out a problem according to the exigencies of that problem, rather than to a predetermined plan.

The meditative structure of the whole gives an overall impression of controlled energies moving towards a solution. From the original stating of a paradox, the characters move through a series of exploratory comments--using the devices mentioned above--to a final statement, usually in the form of a series of metaphoric nouns or adjectives. This tripartite division of the characters can be attributed to the rhetorical training in preparing an oration for delivery. But the emotive intent of the opening paradox and the stunning conclusion of the characters, following a series of contemplative remarks,

---

[13] "The Baroque Style in Prose," *Studies* *in* *English* *Philology,* *A* *Miscellany* *in* *Honor* *of* *Frederick* *Klaeber*, ed. Kemp Malone and Martin B. Ruud (Minneapolis, 1929), p. 435.

indicate the influence of Hall's interest in meditative literature.[14] It is reasonable to assume that Hall, who invented the form of his characters, tried to shape its structure according to his interests in other devotional genres. This does not discount the presence in the characters of the tendency toward epigrammatic statement and the interest in paradox for its own sake. Both of these techniques also help to achieve the flash of sudden insight that Hall sought in his work.

Hall's formula for the character was a moving and inventive one. But it held little possibility for further development along such spare and gnomic lines. The tendency in later practitioners of the character was to expand its form and its interests, thereby bringing it more in accord with the social and literary forces of the age. There was little that Hall could give to the engagé contributors to the Overburian collection.

---

[14] The form and structure of the meditation is fully discussed by Martz. Another explanation for the form and structure of Hall's characters is suggested by Harold Fisch's assertion that it was the style and spirit of the Psalms that influenced Hall's meditative approach. See Jerusalem and Albion: The Hebraic Factor in Seventeenth-Century Literature (New York, 1964), pp. 48-52.

III. The Overburian Characters

The appearance in 1614 of twenty-two characters as part of a volume containing Sir Thomas Overbury's poem "A Wife" set in motion the development of the character form. The work of the Overburian contributors--who include Webster, Dekker, and Donne--is marked, not by the example of Hall and his dimly-perceived exemplar, Theophrastus, but by the experimentation in satiric techniques that affected every aspect of English literature in the last decade of the sixteenth century and the first quarter of the seventeenth. The popularity of the Overburian characters has often been traced to the sensational circumstances surrounding Overbury's murder.[1] The characters are also used to illustrate "how wit was exercised . . . by half-a-dozen or more of the mob of gentlemen who wrote with ease."[2] Considering the Overburian characters as part of the development of satire shows them to be more the natural result of satiric tendencies than a fad emanating from lurid violence or aristocratic condescension.

---

[1] Tucker Brooke in the Renaissance section of A Literary History of England (New York, 1948), p.602, says: "The 'character' owed the beginning of its special vogue to a purely accidental cause."

[2] Henry Morley, ed. Character Writings of the Seventeenth Century (London, 1891), p.27.

The intense interest in satire that burgeoned in the last few years of the sixteenth century is too well-known to require an extended historical survey. Suffice it to say that the epigrams of Jonson and Harington; the formal verse satires of Marston, Hall, and Donne; and the "comicall satyres" of Shakespeare and Jonson were all part of this activity.

For the Overburian characters, the dramas of Jonson were the most important of these satiric experiments. Jonson's early plays, <u>Every Man Out of His Humor</u> (1600) and <u>Cynthia's Revels</u> (1601), provided the closest approximations to the detached character that were then written. In the earlier play they formed the <u>dramatis personae</u>; in the later, they were descriptive set-pieces inserted right into the play. These two early works, along with <u>Poetaster</u>, were part of Jonson's experimentation in the dramatic use of techniques of formal verse satire. Jonson tried to give the characters of these plays a more rational, less savage view of society, thereby producing a Horatian rather than a Juvenalian type of satirist--in effect a "clean" satirist.[3] Jonson abandoned these abortive attempts for the Menippean type of satire that

---

[3] This view of Jonson's work is expressed in Alvin C. Kernan's <u>The Cankered Muse: Satire of the English Renaissance</u> (New Haven, 1959), pp.156-191. Jonson's use of verse satire is also discussed by Oscar J. Campbell in <u>Comicall Satyre and Shakespeare's Troilus and Cressida</u> (San Marino, California, 1938).

stressed the satiric scene rather than the satirist. The result of this change--effected after 1604--was Jonson's great succession of satiric works. He abandoned the allegorical and humours types for the full-fleshed realism that accounts for the remoulding of Every Man In His Humor into an English environment about 1612, and the re-creation of the density of London life in Bartholomew Fair, acted in 1614.

The Overburian characters are part of this change in technique from Marstonian invective to realistic description. They adopted the restrained satirical tone of the characters in Jonson's earlier plays. And as the satiric field broadened in Jonson's Menippean plays, so did the Overburian characters swell to a collection of eighty-three pieces,[4] comprising Dekker's re-creations of an actual environment in his prison characters and Donne's "Character of a Dunce," with its scantily-disguised attack on the deterioration of the scholastic tradition. The characters provided a mirror of English society rendered in prose. Like the drama, the characters employed many variations in the treatment of human character--from the Arcadian idealism of "A Fair and Happy Milkmaid" and "A Franklin," to the rhetorical and ethical tradition of the

[4] For a complete discussion of the additions to the Overbury canon and the problem of authorship, see the introduction by William J. Paylor to his edition of The Overburian Characters (Oxford, 1936), and also two articles by Paylor, "Thomas Dekker and the 'Overburian' Characters," Modern Language Review, XXXI (1936), 155-160; and "The Editions of the 'Overburian' Characters," The Library, XVIII (1937), 340-348.

descriptio in "A Covetous Man" and "The Proud Man," to the pungent realism of "A Waterman" and "An Affected Traveller." The Overburian collection is a repository of varied techniques and approaches partly attributable to the different authors who gave to it and partly to the coexistence of medieval and modern outlooks that inform the thought of this period.

For a work that owes so much to the thoroughly English approach of Jonson, the label "Theophrastan" is inaccurate.[5] The Overburian contributors also found little to interest them in the characters of Hall. They directed their attention to the world around them--a world of usurers, almanac-makers, foreigners, and gallants. The characters were successful because they struck precisely both the chords of stability and change that were part of Jacobean society. To ascribe their appearance or vogue to the Latin translation of Theophrastus in 1592 is to ignore the social and literary forces at work during this age.

Although the choice of subject matter and general approach of the Overburian characters are often noted, their witty style has always been their best known quality. One

---

[5] Wendell G. Clausen, in his article "The Beginnings of English Character-Writing," *Philological Quarterly*, XXV (1946), 32-45, traces the popularity of the Overburian characters to the Jonsonian humors play on their joint interest in the analysis of human behavior; in the assumed friendship of Overbury and Jonson, since they both traveled in the same circles; and in an influence of Theophrastus on Jonson based on rather doubtful borrowings in *Volpone*. Clausen acknowledges a common debt of Overbury and Jonson to the earlier rogue pamphlets, but he does not consider the changes in satiric treatment at this time.

view states that this wit actually worked at odds with the main purpose of the characters--to analyze human motives and actions. Benjamin Boyce commented on this tendency: "The most striking feature of all . . . is the ubiquitous exaggeration of wit and fancy. In some of the Characters this wit seems to become the main method; an effect is achieved not by an accumulation of sentences that describe the habitual, revealing conduct of a representative individual but rather by a series of fantastic, astonishing figures and puns that merely have in common the same starting-point."[6] This is certainly true. But to criticize the Overburian authors for this fault is to expect from them demands that our novel-centered critical method has no right to make.

The explanation for the apparent contradiction between the avowed purpose of the characters and their style can perhaps be traced by citing additional comment on the wit: "We know the subject little better for treatment like this. The striving for wit visible in Hall's writing has in these cases encouraged the author almost to abandon the idea of a portrait."[7] Another comment is also pertinent: "This language seemed particularly suitable for securing the point and smartness for which the early practitioners strove, but it distorted the accuracy of the picture and eventually became the end rather than the means of the production. Veracity and lucidity were

---

[6] The Theophrastan Character in England to 1642 (Cambridge, Massachusetts, 1947), p.143.

[7] Ibid.

sacrificed for the verbal apparatus; the picture became obscured and indistinct."[8] These critical views are similar in their holding up as the ideal striven for the accurate delineation of a visual medium (portrait-picture). The explanation for this is probably the modern "isolation of the visual faculty from the other senses" that Marshall McLuhan has observed in post-typographic culture.[9] The views quoted above are critical of the Overburian wit, because it is based on oral-aural techniques--the principle of <u>ut pictura poesis</u> notwithstanding--that give it a distinctly different result from what the approach of, say, the <u>New Yorker</u> would accomplish.

The Overburian style is an example of what Father Ong calls "oral residue" in prose style. Briefly, this is the presence in a visually-oriented culture of "habits of thought and expression tracing back to preliterate situations or practice."[10] It results, in the case of Tudor--and certainly later--prose, in a retention of linguistic habits formed by an "oral set of mind." The prime requisite for the individual trained in the traditional rhetoric was a free and ready flow of eloquent sayings--the well-known quality of <u>copia</u> as it was formed by the demands of oratory. To insure success in this area it was

---

[8] Maximilian G. Walten, ed. <u>Thomas Fuller's The Holy State and the Profane State</u> (New York, 1938), I. 30.

[9] <u>The Gutenberg Galaxy</u> (Toronto, 1962), page not numbered.

[10] Walter J. Ong, S.J., "Oral Residue in Tudor Prose Style," <u>PMLA</u>, LXXX (1965), 145-154.

necessary to have available a ready stock of linguistic formulas such as sententious phrases, aphorisms, or topoi. Using such ready-made devices resulted in a loose, episodic organization. Sidney's Apology for Poetry, for example, despite the fact that it is literary criticism and specifically meant as written composition, is cast in the form of a classical oration--a form carefully structured along oral, preliterate lines. This "adding" technique is also noticeable in controversial literature, prose fiction, characters, and the essay. The discontinuous form in the Overburian characters has its origin in this "oral residue." The metaphoric style is employed as an aid to memory, enabling the mind to retain a store of well-turned images for future use.

This does not contradict the stylistic explanations of Croll that were mentioned above with regard to Joseph Hall. However, labelling two such different stylistic approaches as Hall's and Overbury's "Senecan" does not help to distinguish between them. But the Overburian style, with its impression of conversational brilliance, becomes clearer when viewed against Hall's meditative dèliberateness. Hall's characters, though divided almost like a sermon text, are meant to be pondered and assimilated slowly. Overbury's technique is, in the words of its own definition, "a quicke and softe touch of many strings, all shutting up in one musicall close: It is wits descant on any plaine song." With Hall it is the written word that is significant; with Overbury "those elements which we learn first, leaving a strong seal in our memories."

The followers of Overbury are dependent for their wit on this verbal fluency. Even Earle, who more than any other of the character-writers accommodated his work to the changing stylistic temper of the time, was known for his "conversation so pleasant and delightful" and was praised for his "witty and sharp discourses."[11] With this knowledge the Overburians can be praised for what they did, rather than be criticized for what they did not intend to do. Webster, Donne, and Dekker were all profoundly medieval in many of their views and literary techniques, even though they are valued most for those elements that align with modern thought and feeling. In their characters will not be found the sudden revelations of character that abound in their works in other genres. But in them one can find the elements of wit that contribute to their greatness.

---

[11] The Life of Edward Earl of Clarendon (Oxford, 1827), I, 57.

IV. The Earlier Character-Writers:
Breton, Stephens, and Mynshul

With the characters of Hall and Overbury the general form, style, and approach of the genre were established. Yet within the apparently circumscribed limits of the character an amazing variety of tones and techniques soon became one of its most attractive features. When Nicholas Breton said that "their natures are divers" he was referring to his own work, Characters Upon Essaies Morall and Divine, but this applies equally well to much of the vast body of characters that appeared in the seventeenth-century. The earlier writers, however, were very much under the mantle of Bacon, whose "dispersed meditations" had appeared in 1597. These ten highly aphoristic and concentrated essays were enlarged and augmented to form thirty-eight more fully-developed pieces in the edition of 1612. The earlier authors of characters hoped to combine some of Bacon's penetrating, analytic insights with the more homespun satirical sallies of Hall and Overbury. Their attempts to give the lineaments of actual experience were most successful when directed towards their own capabilities and backgrounds. Breton, with his protean ability to assume literary attitudes from the ponderously solemn to the naively whimsical, was most successful in the fragile mosaic of the <u>Fantasticks.</u> Geffray Mynshul very barely approached the pathetic intent of his <u>Essayes and Characters of a Prison and Prisoners</u>. John Stephens, the legalistic and verbose author of two books, <u>Satyrical Essayes Characters and Others</u> (1615) and the enlarged <u>Essayes and Characters Ironicall and Instructive</u> of the same year, was believable when he touched on those subjects whose habits he had assimilated through his life at the Inns of Court. There was hardly any aspect of contemporary life--except the genuinely controversial--which these authors did not at least open to further exploration.

In Nicholas Breton's first book of characters, <u>Characters Upon Essaies Morall and Divine</u> (1615), the sententious subject matter and affected brevity of Bacon's essays of 1597 were mated with the metaphoric tendencies of the character to produce a bizarre offspring, a <u>reductio ad absurdum</u> of Senecan style. Breton was praised in a dedicatory poem for his "Lipsian stile, terse Phrase." Here Senecan style is used, not so much to advance thought and to quicken its assimilation through brevity, as to render thought unnecessary and indeed impossible. Breton's technique was to string together in groups of two, three, or four, highly-charged emotive terms such as Reason, Time, Nature, Grace, and Love with the minimum of syntactic connection.[1] Bacon was aware of the danger implicit in the overuse of any style; in a passage added in

---

[1] Chester N. Greenough wrote about this tendency of Breton's, which he termed "quadrumania." See "Nicholas Breton: Character-Writer and Quadrumaniac," <u>Collected Studies by Chester Noyes Greenough</u> (Boston, 1940), pp. 59-67.

the Latin translation of The Advancement of Learning (1623) he commented on Senecan style, in which "words may be aculeate, sentences concise, and the whole contexture of the speech and discourse rather rounding into itself than spread and diluted: so that it comes to pass by this artifice that every passage seems more witty and weighted than indeed it is."[2] In the Characters Upon Essaies, where the subjects were abstract and required the searching intellect of a Bacon, Breton's technique was inadequate. Topics such as wisdom, learning, peace, war, honor, and time require a looser style, one more designed for expatiation. In The Good and the Badde, or Descriptions of the Worthies and Unworthies of this Age (1616), Breton's second character book, the subjects were more clearly suited to the technique of the character.

In this book Breton placed in opposition twenty-five pairs of characters good and bad. The almost incantatory cadence is more suited to the solemn commonplaces of his descriptions than his previous work and is indeed more readable. The balance of oppositions reflects the same order and harmony of thought that informs Hall's Characters of Vertues and Vices. Breton deals with the certainties and verities of Christian humanistic tradition. His characters are arranged so that they offer comprehensive examples of the structural principle

---

[2] The English translation is by Gilbert Watts, 1640. Cited by F. P. Wilson, Elizabethan and Jacobean (Oxford, 1945), p. 36.

behind feudal social structure: the three estates of the nobility, clergy, and commons.[3] This conventional plan was dislocated, however, when he reached far enough down into the social scale and arrived at the parasite, the bawd, and the atheist. Perhaps if read occasionally as a mine for Renaissance commonplaces they might fulfill a purpose, but their deadly regularity--of thought as well as of form--tends to negate any possible emotional effect. The character form does not lend itself well to the exposition of ideology. If it is to be used for propagandistic purposes, it must possess a distinctive, varied style or humorous approach. Breton accomplished this in his less pretentious work, but not here.

Breton wrote one character book that has all the qualities lacking in the other two. The Fantasticks: Serving for a Perpetuall Prognostication (1626; but listed in the Stationer's Register for 1604) combines the brevity of the character with the pictorial appeal of the popular almanac. As a work it seems to be of an earlier date, intended more as a defense of the redeeming qualities of the almanac and prognostication against the mock-prognostication of Thomas Nashe and the fulminations of Philip Stubbes and John Chamber, than as a character book. The unaffected simplicity of the diction and the graceful typicality of the imagery resemble Herrick's homely miniatures of Devon country life. These characters

---

[3] For Breton's use of the "estates" in his work, see Ruth Mohl, The Three Estates in Medieval and Renaissance Literature New York, 1933), pp. 229-237.

seem much more distant from the harsh polemics of sixteen years hence than their publication date indicates. They reflect a world untroubled, unaffected by any change save the rhythmic change and ordered progression of hours, months, and seasons.

John Stephens's two books, <u>Satyrical Essayes Characters and Others</u> (1615) and the much enlarged <u>Essayes and Characters Ironicall and Instructive</u> (1615), indicate the interests of the earlier character-writers and what they considered suitable to the character form. Stephens's earlier book, <u>Satyrical Essayes</u>, contained forty-three characters; seven more were added to the next volume. A collation of the two volumes reveals some interesting, though hardly surprising, facts about an author writing in competition with the Overburian characters. Most of his changes are amplifications of several kinds. In some cases he made the language coarser and therefore more satirical according to early definitions of satire: "And as some sluttish people take pleasure in their owne excrements, and relish the pickings of their nose; so hee, his owne opinion."[4] He made additions in the form of witty similes: "His vices are like <u>Errata</u> in the latter end of a false coppie: they point the way to vertue by setting downe the contrary."[5] Some additions were made in the interest of greater realism: "He is therefore much like a booksellers shoppe on <u>Bartholomew day</u> at

[4] Stephens, <u>Essayes and Characters</u>, sig. M5^v.

[5] Stephens, <u>Essayes and Characters</u>, sig. T1^r.

London; the stalls of which are so adornd with bibles and prayer-bookes, that almost nothing is left within, but heathen knowledge."[6] Stephens also added learned allusions to classical and modern authors with accompanying marginal references: "So that I might almost say of him as Scaliger saith of Locus; that he is Quodammodo ens, quodammodo non ens."[7] Some of these additions can no doubt be ascribed to his running poet's feud with the authors of the Overburian characters over Stephens's unkind character of an actor that had appeared in his first edition. But most of them should be considered as examples of his conception of copious wit. In any case, his work indicates how far and how quickly the early character-writers traveled from the model of Theophrastus, their putative father whom Stephens quoted on the title page of his first edition.

Stephens achieves some of his witty intent when he writes from his experience as a resident of Lincoln's Inn. In his character of "A Pettifogging Atturny" he describes the dominant interest of his subject: "He is indeed the upshot of a proud ignorant Clarke, and retaines his learning from Paenall Statutes, or an English Littleton. He doth multiplie businesse, as a tinker multiplies worke, with mending: and in a Michaelmas tearme, hee will seeme more busie about offices,

[6] Stephens, Essayes and Characters, sigs. Q1^v-2^r.

[7] Stephens, Essayes and Characters, sig. Q7^r.

then a flea at midnight in the midst of summer."[8] But in his other characters, whether of good types or bad, there are few real attempts made to fuse his rather maneuverable Senecan style with the demands of his subject, and the result is the lack of variety of approach characteristic of Breton.

Geffray Mynshul's Essayes and Characters of a Prison and Prisoners (1618) attempted to use the character and the essay for rendering personal experience--in his case, incarceration in the King's Bench Prison in Southwark. His characters, interspersed among restrained essays, are composed of heaped-up metaphors, with no discernible intent except their purely emotive impact. A mixture of the native and the exotic is his usual means of variation, as in this comment on Visitants: "They are like the rings and chaines bought at S. Martines, that weare faire for a little time, but shortly after will prove Alchimy, or rather pure Copper. Lastly, they are like the Apples which grow on the Bankes of Gomorrah, they have crimson and beautifull rindes, but when they come to gather them they crumble all to dust."[9] In the "Character of a Prison" Mynshul compares the prison to a microcosm, a commonwealth, Rosamund's labyrinth, the Inns of Court, the Doctor's commons, the Surgeons' Hall, and purgatory, but these attractive topics are not developed with any intensity of

[8] Stephens, Essayes and Characters, sig. Z2^v.

[9] Mynshul, Essayes and Characters, sig. D4^r.

imagery. His experiences, however vivid they were, remain undigested. These characters, along with those of Breton and Stephens, do not force their way into the consciousness of the modern reader; they are, in fact, poorer in quality than the characters that followed them. But there are scattered moments in their works when their language is equal to the interest of their subject matter. In a limited form like the character, the style assumes tremendous importance. John Earle had both the wisdom and stylistic grace to give the character form permanent value.

V. John Earle's <u>Micro-cosmographie</u>. <u>Or</u>, <u>A</u> <u>Peece</u>
<u>of</u> <u>the</u> <u>World</u> <u>Discovered</u>; <u>in</u> <u>Essayes</u> <u>and</u> <u>Characters</u> (1628)

When John Earle cast his work, he effected a synthesis of the most notable efforts in the character tradition. Hall gave the character its brevity and moral fervor tempered with Stoic reasonableness; the Overburian contributors opened up a vast arena of social types that the drama had also found to be fit targets for satiric barbs. Earle, inherently oriented toward a traditional and conservative cast of thought, pruned the excesses of his predecessors and, through a brilliant act of artistic selection, created a far more effective argument for his Latitudinarian principles than his translations into Latin of the <u>Ecclesiastical</u> <u>Polity</u> and <u>Eikon</u> <u>Basilike</u>. The great problem for the character-writer is how to achieve a satisfactory balance between cold abstraction and didacticism on the one hand, and shallow, wooden caricature on the other. This Earle surmounted through an instinctive, stylistic <u>via</u> <u>media</u>--the gentle force of his personality manifested in the form of ironic humor.

Irony is a term often applied to Earle's characters, for it is the skilled use of this element in his work that separates him from the other character-writers. In the <u>Micro-cosmographie</u> irony implies a sympathetic awareness of the basic disparity between a man's actions and his motives, expressed without stridency or tendentiousness. Behind the gently mocking <u>persona</u> is a strong set of normative values, held by a man confident in the importance and efficacy of right reason. Irony also implies a certain quality of detachment from personal feelings toward the subject; in Earle, as in the other writers of characters, this is a relative point. The act of selecting a particular subject or characteristic for scrutiny is in itself determined by one's total view of the subject. The tendency in the development of the character form was to move further and further from Earle's humane acceptance of folly to the complete exclusion of anyone's ideals that may be different. In order to be effective, the satiric instrument has to be complex, for sheer invective is a self-defeating approach. Earle's characters make use of subtle and varied satiric techniques, but they do not sacrifice an openness of spirit in the process.

Earle's subjects reflect his academic background, for he was, according to Clarendon, "a person very notable for his elegance in the Greek and Latin tongues, and being fellow of Merton College in Oxford, and having been proctor of the University. . . ."[1] He was also in his distinguished career tutor of Lucius Cary, future Lord Falkland, and the young Prince Charles, who amply rewarded Earle at the Restoration

---

[1] <u>The Life of Edward Earl of Clarendon</u> (Oxford, 1827), I, 57.

with the Deanery of Westminster. The characters of the grave divine, the downright scholar, the plodding student and others are, however, only representative players in Earle's "theatre of natures."[2] Their pretentions and affectations are perhaps less excusable than others' and thus more deserving of exposure. But these characters of particular social types are interspersed among others of more universal application-- an insolent man, a vulgar-spirited man, a child, and many others. As in the Overburian characters and in Mynshul, there are also characters of places that almost assume a life process of their own and can thus be charactered: a prison, a tavern, a bowling alley, and Paul's Walk. Together the seventy-eight characters form a comprehensive gallery of types which no character collection can equal in its fairness to its subjects, and in its eschewing of easy satirical targets.[3]

In spite of its frequent appearance in anthologies of seventeenth-century literature and characters, there have been remarkably few critical comments of any kind on the structure and technique of the Micro-cosmographie. There have been, in fact, few real analyses of specific characters in Earle's work, and thus little real appreciation of his achievement. It will

---

[2] From the character of "A Tavern." All citations from the Micro-cosmographie are from the edition of Harold Osborne (London, n.d.)

[3] In the first edition of 1628 there were 54 characters; 23 were added in the 5th ed. of 1629; and 1 more in 1633. Earle's name never appeared on any title page of the Micro-cosmographie during his lifetime, but he was well-known as the author of the work.

become clear that Earle's effectiveness is based on conscious arrangement of organizational patterns for the purpose of achieving variety and appropriateness to subject; and on skillful use of the resources of language.

The temptation to resort to a mechanical formula is an ever-present one for the character-writer, and one usually succumbed to. Breton, for example, was particularly drawn to the idea of a structural recipe. Earle, obviously aware of the need for variety, created several different formal patterns, each adjusted rhetorically to the subject being charactered. In the character of "A Mere Alderman" Earle reduces the pompous city official to a ridiculous comic figure with marvelous economy. The character begins with an innocently neutral clause: "He is venerable in his gown. . . . " This is promptly and riotously overturned in the next phrase, amplified in the following clause, and then concluded in the following sentence: " . . . more in his beard, wherewith he sets not forth so much his own, as the face of a City. You must look on him as one of the Town Gates, and consider him not as a Body but a Corporation." The result is a complete comic reversal and has the effect of a sudden deflation of the alderman's social standing. The entire following section of the character is built on this technique:

> His eminency above others hath made him a man of worship, for he had never been preferred but that he was worth thousands. He oversees the Commonwealth as his shop, and it is an argument of his policy that he has thriven by his craft.

> He is a rigorous magistrate in his ward: yet
> his scale of justice is suspected, lest it be
> like the balances in his warehouse. . . . He
> is one that will not hastily run into error, for
> he treads with great deliberation, and his judge-
> ment consists much in his pace. His discourse
> is commonly the Annals of his Mayoralty, and
> what good government there was in the days of
> his gold chain: though his door-posts were the
> only things that suffered reformation. . . .
> He makes very much of his authority, but more
> of his satin doublet. . . .

The image of the alderman in his gown at the beginning of the character is repeated in the last line as well: "But his scarlet gown is a monument and lasts from generation to generation." This acts to point up the emphasis on the externals of the alderman's position and, indirectly, on his own superficiality. This is reinforced by other references to the external trappings of public office that are, however, not matched by the quality of the man himself: his symbolic scales of justice and his formerly-possessed gold chain.

No less subtle are the local effects of word play. The pun on the symbolic scales of justice and his merchant's scales contributes to the ironic reduction of the alderman. The pun on body and corporation in their public context and in their application to the ponderous alderman's appearance needs no amplification. Not quoted above is a reference to the alderman and his brethren whose heads, when in conjunction, "may bring forth a City Apophthegm, or some such sage matter." The burlesque quality of this strange birth from the ponderous heads of the city fathers is no less effective for its lack of further development within the brief limits of the character form. Evidence that Earle was not unaware of the potential of verbal ambiguity is the skillful position and meaning of the word "suffered" in the passage quoted above. Though comic in its immediate context, the word assumes an intensity, almost a profound seriousness, after a moment of deliberation. Earle possessed an arsenal of witty devices and knew how to employ them with subtle force.

In "A Discontented Man" a different pattern is established. The opening is a brilliant antithesis that sets the character in motion and requires the remainder of the character to analyze its implications: "Is one that is fallen out with the world and will be revenged on himself." Then follows an effective alternation between the conceptual and the concrete: "His life is a perpetual satire, and he is still girding the ages vanity; when this very anger shews he too much esteems it. He is much displeased to see men merry and wonders what they can find to laugh at. He never draws his own lips higher than a smile and frowns wrinkle him before forty." The effect on the reader is a realization that a problem incapable of final solution has been presented and partially explored. Here Earle used the strategy of Donne's intellectually penetrating poetry.

The character of "An Antiquary" is a series of vivid pictorial images that serve to emphasize the irrational basis of his activities. The dominant trait of this man is an immoderate quest for anything ancient that will transport him into rapturous idolatry. The graphic description of the objects of the antiquary's search is Earle's method of showing their utter foolishness and uselessness: a broken statue, a ruined abbey, the rust of old monuments, shekels and Roman coins, the moth-eaten cover of an old manuscript. The character ends with the death of the antiquary, who "likes death the better because it gathers him to his fathers." The word "gathers," summing up as it does the unnatural avidity of the man himself, gives the character added ironic force.

In "A Drunkard," Earle shuns the obvious line of development for this subject--riotous description or anecdote. Instead, he treats it with dignified seriousness and develops it through generalized didactic comment. As in the character of the antiquary, the drunkard's irrationality is stressed. The last sentence gives the character an insight into the nature of the drunkard's weakness: "Indeed he dares not enter on a serious thought, or if he do, it is such melancholy that it sends him to be drunk again."

Earle's character of "A Younger Brother" could easily have fallen into the mould of a lifeless, didactic exercise on family relations. But the result is dramatic and pointed: "If his annuity stretch so far, he is sent to the University, and with great heart-burning takes upon him the Ministry, as a profession he is condemned to by his ill fortune. Others take a more crooked path yet, the King's highway, where at length their vizard is plucked off, and they strike fair for Tyburn. . . . His last refuge is the Low Countries, where rags and lice are no scandal, where he lives a poor gentleman of a company, and dies without a shirt." Earle constantly made shifts from the general to the particular as a means of creating variety and sustaining interest throughout the work. In effect, he united the essay and the character forms, which previously had been mixed indiscriminately or treated as mutually exclusive forms. The character of "A Young Man," for example, has an almost unvaried series of sentences beginning with the usual mark of the character, "He is. . . . He sees. . . . He pursues. . . . " Yet here the form enacts the regularity, discipline, and control reflected in the ordered flow of restrained counsel in the character. Earle modulated the tone and design of his characters to suit the demands of the subjects he selected with obvious care.

There are, of course, lapses of artistic intent in the Micro-cosmographie. When Earle tried to imitate the condescending tone and attitude of the Overburian characters toward lower class figures--the constable, tobacco-seller, cook, baker, and sergeant--his mind and art were clearly not engaged. There are also several examples of Earle's borrowing from other character-writers of subject matter and general approach. But whatever Earle used he changed alchemically to a brighter substance than he received. His is the only character book that shows such consistently purposeful design in its individual characters.

Literary historians, such as F. P. Wilson,[4] have said that the character form was taken up by the eighteenth-century

---

[4] Seventeenth-Century Prose (University of California, 1960), p.18.

periodical writers and then, after experiencing a sea change, passed on to greater things in the novel. First, this view submits, the extravagant wit of the character was brought into line with the rational, scientific temper of the Restoration. The "quaintness" had to be sacrificed to good taste and common sense. Yet, as with most generalizations about the character, this is not entirely accurate--particularly when applied to the <u>Micro-cosmographie</u>. There is little in Earle's work of the quibbling with words that discomfited the next generation of prose writers. The removal and later reinstatement of a remark in the <u>Micro-cosmographie</u> has been interpreted as a change in Earle's attitude toward the Senecan style: at first he criticized the self-conceited man for his choice of "Lipsius his hopping stile, before either Tully or Quintilian." Yet this act should be ascribed to an author's artistic integrity to his text or to an awareness of literary trends, rather than to a stylistic change of heart.

Earle's own style has a neoclassical balance and harmony more typically Augustan than should be thought likely in 1628. The texture of the satirical wit in the <u>Micro-cosmographie</u> is a very close approximation of the raillery of the age of Dryden, not the railing of early verse satire. Earle, for example, achieves some of his witty effects through the use of subtle juxtaposition of words that are not at all unusual in themselves--a device that Pope used to deadly advantage in his satirical verse characters: "He would make a bad martyr, and a good traveller. . . ." ("A Church-Papist"); He [his father] purchased the land, and his son the title" ("An

Upstart Country Knight"); "He makes very much of his authority, but more of his satin doublet" ("A Mere Alderman"). These unobtrusive antitheses are examples of what Earle was capable of achieving in satire. It is much different from the violent political invective of the not too distant future. And it is, unfortunately, a direction that Earle did not pursue further.

The permanent value in Earle's work can be grasped more readily by viewing it against the larger creation of a contemporary fellow Oxonian--Robert Burton. Burton took for his subject, of course, the entire psychological history of the human race. Earle intended his work to be only "a peece of the world discovered." Yet in both authors there is the same gentle, humane, and unsentimental approach to man's shortcomings; the same understanding of the importance of humor as an instrument of moral correction and ethical counsel. In the construction of their art they are at opposite aesthetic poles. But both had that tolerant, ironical, Lucianic temper of mind that can see the world as a combination of various shades and not as absolute colors.

VI. Brathwait and the Character Books of the Early 1630's

The years 1629-1635 are remarkable ones for any discussion of the character to consider. In this short span of years were published no fewer than six separate collections of characters. If the works of R. M., Lenton, Saltonstall, Lupton, and Brathwait, and the anonymous A Strange Metamorphosis of Man are not all equally valuable contributions to character literature, they form together a vivid example of experimentation and variety in a genre that appeared to have rather fixed and static qualities. Their joint efforts indicate a desire to submit everything--from animal life to all of England--to scrutiny by the character form. The results of their efforts were shortly after swallowed up by the controversies of the Revolution. Thus their works form the last genuine additions to the tradition begun by Hall, expanded by the Overburian writers, and mastered by John Earle.

R. M.'s Micrologia (1629) attempted to capitalize on Earle's title, but spoke mainly about the lower working class types--the shoemaker, smith and tinker. Presaging the work of Lupton, there are characters of Bedlam, Ludgate, Bridewell, and Newgate. There is an unflattering picture of an actor, as in John Stephens's book of 1615.

In 1631, Sir Francis Lenton, Henrietta Maria's "Queen's Poet," brought out his Characterismi: Or, Lentons Leasures, containing forty-one brief characters modelled along the lines of the Overburian collection. The work lacks, however, the sharp metaphoric bite of the earlier book; most of Lenton's characters are untouched by a distinctive style or approach. He had a lively eye for singling out typical qualities that were most interesting in a subject, but he lacked the wit to exploit their possibilities. Only rarely did he strike the right chord of humor to fit his subject, as in this passage from the character of "A young Schoolmaster": "Is a new Commenc'd Bachelour, who hath suckt so long at the paps of his Nurse (the University) that shee hath almost pin'd him: and therefore his fortunes denying him the degree of Master, in a resolution leaves his Nurse to rocke the Cradle her selfe, and boldly adventures into the broad world, (like a Lapwing with its shell o'th Crowne) with Lilly in's head, and Ramus in's hand, where in some small Village hee first exerciseth the Art of a Pedagogue, for instruction of infants."[1] Lenton's work suffers from an over-dependency on his predecessors, Overbury and Earle--who are mentioned by name in a commendatory poem prefacing the <u>Characterismi</u>. By assiduously copying their choice of subjects and stylistic approach, he sacrificed the individuality of technique that is the <u>sine qua non</u> of the successful character book.

In the same year as Lenton's work appeared Wye Saltonstall's <u>Picturae Loquentes</u>. Twelve more characters were added to the

---

[1] Sigs. Dl^v-2^r.

original twenty-six in a second edition of 1635. Saltonstall wisely eschewed the temptation to follow the well-marked paths of the earlier writers without making some excursions of his own. By substituting a distinct narrative tendency for the usual conceited approach, he created an amusing series of miniature sketches. His character of "A young Heire" takes the subject through his entire career-from his arrogant condescension toward his father's tenants, to his unmourned death after years of self-indulgence. The character of "A Countrey Bride" describes a rural wedding, ending with an invitation to the reader to think out the rest of the post-hymeneal activities for himself.

The character of "A True Lover" views its subject through the clouded lens of Caroline Platonic love: "Thus he lives like a man tost in Cupids blanket, and yet is so constant to his sufferings, that he could be content to be Loves martir, and dye in the flames of love. . . . "[2] Just as stylized in its approach is the character of "A mower," which provides a conventional background for Marvell's poems on the theme: "Is one that barbes the overgrowne fields, and cuts off the green lockes of the meddowes. Hee walkes like the Emblem of Tyme, with a Sith upon his backe, and when he cuts the grasse, hee shewes the brevity of mans life, which commeth forth like a flower, and is cut downe."[3]

[2] *Picturae Loquentes* (1631, 1635), ed. C. H. Wilkinson (Oxford, 1946), pp. 25-26.

[3] *Picturae Loquentes*, p. 72.

Two characteristics of his work were developed further by Lupton and Brathwait. Saltonstall's lively character of "The Tearme" attempted to render the activity of all London during the busiest time of the year--the court sessions. The taverns are painted, the coaches hurry to a new play at Blackfriars, and centers of gossip come alive: "It sends forth new bookes into the world, and replenishes <u>Pauls</u> walke with Fresh company, where <u>Quod novi?</u> is their first salutation, and the weekely newes their chief discourse."[4] This character was an addition of 1635, after Lupton's broad treatment of the London satiric scene.

Another aspect of Saltonstall's narrative manner is his ending a character with the subject's death. Begun by Earle, this tendency was given fuller treatment by Brathwait in his <u>Whimzies</u>. The deservedly unhappy end of the young heir has already been mentioned. A more sympathetic attitude is afforded the "Country Dame," whose plainness and simplicity are contrasted with the ostentation of the fine city dame. The country dame's death is a happy one: "Lastly, her life is nothing but a continuall stirring about businesse and huswifery, till shee be laid in her grave, and then shee rests from her labour."[5] Although Saltonstall never looked beneath the surface of his subjects, he rendered that surface with a filmy pastoral charm rarely achieved by the character-writers.

---

[4] <u>Picturae Loquentes</u>, p. 71.

[5] <u>Picturae Loquentes</u>, p. 62.

One of the most interesting of character books is Donald Lupton's <u>London and the Countrey Carbonadoed and Quartred into Severall Characters</u> of 1632. He attempted nothing less than a comprehensive treatment of all English society through its two great social and geographic divisions. In London, the author ranges all through the city, rendering its energy and movement, commenting upon its glories and shortcomings. As a travel guide or as an antiquarian mine it is less valuable than Stow; but as the response of a personality to his environment, <u>London and the Countrey</u> is a fascinating social document.

Lupton begins his account with an expression of London's teeming movement: "She is growne so Great, I am almost affraide to meddle with Her; She's certainely a great World, there are so many little worlds in Her: She is the great Bee-hive of Christendome, I am sure of <u>England</u>: Shee swarmes foure times in a yeare, with people of al Ages, Natures, Sexes, Callings: Decay of Trade, the Pestilence, and a long Vacation, are three scar-Crowes to her; Shee seemes to be a Glutton, for shee desires alwayes to bee Full. . . . "[6] Lupton frequently injects personal comment on religious and social matters of great importance. In the character "Of S. Paules Church" he expresses his concern for the church, which needed reparation--both physical and spiritual. He also has unkind words for the Puritans and for the "Company of Hungarians" who frequent the middle aisle.

[6] <u>London and the Countrey</u>. . . , sig. Bl^{r}-^{v}.

Other social institutions that draw his comment are Bedlam, Christ's Hospital, and the Charterhouse. Lupton sides with the enlightened thought of the day on preventing the rise of beggars and vagabonds, by approving the work done at Christ's Hospital. And he affirms the social benefits to be derived from giving relief to the "decaied Gentlemen, old Souldiers, and auncient Servingmen," the deserving poor of the land. Regarding Bedlam, he sees nothing but unfortunate misery in its inhabitants and doubts how anyone could regain his wits in such an atmosphere of frenzy.

Lupton continues the pattern of description and social commentary in the rural characters, where he touches upon some of the ranking social problems of the age--the injustices of landlords, the enclosures, and the venal apparitors. The latter subject was treated in the same year as Lupton's work by Brathwait--who also discussed the corantos, as does Lupton. London and the Countrey is a genuinely interesting work--for its insight into the important concerns of the time and for its sprightly pace and liveliness. And it aptly illustrates how easily the character could become a medium of social criticism--a function it was shortly to serve during the disruptions of the Revolution.

Richard Brathwait's Whimzies: Or, A New Cast of Characters, published in 1631, is the best of the character books that appeared between Earle's Micro-cosmographie in 1628 and the beginnings of the Revolution in 1642. And if it could somehow be dissociated from the bulky canon of Brathwait's works, it would be recognized as one of the best of all the character books of the century. Whimzies is one of the few of Brathwait's works that makes any attempt to live up to the promise of the title; for it is, despite the excesses of style and tone for which Brathwait is usually soundly clubbed, a whimsical work, free of the asperity that affects many of the characters written in the century. With the exception of the greater work of Earle, Brathwait's Whimzies alone makes such extended and effective use of humor as a characterizing technique.

Criticism has fallen rather harshly on the literary reputation of Richard Brathwait. The reasons are not hard to find. Brathwait directed his works to the growing ranks of the middle class, a dynamic group hungry for popularized information on practical morality, culture, and social behavior. Although himself a country gentleman by birth, and, having received a classical education at Oxford, a man of some learning, Brathwait keyed his intellectual talents to the vast number of Londoners aspiring to the status of gentry. From his first published work in 1611, a farrago of verse on classical and religious subjects called The Golden Fleece, to his last, The History of Moderation, a didactic allegory that appeared in 1669, Brathwait knew how to please his broad but not overly-discriminating public.[7] As a result, most of his more than fifty literary works are marred by careless workman-

---

[7] Matthew W. Black, Richard Brathwait, An Account of His Life and Works (Philadelphia, 1928).

ship and superficial expressions of moral sentiment. "It is a good market where all are pleased," Brathwait said of the Exchange and its patrons; he could have been referring also to the motive that underlies his prolific literary activity.

There were different sides to Brathwait's work; and just as John Donne's protean nature caused his work to be divided by others into two artificial and alien camps--that of Jack Donne, the London gallant, and that of Dr. Donne, Dean of St. Paul's--Brathwait's work has been more often criticized for its plodding morality and tedious didacticism than praised for its keenly descriptive powers and genial humor. Don Cameron Allen, anxious to prove the absence of Brathwait's pen in A Strange Metamorphosis of Man (1634)--a work that has been ascribed to the author--goes to great length to stress the qualities in Brathwait's work that sort ill with modern critical opinion: "Brathwaite belonged, I am afraid, to that hardy race of mortals that will always be with us. He mistook piety for religion, prejudice for wit, learning for wisdom, and Brathwaite for God. Like all men who believe that there is but one form of moral conduct, he was a little wanting in human understanding, too long on will, too short on heart."[8] One might add that even a John Milton was not always able to distinguish accurately between Professor Allen's categories. And if these comments are true regarding Brathwait's

---

[8] A Strange Metamorphosis of Man, Transformed into a Wildernesse, ed. Don Cameron Allen (Baltimore, 1949), p.xi.

<u>Essaies</u> <u>Upon</u> <u>the</u> <u>Five</u> <u>Senses</u>--a work Professor Allen cites as an example of Brathwait's ponderous insensitivity to worldly pleasures--they are not true when applied to the <u>Whimzies</u>. <u>Whimzies</u> belongs to that other side of Brathwait's nature, a side best represented by <u>Barnabees</u> <u>Journall</u>--a warmly discursive account of a bibulous journey from Kendal to London. This work of 1638, with its accompanying version in Latin rhymed verse, is born of Brathwait's love for the English countryside, expressed in his humorous catalogs of taverns and place-names. It is the only one of Brathwait's works that has been reprinted with any consistency, even if it is known for only one quotation. Yet the four lines are sufficient evidence for refuting Professor Allen's charges of moral obtuseness in Brathwait; and they reveal a talent for irony that can perfectly hit its mark:

>To <u>Banbery</u> came I, O prophane one!
>Where I saw a Puritane-one,
>Hanging of his Cat on Monday,
>For killing of a Mouse on Sonday.

Brathwait's moral sense, of course, is never separated from his less sober impulses. But even when he assumes his most grave and morally-outraged <u>persona</u>, he is fascinated by the potential for realistic, vivid narrative inherent in the situation:

>For all your pretious Morning-houres are given
>For you to paint and decke you till eleven;
>And then an houre or two must be the least
>To jeere your foolish Lover, or to feast,
>Or court your amorous cringing Favorite
>With a bare-bathed breast to feed delight,
>And purchase more Spectators:-but time's lost

> Till a Play-bill be sever'd from the Post
> T'informe you what's to play; then comes your Coach,
> Where numerous light-ones, like your selfe approach,
> But where's Devotion all this while? Asleepe. . . . [9]

Brathwait had a sense for the dramatic--surely not surprising in a man born in the year of the Armada, and a gentleman of means attuned to the literary fashions of the time.

Brathwait's approach to charactery is determined by this dramatic sense. If the genuine technique of the character requires the author to relate his subject's qualities rather than his actions, then Brathwait wrote no characters. Constantly Brathwait leaves his subject in order to render the satiric scene in which the subject moves and responds. The character of "An Exchange-man" shifts its discussion from the man to the finely-regaled customers who take their stroll down the long gallery of the Exchange. The reader's position shifts as well; he is no longer merely an observer, but a participant in the satiric action: "But were all that traffick with him as well-lin'd in pate as purse, wee should finde many emptie shoops before the next vacation. By this, a new troope of ruffling plum'd Myrmidons are arrived; and these will swoope up all before them; Not so much as a phantastic tyre, be it never so ougly, shall escape their encounter. Now out with your lures, baites, and lime-twiggs, my numble Didapper. Your harvest is not all the yeare. See how hee shruggs; and with

---

[9] Anniversaries upon his Panarete; Continued (1635), sig. A6. Quoted in Black, pp. 72-73.

what downeright reverence hee entertaines them!"[10] The next logical form that Brathwait's charactering technique could assume is simply dramatic action itself, letting the subject reveal himself through his own speech, as in the character of "A Gamester": ". . . casting his Cloake carelesly on his left shoulder, hee enters into some complementall discourse with one of his <u>ordinarie Gallants</u>. The argument of their learned conference is this; <u>Where shall we suppe, or how shall we trifle away this night? Where shall we meete tomorrow; or how bestow our selves?</u>"[11] There is no need to cite in proof a series of quotations from <u>Whimzies</u>; as often as not, Brathwait wants his readers to hear, as well as to see, his subjects. There is hardly any element for securing attention that he does not employ in his characters; in effect, "anything goes."

The characters take as their concern only the lower types of society. The approach that Brathwait takes is only befitting the demands of decorum. He includes, therefore, material from the coney-catching pamphlets, the jestbooks, proverbs, and street vendors. He does not hesitate to move from description to direct exhortation, as in the character of "A Hospitall-man." The only stylistic and formal rule is to include whatever will be most effective. The characters have what Father Ong calls "rhapsodic structure," the tendency to stitch together in episodic fashion a variety of

---

[10] <u>Whimzies</u>, p.164. Page references are to the text of this edition.

[11] <u>Whimzies</u>, pp.171-172.

stylistic elements.[12] This has already been mentioned with regard to the Overburian characters, but it is a much more noticeable element in Brathwait's extended, seemingly formless characters. Brathwait uses the character form as a convenient mould in which to pour anything that will secure an immediate emotive effect. Appropriately, all his characters conclude with the death of the subject, whose end is often ironically tied to the ignoble means by which he lived. The result is a unity of effect, rather than of form.

The various characters are linked to each other in a more significant way than their order in the alphabet. Almost every one of the subjects is characterized by his grinding poverty. This does, one must admit, take a slight edge off the whimsical intent of the work. But Brathwait, as he portrays his subjects scratching out a meager level of subsistence, catches them in odd poses and stresses their idiosyncratic features. The result can be both moving and humorous as in the character of "A Hospitall-man," a genial, compassionate picture of a man spending his last years in venial self-indulgence. More often, Brathwait renders the economic outsiders of society--the almanac-maker, ballad-maker, coranto-coiner, painter, peddler, piper, and alchemist--with an uncritical acceptance of their position in the social structure. Their poverty is life-long, and at their end nothing is left to pass on to family or friends.

[12] Walter J. Ong, S. J., "Oral Residue in Tudor Prose Style," PMLA, LXXX (1965), 150.

In the midst of these unfortunates stands the sturdy figure of the country-house keeper, a remnant of the old spirit of hospitality--a spirit that will die with the death of its last true adherent. The keeper holds fast to those anti-acquisitive principles of medieval Christianity that were threatened with extinction, according to L. C. Knights, with the rise of capitalist competition and expansionist economy.[13] Brathwait asserts the older values of the country gentry, shunning the idea of the profit motive: "He preserves that relique of Gentry, the honour of hospitality, and will rather fall, than it should faile. He revives the Black Jack, puts beefe in his pot, makes poore passengers pray for him, his friends to love him, his foes to prayse him. Hee wonders how any one should bee so voyde of pitty as to leave his smoaklesse house in the Countrey, where he has his meanes, to riot in the Citie, and estrange himselfe to his friends."[14]

Brathwait's characters deal with the surface world of Jacobean and Caroline society, the crowded, rank environment of Jonson's and Middleton's London comedies. It is Brathwait's ability to render this theatrum mundi with pungently realistic detail that makes his Whimzies still quite worth reading. Like Thomas Dekker, Brathwait was a keen observer of surface detail, on intimate terms with those subjects who make up his cast of characters. Despite his sometimes exhaustive wordiness, his unconcern for form, his frequent changes of tone ranging

[13] Drama and Society in the Age of Jonson (London, 1937).

[14] Whimzies, pp. 182-183.

from the whimsical to the hortatory, he succeeded in his
purpose--to portray his subjects in a pleasant, amiable
fashion. "Many Characters," said Brathwait in his dedicatory
epistle to Sir Alexander Radcliffe, ". . . have been published
both in former times, when the ignorance of the age could
scarcely render the ambiguitie of the word: as likewise in
these more refined times of ours, wherein, as in habit and
attyre, so in discourses of this nature, nothing but rarities
(bee they never so light) can afford delight. But to give them
their true and native Character, they relished more of Aphorisme
than Character. For to suite them with their approvedst and
retentivest title, what else are Characters but stampes or
impressures, noting such an especiall place, person, or
office. . . ."[15] He goes on to state that the character
should avoid dullness throughout and bitterness at the end.

Brathwait is also conscious of the character style of his
predecessors. His own style--discursive, rambling, often
maddeningly punning, and tending toward the descriptive--is
usually free of the excesses he finds in the works of others:
"Strong lines have beene in request; but they grew disrelishing,
because they smelled too much of the Lampe and opinionate
singularitie. Clinchings likewise were held nimble flashes;
but affectation spoyl'd all, and discovered their levitie."[16]
And if the reader should think Brathwait's characters too long,
he misunderstands the author's intent: "Characters in this age,

---

[15] Whimzies, sig. A5^{r-v}.

[16] Whimzies, sig. A6^{r}.

may be properly resembled to Squibbs or Crackers; they give a Cracke and a Flash, and so dye. . . . Or to raw and ill-drest meat, which procures in the longing appetite a loathing; being to be egested long before it come to bee digested. . . . But here be fruits . . . of firmer setting, deeper rooting and longer promising."[17]

Brathwait's view of the character, then, was not that of Hall or Overbury. As the author of essays and courtesy books--The English Gentleman (1630) and The English Gentlewoman (1631) were probably Brathwait's best-known works--he had a natural tendency to dilate his material, expatiating at will upon his subject. But one of the most attractive qualities of the character is its plasticity, as it yields to the style and temperament of the individual author to create a distinctive work. Brathwait remade the briefer character into a pageant of memorable scenes: the almanac-maker on his back, staring up into the summer sky; the ballad-monger displaying his wares on Holborn Hill; the ruffian and his troop forcing their way into the theater; and the tavern painter trudging with his paints on his back looking for a commission. The nineteenth century relished Brathwait for his racy style and quaint preservation of lost traditions.

[17] Whimzies, sig. A9^{r-v}.

There is still room to value him as a highly interesting--and entertaining--figure in the history of the character genre.[18]

The last noteworthy development of the character in the early 1630's is the unusually observant Strange Metamorphosis of Man of 1634. Don Cameron Allen aptly compared its delicate yet vigorous approach to Breton's Fantasticks of 1626. Professor Allen's description of the anonymous author's method needs no amplification: "He has . . . a central philosophy; for whereas the Renaissance had been given to seeing nature in man and to searching for the macrocosm in the wilderness of the body, this man saw man in nature and surveyed the creatures for those particular qualities that made them singularly human."[19] Only through the quoted passage can his method be really shown: "The Mustard-seed Seemes to be a thing of nothing. It is even the dwarfe among the rest of seeds; and yet is a Giant if you deale with him. Hee is very snappish, for if you meddle with him, he will strait take you by the nose. He is full of his jests, which are so quicke and sharpe, as you will not know how

---

[18] Although Whimzies is Brathwait's best work in the character form, there is also a later effort, The Captive Captain (1665), discussed briefly in Black, pp.96-98. In addition to a few other characters inserted into various works, he also wrote a roman à clef on the Commonwealth period that employed elements of the character. See Benjamin Boyce, "History and Fiction in Panthalia: Or the Royal Romance," Journal of English and Germanic Philology, LVII (1958), 477-491.

[19] A Strange Metamorphosis of Man, Transformed into a Wildernesse (Baltimore, 1949), p.xvii.

to relish them, for they bite shrewdly."[20] How strangely anachronistic this work appeared only eight years later will readily be seen. The Puritan that the ardent Royalist Brathwait humorously conceived after some borrowing from Jonson's <u>Bartholomew Fair</u>, would then himselfe be cast in animal form--but in the much less flattering guise of a destructive locust.

[20] <u>A Strange Metamorphosis of Man</u>, p. 22.

VII. The Character of Argument

The character in the manner of Overbury and his successors must be forgotten. The sensitive, often profound, understanding of Earle; the amiable discursiveness of Brathwait; and the sprightly ingenuousness of *A Strange Metamorphosis of Man*—these are some of the most prominent features on the map of charactery as it has thus far been traced. As guides to the confused topography of the Interregnum character, they offer little assistance. The character of argument, fashioned from the current ideological materials of English society, can be recognized by its jagged, often treacherous paths that seem to have no definite direction or end; by contrast, the rather well-traveled roads of the older character offer little difficulty, for the trip is generally a short one and the destination is always clearly in view. With the traditional character there was little danger of tedium and loss of breath, but there was also little opportunity for further exploration and novelty.

The events that precipitated the character of argument were, of course, those that profoundly affected the course of English history. With the final and complete polarization of attitudes that had long been at odds, the character was utilized as a vigorous polemical weapon. It took its place among the other types of pamphlets that were loosed from the press after the abolishing of Star Chamber censorship in 1641. The greater part of these argumentative or pamphlet characters are ephemeral--by nature of the events that occasioned them and in their literary quality. They have, of course, historical interest, being valuable barometers to the political and religious feelings of the time. Less recognized as a reason for discussing the pamphlet character is the intrinsic literary interest that several of them possess.

Artistic unity, however, is a formal principle that it is inappropriate to demand of these works. They are perhaps best viewed in light of one possible Renaissance definition of satire--as a <u>satura</u> or medley of stylistic ingredients held together by the rhetorical energy of the author. In order to enforce a point upon the reader the author often resorted to purposeful misrepresentation of the opposing view. The verbal form that this misrepresentation assumed was often invective; but for this to be successful it was necessary to contain it within a stylistic mould. The most interesting of the pamphlet characters recognized this need; and the result was surprisingly effective satire.

Engaged in a powerful struggle for control of the nation, it is to be expected that the conflicting forces would resort to a strident tone of argument. First Roundhead against Cavalier, then Presbyter against the sects--these were the oppositions that called forth characters during the period. Most of the characters were written by the Royalist side. This is the natural reaction of a group who feels its privileges and beliefs--its very existence--threatened by another group whom it believes to be socially inferior. Several characters, usually written by the rising religious groups, are the expressions of their own beliefs or platforms; these characters are generally plain expositions, relying upon strength of principles, not wit. During these offensive and defensive engagements the form of the character practiced by Earle and Brathwait was usually quickly discarded as an unwelcome restraining force. Long, rambling analytical descriptions of groups, individuals, and places still received the name "character." The works discussed here attempted, for the most part, to describe--and to vilify--the stereotyped characteristics of some group.

When the anti-Puritan characters appeared, there already existed an established tradition for satiric representation of Puritan characteristics.[1] In pamphlet and broadside, in poetry, prose, and the drama, the Puritans were attacked for their radical political beliefs, their supposed hypocrisy, and their alleged sexual promiscuity. As a literary form well-suited to express prejudices and preferences, the character became a rather effective weapon of denigration. Printed in 1640 as part of <u>A Dialogue, Wherein Is Plainly Layd Open the Tyrannicall Dealing of Lord Bishops Against Gods Children</u> is a brief verse character that managed to attach itself to the reprinting of a Martin Marprelate polemic. In 1643 it appeared

---

[1] See William P. Holden, <u>Anti-Puritan Satire 1572-1642</u> (New Haven, 1954). Characters are briefly discussed on pp. 76-79.

under the title of <u>The Character of A Puritan; And His Gallimaufrey of the Antichristian Clergie</u>. The character, then, was viewed as another means through which a controversy originating in 1588 and 1589 could be maintained. The stereotype of the Puritan remains unchanged in this version of him:

> Long hath it vext our learned age to scan,
>   who rightly might be termed a <u>puritan</u>.
> A puritan both layic and divine.
>   I will according to my skill define.
> A puritan, is he, that when he prays,
>   his rowling eyes up to the heavens doth raise.
> A puritan, is he, that cannot fare,
>   to deck his round head with a bonnet square.
> Whose Turkey robe, in his fair furred train
>   above his ankle, turneth up again:
> That at his belt a boss-clad Bible bears,
>   stampt with the true Geneva characters;
> Whose thin beat volume scorneth to admit,
>   the bastard monuments of humane writ.
> Whose hair, and ruffs, dare not his ears exceed:
>   that on high saints days wears his working weed. . . .[2]

The character entered the Puritan controversey almost from its first appearance as a distinct literary genre. Hall did not write a character of a Puritan, but his "Character of the Hypocrite" has several of the necessary vices often ascribed to the Puritan, and the character "Of the Inconstant" mentions the "giddy Anabaptists." In 1609 the Puritan is mentioned by name in W. M.'s <u>The Man in the Moone, Telling Strange Fortunes, Or The English Fortune Teller</u>, which, though not primarily a character book, has recognizable characters interspersed in the

---

[2] Printed in <u>Complaint and Reform in England 1436-1714</u>, ed. William H. Dunham, Jr. and Stanley Pargellis (New York, 1938), pp. 597-599.

frame of a dialogue.³

The Overburian collection has several characters with the biting tone of the later attacks of the 1640's. There is the character of "A Puritane": "Is a diseas'd peece of Apocripha, bind him to the Bible and he corrupts the whole text; Ignorance, and fat feede, are his founders, his Nurses, Raylings, Rabbies, and round breeches; his life is but a borrowed blast of winde; for between two religions, as betweene two doores hee is ever whisling." Included in the collection are also characters of "A Precisian" and "A Button-Maker of Amsterdam."

In Thomas Scott's The Interpreter (1622) the Puritan is among the three "principal Terms of State"--the others being the Protestant and Papist--that the author unfolds in rhymed verse characters. Here, however, the Puritan clearly comes out the best of the three:

>   A Puritan is such another thing
>   As says, with all his heart, "GOD save the King
>   And all his issue!" and to make this good,
>   Will freely spend his money and his blood. . . .
>   . . . .
>   A Puritan is he, that rather had
>   Spend all, to help the States (he is so mad!),
>   Than spend one hundred thousand pounds a year
>   To guard the Spanish coasts from pirates' fear. . . .
>   . . . .
>   A Puritan is he that would not live
>   Upon the sins of other men; nor give
>   Money for Office in the Church or State,
>   Though 'twere a Bishopric. . . .
>   . . . .
>   A Puritan is he, that, twice a day,
>   Doth, at the least, to GOD devoutly pray,
>   And twice a Sabbath, he goes to church. . . .
>   . . . .

---

³ Ed. James O. Halliwell (London, 1849).

> A Puritan is he, that speaks his mind
> In Parliament: not looking once behind
> To others' danger; nor yet sideways leaning
> To promised honour, his direct true meaning.
> . . . .
> His Character abridged, if you would have,
> HE'S ONE, THAT WOULD A SUBJECT BE, NO SLAVE![4]

Other allusions to Puritans are in Mynshul, Earle, Lenton, Lupton, and Brathwait. Brathwait's character of "A Zealous Brother" is much indebted to the figure of Zeal-of-the-Land Busy in Jonson's *Bartholomew Fair* (1614); Jonson's Rabbi, however, is more a symbol of all hypocritical excesses than a particular attack on Puritans. In the 'forties the ability to transcend one's own firmly-held tenets was decidedly limited; and there was hardly the presence of an artist of Jonson's stature working in the character form.

The anti-Puritan characters are never very far from being war reports dispatched by a slanted correspondent at the front lines. The author of *The Anatomy of the Separatists* (1642)-- John Taylor, according to the Thomason Catalogue, but this piece lacks the friskiness of the Water Poet's other works-- completes his description of these "Egyptian Locusts" with a factual account of an incident in a church, where certain "rude rascals" disturbed the service by crying "A Pope, a Pope, a Pope" at the preacher. In another piece attributed to Taylor--and this has Taylor's liveliness--the author reports an incident in a style that combines propaganda with ironic humor:

---

[4] Attributed to Scott by Gwendolen Murphy in *A Bibliography of English Character-Books 1608-1700* (Oxford, 1925). The text is printed in *Stuart Tracts 1603-1693*, ed. C. H. Firth (London, 1903), pp. 233-247.

> And yet are there amongst this holy assembly (as they tearme themselves) as many severall opinions as men, which will easily be made manifest by their last Congregation in the Malt-house of one Fob a Brewer, the number being about sevenscore, there had every one a Religion by himselfe, and every one a nigher way to Heaven than the other, each shewed his opinion, which to relate it would be too tedious, but their ambitious zeale was so hot, that in snuffe each left the other, but not long after the Reverend Box-maker elevated as high as little St. Bartholomewes Pulpit, where he threw more stones against the Bishops and the booke of Common Prayer, then little Boyes use to doe Snow-balls in the time of Winter.[5]

The borderline here between fact and fiction is indistinguishable amidst the tumbling rhetoric of the narrative.

A number of the argumentative characters retained the descriptive pattern and wit--if not the brevity--of the older character. Hogs Character of a Projector, Being a Relation of his Life and Death, with his Funerall (1642), a reprint of Thomas Heywood's "A Projector in General," from his Machiavel of 1641, focused its attack on the new breed of economic opportunists:

> Hee is one that hath always more money in his mouth then in his purse, and feeds as heartily upon his ayery hopes as the Newes-mongers in Pauls, upon Duke Humphreys Cates. . . . He is made all of complements, as if he dropt out of the Dock of a Courtier, and can change himself into as many shapes as Proteus can doe colours, either a decayed Merchant, a broken Citizen, a silent Minister, an old maymed Captain, a fore-judg'd Attourney, a busie Solicitor, a crop-ear'd Informer, a Pick-thank Pettifogger, or a nimble pated Northern Tyke, . . . these are the only men that make your bravest Projectors, who in short time may be dignified with title of Knight of the Post or Canker Generall of the Common-wealth.

In The True Character of an Untrue Bishop (1641), the author arraigns the Bishop in thirty-eight paragraphs that usually

---

[5] Lucifers Lacky, Or, The Devils new Creature (1641), sig. A3^r.

follow the character pattern, as does this ironic, punning commentary: "Hee is learned in almost all arts and sciences: Hee is an excellent judiciall Astrologer; for wheras Picus Mirandula, Julius Caesar, Cornelius a Lapide, cum multis aliis, deny any certaine knowledge of our condition, by the influence of celestiall bodies, hee saith boldly and truly, Let him bee but under the gracious aspect of Charles his Waine, and hee is confident all will doe well."

The character pattern is barely retained in Tyrants and Protectors (1654). It consists of short paragraphs in the character manner followed by lengthy Biblical citation. The character of the Protector ends in the conventional metaphoric peroration: "He is the poor mans Patron, the widows Husband, the Orphans Father, the good mans pleasure, the bad mans terrour, affable in speech, facile in access, amiable in countenance, respecting no mans person, but every mans cause, thereby he becomes the desire of all." Few of its fifty-two pages utilize the character to any purpose; and wit is not appropriate for its panegyrical exegesis of the Protector.

Many of the pamphlet characters echo Biblical words and phrases, and it is not unusual, therefore, to have a character that bases its description upon Biblical analogy. A Short, Compendious, And True Description Of the Round-Heads . . . (1642) traces the origin of the noble Roundheads to the last day of creation and, therefore, "going before that of the locust shag-polls, being of more antiquity." The "shag-poll locusts" originated in the smoky pit, were made of dust by the devil, and in numbers "they darken the light of the Sun with their multitudes, as did the Flyes of Egypt." Within such a strict genealogical pattern, there can naturally be little room for the wit that might temper this apocalyptic invective.

Biblical wrath was not the property of one faction. In *Independency Stript and Whipt* (1648), an Independent is viewed as "an incarnate *Devil*, spawn'd by *a broaken rib of Adam*, a holy Sister in the height of *zeale*, his *Syre* is (of an ancient family, and hath large dominions) *Don Lucifer the Prince of darknesse*, the first *Independent* that ever was." The Bible was not the only authority that could call forth the stock response. On a more restrained note the author of *A Puritane Set forth In his Lively Colours: or K. James his description of a Puritan* (1642)—attributed by Halkett and Laing to the ubiquitous John Taylor—invoked the image of James I, "the **King** of Prophets in these later times, and a Propheticall King. For he wisely fore-seeing with the Promethean eye of judgement, what miserable consequents, and dangerous effects, would ensue and happen unto this Kingdome, if these turbulent spirits should get a head, or come into any place of authority." The reader is referred to the second book of James's *Basilikon Doron*, "that Kingly gift."

Not all the argumentative characters wore such mournful garb. The demolishing of opposing views could also be achieved through the knowing grin, called forth by the skillful use of irony. Two of the most successful characters were *Saint Hillaries teares* (1642) and *The Reformado, Precisely Charactered by a Transformed Churchwarden, at a Vestry* (1643). *Saint*

<u>Hillaries teares</u> is both a character of London and of the narrator. The purpose of the author is to show the utter desolation of London during a term when the law courts are in session and the streets would ordinarily be teeming with litigious citizens. Rather than thunder out his condemnation in the expected manner, the author lets his narrator roam through the streets and make pertinent comment on what he sees. The result is a subtle piece of ironic satire.

The character begins with the opening questions of the <u>persona</u>: "What? Middsomer?" As he proceeds from Westminster Hall to the Chancery, then to the Court of Requests and Court of Wards, he notices that there is absolutely no activity. He then continues on his way:

> And you are no sooner out of the Hall-yard but entring into Kings streete, you finde the Cookes leaning against the Dore-postes, ruminating upon those Halcion Termes, when whole herds of Clerks, Solicitors and their Clyents, had wont to come with their sharpe-set noses, and stomacke, from the Hall, and devoure the Puddings, and minc't Pyes by dozins, as swiftly as a kennel of Hounds would worry up a dead Horse.

Everything is so idle that the proud London ladies cannot even get pomatum or fucus for their faces. The pedestrian continues:

> Well from you, I must follow the steps of many an old Letcherous Citizen, and walke into <u>London</u>, where at the <u>Exchange</u>, the onely question that is ask't is what <u>newes?</u> not from <u>Aleppo</u>, <u>Constantinople</u> the <u>Straits</u>, or <u>Indies</u>, but from <u>York</u>, <u>Ireland</u>, and <u>the Parliament</u>. . . .
> From hence I travell to Guild-Hall, where I finde the Lawyers complaining of infinite numbers of Bankerouts, men so far decayed in estate, that they will compound to pay more than halfe, confesse judgments, render their bodies to prison, prostitute their wives, or any thing rather than stand out the prosecution of a suit at Law.

The persona has something of the naïf about him—as
Maynard Mack classified the satiric persona who observes but
yet does not seem to fathom the significance of everything
about him.[6] But the ironic import of the scene is quite
clear to the reader, who sees through the eyes of the persona
and comprehends the reason for the deathly idleness. The tone
of the narrator becomes harsher:

> It is not pitty to see them (poor soules) who
> had wont to shine like so many constellations in
> the Firmament of the suburbs, and be hurried in
> Coaches to the Tavernes, and Sparagus Gardens, where
> ten or twenty pounds suppers were but trifles with
> them, should now goe to the Chandlers, and herb-wives
> in slip-shooes, for Cheese and Onions to dinner?
> Well content your selves, (you attractive
> Load-stones, of delicious and smooth damnation) And
> doubtlesse the Arch-angell my successor, will bring
> your angells to redeeme all, And your Champions
> and Davaliers, will returne with their pockets doubly
> furnisht, for you are as sure of them as they are
> of your diseases.

He concludes the character with a description of the "Masterpiece
or Idea of dissimulation which nature made her example to
portraicture a Rogue by, the Round-head. . . . " The tone is
even harsher, taking the form of a curse: "May his wife be
catch't in the spirituall act of her next carnall copulation."
The peroration is one that promises hope, for when the Roundhead
is finally harrowed, "S. Hillary will make a Holiday, and in
stead of his Teares will send you himnes and madrigalls for joy
of the Roundheads confusion, and your more full enjoyment."
The result is a rather morally puzzling but effective piece of
satire.

[6] See "The Muse of Satire," Yale Review, XLI (1951-52), 80-92.

The <u>Reformado</u> has a simpler frame, resembling the parodies of Puritan sermons. The Reformado addresses his congregation and describes his method: "First, that I will follow the present <u>Fashion</u> so far in my <u>Discourse</u>, as to keep no <u>Order</u>." He then proceeds to reform every part of the church, including the prayer books and preacher himself. The Reformado reveals himself, through the rhetorical thrust of the monologue, as a truly mad reformer: "Away with it, this <u>Font is abhominable</u>. . . . And these lofty <u>Pewes</u> which are higher by the <u>head</u> and <u>shoulders</u>, than their <u>Inferiours</u>, shal be <u>circumsised</u>, that our grave Matrons, and <u>sweet</u> <u>heavenly</u> <u>minded</u> <u>sisters</u>, (whose <u>posture</u>, turning their faces <u>westward</u>, is most <u>amiable</u>) may have a more cheerfull <u>influence</u> upon us their <u>Governours</u>." The parenthesis gives an immediacy to his vivid--if not trustworthy--discourse. Both <u>Saint Hillaries teares</u> and <u>The Reformado</u> severely strained the limits of the character. They deserve, however, a different fate from that obscurity which so quickly overtakes the vast bulk of occasional pieces--particularly pamphlets.

All of the pamphlet characters described above belong to the shadow world of hasty journalism. Their authors are unknown; their role and importance in the development of later satire difficult to determine. One name manages to stand out from the huge bulk of satiric writings produced during the period of the Civil Wars--that of John Cleveland. A large part of his work was concerned with the daily shift in political events and the personalities that took part in them. Eleanor Withington aptly described the course of Cleveland's work: "Cleveland's satire flowered in a bramble bush of anonymous political broadsides, pamphlets, mercuries, and counterfeit mercuries; when plucked for a keepsake, it was left to dry in those grab-bag omnium gatherums of interregnum wit which flourished under his name after 1647."[7]

Although Cleveland was so thoroughly engaged in political controversy of a transient nature, his work has the impress of a powerful satirical intelligence. The three characters reliably attributed to him--Character of a London Diurnall (1645), Character of a Country Committee-Man (1649), and Character of a Diurnal-Maker (1654)--are not simply chips from his satiric workshop. They are of a piece with his most biting political verse satires--"The Mixed Assembly" and "The Rebel Scot."

Cleveland's political poetry is more often considered for its influence on later verse satirists than for its innate value and uniqueness. It was an important formative element in Dryden's poetry, passing on to him a supple heroic couplet that could easily range from the burlesque to the ferocious. Cleveland also contributed to Oldham and Butler an accomplished burlesque style that could manipulate meter, rhyme, accent, and diction for brilliantly satirical purposes.[8] As Harry Levin said, "His poems, or--in other words--his collected conceits,

[7] "The Canon of John Cleveland's Poetry," Bulletin of the New York Public Library, LXVII (May, 1963), 307.

[8] John L. Kimmey, "John Cleveland and the Satiric Couplet in the Restoration," Philological Quarterly, XXXVII (1958), 410-423.

constitute a complete anatomy of wit. . . ."[9]

Cleveland's work reflects the crisis of language that occurred during the period of the Civil Wars and the Protectorate. The political struggles evoked harsh invective that seemed to strengthen one's opponents rather than destroy them. There arose the need for a more subtly devastating stylistic instrument, one that could penetrate the satiric object but leave the satirist morally unblemished. Kimmey sees "a mixture of the old discords and new harmonies" in Cleveland's poetry. Certainly his satiric theory reverts to that of an earlier period--the scourging roughness of Marston, for example. Of course, Cleveland would justify his method by citing the horrors of the age:

> Come, keen iambics, with your badger's feet
> And badger-like bite till your teeth do meet.
> Help, ye tart satirists, to imp my rage
> With all the scorpions that should whip this age.
> ("The Rebel Scot")

A poem in the Lansdowne MS., which contains poems attributed to Cleveland, gives a vibrant and concise description of Cleveland's method:

> Satyres run best when Clashing tearms do meet,
> And Indignation makes them knock their feet.
> To bee methodical in Verse & rhime
> In sutch invertives is the highest crime.
> Who Ever saw a firy passion breake
> But in abruptness? Thus my pen must speak
> Make at Each word a period, which may show
> As Cornes of pouder, & then fire the row
> With sharp artic'late blasts, which breathing on
> Those lines, may 'nflame each hot expression.[10]

---

[9] "John Cleveland and the Conceit," *Criterion*, XIV (1934), 50.

[10] From "On the Pouder Plot." The whole poem is quoted in Eleanor Withington's "The Canon of John Cleveland's Poetry," Part II, *Bulletin of the New York Public Library*, LXVII (June, 1963), 385-367. In the above quotation modern "th" has been substituted for "y" and "u" for "v."

Thomas Fuller described Cleveland's "epithets" as "pregnant with metaphors, carrying in them a difficult plainness, difficult at the hearing, plain at the considering thereof."[11] Fuller's and, possibly, Cleveland's own assessments of the critical basis of the poetry, also apply to the three prose characters.

The Character of a London Diurnall (1645) is the first of Cleveland's important prose satires. It begins in the usual manner of the character with a definition of the subject: "A Diurnal is a puny Chronicle, scarce Pin-feathered with the wings of Time. It is a History in Sippets: The English Iliads in a Nutshel: The Apocryphal Parliament's Book of Maccabees in single sheets."[12] Next follows a discussion of the diurnal's contents. The news sheet begins with an Ordinance, then a recitation of current plots, followed by the adventures of the Roundheads. Exhausting these ingredients, the diurnal turns to a panegyric of Cromwell. The character then falls into a general condemnation of Cromwell and other Roundheads.

The general formula, then, is a simple one, not differing to any great extent from many of the other Royalist pieces. What distinguishes Cleveland's work is the tremendous impression of disorder and irrationality he manages to produce within the

---

[11] The History of the Worthies of England, ed. P. A. Nuttall (London, 1840), II, 240.

[12] Clievelandi Vindiciae (1677), p.108. All quotations from Cleveland's characters are from this edition.

simple framework of the character. There is a constant transformation of images--of "Clashing tearms"--that pushes the reader nervously towards the close. The personages who make fleeting appearances in this surreàlistic drama reflect the lack of reason in their actions and follow a path--sometimes whimsically, sometimes grotesquely--of their own creation: "The Countess of Zealand was brought to bed of an Almanack, as many Children as days in the year. It may be the Legislative Lady is of that Linage, so she spawns the Diurnals. . . . The Country-carrier, when he buyes it for the Vicar, miscals it the Urinal; yet properly enough, for it casts the Water of the State ever since it staled Blood" (pp.108-109). There is also "the old sexton, who swore his clock went true, whatever the sun said to the contrary." Cleveland invokes the archetypal example of the man possessed by unreason: "Thus the Quixots of this Age fight with the Windmils of their own heads, quell monsters of their own Creation, make Plots, and then discover them; as who fitter to unkennel the Fox than the Tarrier that is part of him?" (p. 112)

When at last Cromwell is called onto the scene, he represents the fulfillment of the heightened misrepresentation of Roundhead exploits. Cleveland's attack on him is an attempt to strip him of the spurious glory attributed to him by the diurnals: "This Cromwel is never so valorous as when he is making Speeches for the Association; which nevertheless he doth somewhat ominously with his Neck awry, holding up his ear as if he expected Mahomet's Pigeon to come and prompt him. . . . What we wonder at in the rest of them is natural to him, to kill without Bloodshed; for the most of his Trophies are in a Church window, when a Looking-glass would shew him more Superstition" (p.115). In this context the attack on Cromwell is part of Cleveland's larger vilification of all those irrational forces that result in the destruction of man's noblest creations: "Believe him as he whistles to his Cambridge-Teem of Committeemen, and he doth wonders. But holy Men, like the holy Language, must be read backwards. They rifle Colleges to promote learning, and pull down churches for Edification" (p.116). The lesser sins of the diurnal can be treated with a humorous distortion, but Cromwell is an embodiment of the evils besetting the entire state and must be purged from the body politic. The tone and imagery of the character are adjusted to fit the crime.

Another viewer, Ruth Nevo, sees the philippic on Cromwell as part of the larger problem of Interregnum satiric attitude:

> The desire to express contempt in burlesque or farcical images clashes with the need to present the enemy in terms larger than life. Instead of comic exaggeration, . . . Cleveland verges towards the exaggeration of invective which raises the object to heroic proportions, though of a monstrous, not virtuous, kind. Thus the defacer of the image of God in his own countenance sorts ill with the orator holding up his ear to catch the prompting of Mahomet's pigeon. . . . The dual impulse towards ridicule and invective is one not brought into focus or unified easily.[13]

Miss Nevo cites Cleveland's character as an example of the difficulty which Interregnum and Restoration satire faced when it attempted to treat heroic subject matter with stylistic techniques inherited from an age oriented toward the low style of satiric treatment.

---

[13] *The Dial of Virtue: A Study of Poems on Affairs of State in the 17th Century* (Princeton, 1963), p.55.

Certainly there is a bizarre jostling of rhetorical effects in Cleveland's character. To explain this one might justifiably look to the author himself--Reader in Rhetoric at Cambridge and staunch Royalist. Faced with a series of revolutionary movements he did not understand, Cleveland reacted in the instinctive manner of his social class: he tried to deny the significance of the "new men" and their ideas. Burlesque ridicule is the natural stylistic course for the author's contempt: "The victories of the rebels are like the magical combat of Apuleius, who thinking he had slain three of his enemies, found them at last but a triumvirate of bladders. Such, and so empty are the triumphs of a diurnal, but so many bladders of their own blowing."

In spite of the contemptuous shrugging-off of his inferiors that motivated Cleveland to write his attack, the author rarely lapsed into the kind of approach that deemed "Egyptian Locusts" an adequate label for the Roundheads--and an array of similar epithets the ideal rhetorical method for confounding one's enemies. Cleveland's talent for ironic statement is most obvious in his poetry; but in the character it is employed with similar force. As the object of the author's ridicule, the diurnal's journalistic methods elicited some of the most incisive examples of "Clevelandified" wit: "Thus they kill a man over and over, as Hopkins and Sternhold murder the Psalms with another of the same; one chimes all in, and then the other strikes up as the Saints-bell. . . . Thus these Artificers of death can kill the Man without wounding the Body, like Lightning, that melts the Sword and never singes the Scabeard"(pp.113-114). And when discussing Cromwell: "Time's Voyder, Subsizer to the Worms, in whom Death, who formerly devoured our Ancestors, now chews the cud" (pp.115-116). Cleveland takes a parting shot at the Quaker, George Fox: "And now I speak of reformation, Vous Avez, Fox the Tinker, the liveliest Emblem of it that may be: for what did this Parliament ever go about to reform, but, Tinkerwise, in mending one hole they made Three?" (p.119) The burlesque quality of the meiosis and the falling rhythm of the sentence brings each statement perilously close to shattering into a ridiculous effect; but Cleveland had the satiric skill to prevent this. To his rhetorical ability can be added the emotional detachment that one often notices in Cleveland's work, even in the midst of his obviously partisan philippics.

The Character of a Country Committee-Man (1649) is an attack on the county committees, which took control of the confiscated estates of the Royalists. Royalists who could produce enough capital were allowed to "compound" their estates, that is "buy them back for a fine, assessed in relation to the degree of their delinquency, at anything from a half to a tenth of the capitalised value."[14] As a character it is not very successful, perhaps because the subject is hated too much for it to be treated with any degree of satiric indirection. Cleveland finds the name of the committee a fruitful source for invective: "A Committee-man by his Name

---

[14] Christopher Hill, The Century of Revolution 1603-1714 (London, 1961), p.146.

should be one that is possessed, there is number enough in it to make an Epithet for <u>Legion</u>. He is <u>Persona in concreto</u> (to borrow the Solecism of a Modern Statesman). You may translate it by the <u>Red-Bull</u> Phrase, and speak as properly. Enter seven Devils <u>solus</u>. It is a well-truss'd Title that contains both the Number and the Beast; for a Committee-man is a Noun of Multitude, he must be spell'd with Figures, like Antichrist wrapp'd in a Pair-Royal of Sixes. Thus the Name is as monstrous as the Man, a complex notion, of the same Lineage with Accumulative Treason" (p.93). Here is the same rush of similitudes as in the character of the diurnal, but also a diffuseness that subtracts from the satiric intent. The committee-man was too much of an economic threat to be treated in burlesque tones. The end of the character expresses real anguish: "A Committee-man is the Counterpoint, his Mischief is Superfetation, a certain Scale of Destruction; for he ruines the Father, beggars the Son, and strangles the hopes of all Posterity" (p.101).

    Cleveland's last character, <u>The Character of a Diurnal-Maker</u> (1654), marks a turning away from the harsh social realities of the preceding characters to an absurd fantasy world of irrationality and diminishing size. The normal order of the sensible world is transmogrified into a distorted lump of images. There are images of size: "He is swallowed up in the phrase, like Sir S. L. [Samuel Luke] in a great Saddle, nothing to be seen, but the Giddy Feather in his Crown. They call him a <u>Mercury</u>, but he becomes the Epithet, like the little Negro mounted upon an Elephant, just such another Blot Rampant" (pp. 101-102); and images of disorder: "To call him an Historian is to knight a Mandrake: 'tis to view him through a Perspective, and by that gross Hyperbole to give the Reputation of an Engineer to a Maker of Mouse-traps" (p. 102). The diurnal maker is placed in grotesque positions: "They tug at the Pen like slaves at the Oar, a whole Bank together; they write in the Posture that the Suedes gave fire in, over one another's heads" (p. 105). Cleveland created his own vision of Dullness, but according to his own predisposition toward the grotesquely hyperbolic. He failed, however, to give for his absurdity a consistent, moral alternative. The reader is left with the dazzling procession of verbal antics, but with no understanding of their deeper significance.

Another prose character was attributed to Cleveland in J. Cleaveland Revived (1660), an edition of Cleveland's poems to which works of other poets were added without canonical authority. At the end of this volume appears "Mid-sommer Moon: Or, Lunacy Rampant, Being an University Character, and a short Survey of some of the late Fellowes of the Colledges." It also appeared by itself in 1648 with the information Being a Character of Master Cheynell as part of the title. Francis Cheynell, Parliamentary visitor to Oxford, was, as might be expected, vehemently disliked by the Royalists. The author of "Midsummer," most probably Thomas Winyard,[15] obviously followed

---

[15] See Eleanor Withington, "The Canon of John Cleveland's Poetry," Part I, 322-323, for a discussion of the evidence for ascribing this character to Winyard.

in the Cleveland vein of grotesque attack. The character begins in a breathless rush:

> Is Bedlam seven Stories high, or Sir. T. T. his gouty Leg Wire-drawer? his head is shut up, as if he would onely converse with the Prince o' th' air, and what we mistake for the Man i' th' Moon, is but a piece of him. Hee's an Index Expurgatorius in the largest Folio, or was intended for Hoops for the Tun at Hiedelberg: you may take him for the 119 Psalm, lashing the Execution of a whole University, or the Pinacle from which the Devil would break the neck of it.[16]

Following this is a series of strained images of birth resembling Cleveland's Character of a London Diurnall. The actual criticism of University practices does not begin until about three quarters of the character has been spent in references to classical heroes, the trades of alchemy and textiles, and ballad material.

Despite the derivative Clevelandisms, the character has an ironic bitterness that places it in the tradition of the great railers of the earlier period--Marston's Kinsader, Webster's Bosola, and Shakespeare's Thersites: "Why should the Muscovite worship painted images, and reject carved ones? why should my Lady expose her childe, and nurse her dog? be divorced from her Lord, and wanton with her Catamite Monkey? But alas, a slip may break a sober mans neck, whiles drunkards tumble and have no hurt." The work continues in this exposition of the ways of the world: "Thus of Theophrastus Characters, the vices onely survive, the vertues are expelled the world. . . .

---

[16] J. Cleaveland Revived (1660), p.183.

Colledges are converted into Hospitals, Lodges for Diseases, scab'd heads and crutches, 'tis the onely expulsive Crime here, to be wholesom. . . . O that Lice should be humane offspring as well as men! but the happiest Mothers may have abortions. The Kings Image is sometimes stampt on Lead, and Natures Mint coynes Monsters. As this Ostracism proves the University a true Athens, so some Apostates make her a Heaven." Finally, the character gets to specific criticisms of the new occupants of the University: they know neither Latin nor Hebrew, and "Mothes and Worms are acquainted with more Authors. . . . " Winyard had a talent for strong invective as did his intended model, Cleveland.

The Cleveland manner was appealing to other authors as well. John Birkenhead, a minor Royalist author and acquaintance of Samuel Butler, wrote The Assembly-man, a bitter personal attack on Parliament, written in 1647 but not published until 1662. He was most effective when he assumed the character manner and directed his abuse at the Assembly-man's stereotyped qualities:

> The Assembler's only ingenuity is, that he prays for an extempore spirit, since his conscience tells him, he has no learning. His prayer thus ended; he then looks round, to observe the sex of his congregation, and, accordingly, turns the Apostle's men, fathers, and brethren, into "dear brethren and sisters." . . . He divides his text, as he did the kingdom, makes one part fight against another. . . . Yet sometimes, to shew his skill in Keckerman, he butchers a text, cuts it (just as the Levite did his concubine) into many dead parts, breaking the sense and words all to pieces; and then they are not divided, but shattered, like the splinters of Don Quixote's lance.[17]

---

[17] Harleian Miscellany, ed. William Oldys and Thomas Park, V (London, 1810), 102.

The restraining influence of the character form had a mild effect on Birkenhead, who reminded himself at the conclusion that "a character should be brief."

The Royalists did not have exclusive rights to the Cleveland style of attack. <u>The Character of an Oxford Incendiary</u>--dated 1645 in Thomason's Catalogue--begins as a character with a vituperative metaphor: "An Oxford Incendiary is a court-salamander, whose proper element is fire: an Englishman, yet lives by antiperistasis to his native climate; and turns our Northern Temperate into the Torrid Zone."[18] After a short discussion of the incendiary's lineage and birth, the character becomes a procession of all the hated court figures; the repulsive pageant offers a convenient method for singling out the major victims of abuse: "As the prologue before the play, enter Canterbury, the pigmy-champion, the meritorious traitor, the Cathoic demi-culvering, the reverend granado; who lived to set all on fire, yet escaped the martyrdom of hanging, to be quenched upon a scaffold; whereas the other kind of death had been more suitable to his life, having always been a pendant in the ear of majesty." This attack on Laud gives way to similar sallies on court notables such as Heylin and Jermyn, even including Henrietta Maria, whom "the Irish rebels call their generalissima." The scenic form was also used by another anti-Royalist polemic, <u>The Lively Character of the Malignant Partie</u> (1642). More aware of political forces than the <u>Oxford Incendiary</u>, it passed for review the

---

[18] <u>Harleian Miscellany</u>, V (1810), 498.

dominant Royalist groups--Papists, Prelates, corrupt members of the nobility and gentry, "Evill Counsellors, with corrupted Judges and ambitious Lawyers," and the "Hotspurres of the times, who are call'd the Cavaliers."

Although the character form presented a neat container for both Puritan and Royalist corrosives, it was utilized--but rarely--for more nobly-motivated purposes. Probably the best known Puritan character was John Geree's The Character of an old English Puritane, Or Non-Conformist (1646), being reprinted several times during the century.[19] Its idealized description prohibited the rhetorical excesses of the argumentative character: "He accounted preaching as necessary now as in the Primitive Church: Gods pleasure being still by the foolishnesse of preaching to save those that beleeve. He esteemed that preaching best wherein was most of God, least of man, when vaine flourishes of wit, and words were declined, and the demonstration of Gods Spirit and power studyed: yet could hee distinguish between studied plainnesse and negligent rudenesse."[20] The character itself reflects this studied plainnesse in its brief exposition of Puritan simplicity and discipline.

A longer, yet still plain, exposition of religious principles is John Cook's What the Independents Would Have (1647). Cook--

---

[19] Chester N. Greenough's indispensable Bibliography of the Theophrastan Character (Cambridge, Massachusetts, 1947) lists other reprintings in 1649, 1659, 1660, 1670, 1672, and 1673.

[20] The character is reprinted in the Appendix of Benjamin Boyce's The Polemic Character 1640-1661, pp. 128-133. The passage cited above is on p. 129.

the attorney for the prosecution during King Charles's trial--
believed in reasoned discourse: the character reflects this in
its plain language and in its stress on the Independents'
rationality and tolerance: "A solid Reason will at any time
convince him, and hee loves to read discourses which are
rationall. . . ."[21] Rational discourse, however, is anti-
pathetic to the metaphoric wit that is the character's life
force.

Another pamphlet character, The Leveller (1659), used
the character pattern to express its political program. The
character form largely recedes, however, as the political
treatise advances: "First, they assert it as fundamental that
the government of England ought to be by laws, and not by
men. . . ."[22] For members of the New Model Army the character of wit could have little significance.

The Royalist could also express his beliefs without
rancor--but on very rare occasions. Sir Francis Wortley wrote
a character of "A true English Protestant" in his Characters
and Elegies (1646). It exercises restraint in its praise of
the traditional hierarchy, in contrast to the fervid prophetic
tone of "Britannicus his Pedigree," another character in the
same collection, that traces the Puritan to the tribe of
treacherous Saul.[23] In Dudley, Lord North's A Forest of

---

[21] This character is also reprinted in Boyce, pp.134-147; the passage quoted above is on p.147.

[22] Reprinted in Complaint and Reform in England 1436-1714. The quotation is on pp.680-681.

[23] Quoted in A Book of "Characters," ed. Richard Aldington (London, 1924), p.371.

Varieties (1645), a character of "A King" is more a wistful reminder of James I than a didactic character written along the lines of Fuller's Holy and Profane State of 1642. North's king "must esteem his happiness and safety to depend on the love of his people, and, therefore, like a good shepherd he will chiefly be pleased in procuring their contentment and welfare."[24] North's and Worley's characters are anachronisms, appearing in a decade when the traditional type of character could no longer flourish. Thomas Ford, another Royalist who wrote a collection of characters--The Times Anatomiz'd in 1647--described the new medium of analysis in his character of "Pamphlets": "They are the silent traitors that affront majesty, and abuse all authority, under the colour of an imprimatur. Ubiquitary flies that have of late so blistered the ears of all men, that they cannot endure the solid truth. The echoes, whereby, what is done in part of the kingdom, is heard all over. They are like the mushrooms, sprung up in a night, and dead in a day; and such is the greediness of men's natures (in these Athenian days) of new, that they will rather feign than want it."[25] For Ford and the other Royalists, the echoes of the pamphlets were soon replaced by the louder and harsher echoes of 1649.

[24] A Book of "Characters," p.370.

[25] A Book of "Characters," p.373.

VIII. The Last Phase

Writing in 1668, David Lloyd said that the result of Cleveland's work was "on the one side to draw out all good inclinations to vertue; and . . . on the other, to shame the ill from Vice. . . ."[1] Such were the intentions of all the character-writers throughout the century. In the 'forties and 'fifties the vehemence with which one held his parti pris determined the style and direction of the pamphlet character. Lloyd, writing--as he stated in the title of his work--to commemorate "those noble, reverend, and excellent personages that suffered by death, sequestration, decimation or otherwise, for the Protestant religion . . . ," praised Cleveland for his "blows that shaked triumphing Rebellion, reaching the soul of those not to be reached by Law or Power, striking each Traitor to a paleness beyond that of any Loyal Corps that bled by them; the Poet killing at as much distance, as some Philosophers heat-scars lasting as time; indelible as guilt-stabs beyond death. . . ."[2] Lloyd singled out Cleveland's Character of a London Diurnall and Character of a Country Committee-man as examples of these soul-reaching blows.

[1] Memoires of the Lives, Actions, Sufferings and Deaths . . . , p. 618.

[2] Ibid.

The characters of the Restoration did not call forth such passionate praise; they ceased to be an important polemical force in the latter part of the century, yielding to the influence of periodical journalism and the heroic mode of satire. A spate of characters appeared in the years 1679-1683 with the panic that accompanied the Popish Plot. But it was the heightened ironic verse of Dryden in which the reader evinced an interest, not the dull, leaden prose of third-rate authors.

Another reason for the diminishing importance of the character is the growing interest during the century in the individual *qua* individual. In France, this tendency reached its apotheosis in the formalized portraits of Louis XIV; in England, the interest in biography changed from a preoccupation with impersonal, typical narrative[3] to the idiosyncratic treatment of the eighteenth century. As England became more and more a secularized society, the importance of typicality decreased. The subjects of the character were subsumed under the newer mediums of the periodical essay and the novel.

Significantly, the largest body of characters produced during the Restoration by one author came from Samuel Butler. Why this popular writer kept his work from publication during his lifetime is a difficult question to answer. Butler was a passionate conservative. He saw, perhaps, that the Restoration temper was inimical to the establishment of typical,

---

[3] Donald A. Stauffer, *English Biography Before 1700* (Cambridge, Massachusetts, 1930), p.283.

ethical modes. His silent condemnation seems almost obscurantist in intention. The character--basically a Royalist genre--cannot flourish amidst Hobbesian individualism, which, although used to strengthen sovereignty, denied the existence of fixed, ideal types by denying the validity of traditional right reason and its belief in natural law. Butler's work was anachronistic, being written in a period when men were beginning to be characterized by their party affiliation, not their membership in a group of good men, covetous men, or proud men.

A perceptive remark by Ricardo Quintana on Butler's intellectual outlook is also helpful in explaining the reason for the demise of the character: "Had he not witnessed two living burlesques--the Commonwealth and what had succeeded to it? What had the Commonwealth been but a romance, with the Saints joyfully assuming the duties of Knights Errant? And if recent poets were to be believed, what was the Restoration period but an epic?"[4] If in the earlier period the major preoccupation of the author of pamphlet characters was either attacking or defending the romance of Puritan beliefs, in the Restoration the author was concerned with the epic treatment of character--implicit in the drama and heroic couplet, but not in the character sketch. The sharp differentiation between the heroic and low styles in the period was the death blow for the character, which had always tended toward a humorous treatment of lowly types. The prose character could no longer be of

---

[4]"Samuel Butler: A Restoration Figure in a Modern Light," ELH, XVIII (1951), 28.

interest to a major author. When John Oldham attempted to write one in 1678, the result was a strange--though interesting-- literary distortion. The Marquis of Halifax's Character of a Trimmer (1688) is an expression of a pragmatic political philosophy given a certain degree of impersonality through the employment of the character form. But his fellow politician, William Temple, following in the tradition of Montaigne, was writing in the more viable form of the personal essay.

One development of the character in the 'fifties should be noted--the character of nations. Owen Felltham's A brief Character of the Low-Countries under the States (1652) was the first, perhaps in a pirated briefer version in 1648.[5] Felltham divided his subject into a treatment of its vices and virtues, giving each division a sane, balanced discussion that makes for an often moving and entertaining work. Felltham assumes the role of genial traveler, noticing small details and reflecting on their significance:

> Where the Women lyes in, the Ringle of the door does penance, and is lapped about with linnen, either to shew you that loud knocking may wake the child; Or else that for a moneth the Ring is not to be run at. But if the child be dead there is thrust out a Nosegay tyed to a sticks end; Perhaps for an emblem of the life of man, which may wither as soon as born; or else to let you know, that though these fade, upon their gathering, yet from the same stock the next year a new shoot may spring.[6]

---

[5] The CBEL lists an edition of 1648, Three Months Observation of the Low Countries, Especially Holland. Quotations here are from the British Museum copy of 1652.

[6] Felltham, pp. 53-54.

For wit, there is a short discussion of comparative imbibing of the Englishman and Dutchman. The latter "drinks as if he were short winded; and as it were eates his drink by morsels, rather besieging his brains then assaulting them. But the English man charges home on the sudden, swallowes it whole, and like a hasty tide, fills, and flowes himself, till the mad brain swims, and tosses on the hasty fume."[7] Felltham was also a shrewd political analyst, recognizing the reason for Dutch strength and influence: "There is none have the like intelligence; Their Merchants are at this day the greatest of the Universe. What Nation is it where they have not insinuated? Nay, which they have not almost anatomized, and even discovered the very intrinsick veins on't?"[8] Felltham's work opened an attractive field to other writers: John Evelyn wrote A Character of England in 1659; and this was followed by characters of France (1659), Italy (1660), and Spain (1660), written anonymously. Evelyn's character, written in the form of a letter by a French traveler, gives the author the opportunity to make invidious comparisons of England to France. With shocked wonder the persona of the bonus vir comments on the deplorable activities that occur in St. Paul's, the canting of the Presbyterians, the coarse conversation of the alehouses, and--as one might expect from the author of Fumifugium--comment on the "pestilent smoke, which corrodes the very iron and spoils

[7] Felltham, p.59.

[8] Felltham, p.71.

all the moveables; leaving a soot upon all that it lights, and so fatally seizing on the lungs of the inhabitants, that the cough and consumption spare no man."[9]

The years 1660 and 1661 offer an interesting cross-section of the types of characters that were written in the preceding years and in the remaining years of the century. In the year of the Restoration were published several characters against the ubiquitous sectaries, ranging from the very brief Character of a Phanatique to the fifty-two page indictment of many sects in A Briefe Description Or Character of the Religion and Manners of the Phanatiques In Generall. The Character of a Presbyter begins in a lively manner, but, as with many pamphlet characters, promises more than it delivers: "I will first present him in Grosse, and then give you him in his Anatomy: but I am afraid he will stink before I have read through every part of him. Let us unkennel the Fox, and we shall find him no better than a Crab-louse crept out of Luthers Codpiece when he unbutton'd to Katharin Bora. . . ." The Character of the Parliament Commonly Called the Rump discussed actual members of the Rump Parliament without naming them--including a biting reference to Milton, the Secretary for Foreign Tongues. The probable author of the character, John Tatham, also wrote a play called The Rump in 1660.[10] The next year Marchamont Nedham filled in a section of his True Character of a Rigid

---

[9] Harleian Miscellany, X (1812), 193.

[10] See Alfred Harbage, Cavalier Drama (New York, 1936), pp. 185-186.

Presbyter with unacknowledged lines from the Overburian character of "A Puritan"; and another author, possibly John Denham, wrote a verse character, The True Presbyterian without Disguise, beginning "A Presbyter is such a Monstrous thing / That loves Democracy, and hates a King."

For the reader surfeited with a diet of polemical characters there were other diversions. In addition to the characters of countries mentioned above, there was Clement Ellis's The Gentile Sinner, Or, England's Brave Gentleman, designed to fashion a gentleman along true Christian lines. In order to achieve his noble aim he decked out his work with characters of the gallant, seen in various activities; and with various kinds of gentlemen, culminating in an analysis of the true gentleman. Ellis's purpose was much the same as Fuller's earlier manual of 1642: ". . . Whilest I goe about to give you the Character of a true Gentleman, I am faln into that of a Christian; and indeed no wonder, for there is such a necessary Connexion betwixt these two, that they seem to be no more then the Different Names of the same man."[11] Undoubtedly many viewed Ellis's work as an irenic, in light of the earlier pamphlet characters.

One of the last character books appeared in 1661, a zany combination of the traditional character form and pamphlet appropriately named Confused Characters of Conceited Coxcombs. What these twenty-three breathless pieces lack in subtlety they more than match in energy and sheer scurrility. The

---

[11] Page 178. The quotation is from the third edition of 1664.

character of "A Pune Pragmatick Pulpit-filler" says nothing new, but seems to re-create rhetorically the fountain of nonsense it is attacking:

> And me thinks these John Lacklatines creep into benefices, like foxes into henrousts, only to fill their empty guts (starved as much for want of food, as their poetical faculties devoid of all philosophick irradiations, and as their perecranium dark and gloomy, dismall and obscure, for want of the gilding and glistering rayes of the sun of good eruditon). . . . T'would grieve your heart to hear what work these sand rope makers make with an easy and facile text, into what far fetcht notions they dissolve it, and how miserably they are forced to wander from their businesse, to patch up their piece of stuff to the length of the houre glasse. And yet this apothegmaticall licosthenes will bring you up whole legions of examples, and quote you those authors he never saw, much lesse read: and his Greek and Latine spouts from his originall jaws as water from a cesterne redundant with that element.[12]

A more forward-looking work appeared in 1660. Richard Flecknoe, always eager to make literary capital out of current social trends, shrewdly combined the character with the new portrait, which he was anxious to establish as his own import: "The Portrait has this advantage of the Character, that it gives you the Bodies resemblance together with the disposition of the Mind; and the Writer of the Painter, that he both paints the Minde, and Body too. This manner of writing is altogether in fashion in France, and I should be glad to bring it into England."[13]

---

[12] Ed. James O. Halliwell (London, 1860), pp. 83-84. Two obviously typographical errors have been emended in the quotation.

[13] Heroick Portraits, The Preface. Quoted in Gwendolen Murphy, A Cabinet of Characters, p.vii. For a discussion of the portrait character, see Boyce, The Polemic Character, pp. 46-61; and D. Nichol Smith, ed. Characters from the Histories and Memoirs of the Seventeenth Century (Oxford, 1918), pp. xxiv-xxviii.

In spite of the coexistence of these several kinds of characters, the character as a literary form was indeed moribund. A brief discussion of the main drift of the form in the remaining decades of the century should suffice, for most of the minor pieces are hardly worth more than bare enumeration. In the 'seventies and 'eighties there was a slight spark of interest in the types of low comedy. Characters of a town gallant, town miss, quack astrologer, quack doctor, and an ugly woman appeared. Poor Robin's True Character of a Scold (1675) conveniently lifted most of its witty narrative from Brathwait's character of "A Xantippean."

The Character of a Coffee-House, with the Symptoms of a Town-Wit (1673) has some amusing details about this new social institution, frequented by the libertine Restoration gallant, whose conversational equipment includes "an odd metaphor, a conceited irony, a ridiculous simile, a wild fetch, an unexpected inference, a mimick gesture," and who "holds his gospel from the apostle of Malmsbury; though it is more than probable, he never read, at least understood, ten leaves of that unlucky author. . . . "[14] This unfavorable report of the coffee-house was inevitably countered by another pamphlet, Coffee-Houses Vindicated (1675).

The years surrounding the Popish threat produced a number of characters expressing the hopes and fears of that anxious period. There was little sympathy for the Jesuit, charactered in the Character of a Turbulent Pragmatical Jesuit (1678) as

[14] Harleian Miscellany, VI (1810), 468.

"the <u>Bell-weather</u> of the <u>Roman</u> Shepherds Flock; a most trusty Janizary to the Triple-Crown." <u>The Character of a Rebellion</u> (1681) is more a warning about the disorder that would result if the sectaries gained power than a genuine character. There are also characters of a Tory, a modern Whig, a true Protestant, a sham plotter, and a disbanded courtier in this period which produced great verse satire, but mediocre characters.

John Oldham's <u>Character of a certain Ugly Old P-----</u> (1684) is a peculiar combination of scatology and hyperbolic distortion quite out of keeping with the new polite raillery of the age. Adding to its interest is the author's emulation of Rabelais, to whose work the character "contains allusions both open and veiled. . . ."[15] More surprising is the possibility that Oldham's besieged subject may be his own father.[16] The character, however, is not merely purposeless rant. It is written along theoretical lines: "To draw a <u>Thersites</u>, or <u>Aesop</u> well, requires the <u>Pencil</u> of <u>Vandyke</u> or <u>Titian</u>, more than the best <u>Features</u> and <u>Lineaments</u>. All the Thoughts I can frame of him are as rude and indigested as himself. The very <u>Idea</u> and <u>Conception</u> of him are enough to Cramp <u>Grammar</u>, to disturb <u>Sense</u>, and confound Syntax. . . . I

---

[15] Huntington Brown, <u>Rabelais in English Literature</u> (Cambridge, Massachusetts, 1933), p.142. Oldham's character is printed in Appendix D, pp.223-228. Quotations are from this reprinting.

[16] According to Robert Bell, in his edition of Oldham's poems (London, 1854), p.7. Cited by Anna J. DeArmond, "Some Aspects of Character-Writing in the Period of the Restoration," <u>Delaware Notes</u>, Sixteenth Series (1943), 70.

could call him <u>Nature's</u> <u>Bye-Blow</u>, <u>Miscarriage</u> and <u>Abortive</u>, or say, he is her <u>Embryo</u> slink'd before Maturity; but that is stale and flat, and I must flye a higher Pitch to reach his <u>Deformity</u>."[17] Oldham's description really has no relation to his feelings about the subject; the whole piece is almost entirely experimental--and excremental--name-calling, a one-way flyting, or a stylistic exercise in decorum. The conventionality of Augustan personal attack has only recently been recognized. Oldham strives for the exact grotesque, equivalent image to fit his satiric object: "His damn'd squeezing <u>Close-stool-Face</u> can be liken'd to nothing better than the <u>Buttocks</u> of an old wrinkled <u>Baboon</u>, straining upon an <u>Hillock</u>."[18] Subsequent description covers most other prominent physical features. Only rarely does Oldham give an actual view of the man as a real person in a real environment: "When I came first to his <u>Church</u> and saw him perch'd on high against a <u>Pillar</u>, I took him by his gaping for some <u>Juggler</u> going to swallow <u>Bibles</u> and <u>Hour-Glasses</u>. But I was soon convinc'd that other <u>Feats</u> were to be play'd, and on a sudden lost all my <u>Senses</u> in <u>Noise</u>."[19]

Richard Head, author of <u>The English Rogue</u> (1665), combined the popular psychological manual, the essay, the character, and

[17] Brown, p. 223.
[18] Brown, p. 224.
[19] Brown, p. 228.

narrative in his later book, Proteus Redivivus: or the Art of
Wheedling, or Insinuation (1675). He used extended quotations
from Earle, building his characters around those from the
Micro-cosmographie. Head had a sharp eye, however, and many
of his lengthy descriptions reveal the popular novelist's ability
to exploit his subjects.

The two most prolific writers of characters in the
Restoration—indeed in the century—are Richard Flecknoe and
Samuel Butler. Butler is a major author of the period; Flecknoe,
a major clown. In light of Dryden's treatment of him, it is
difficult to discuss Flecknoe seriously. Yet he deserves
consideration on several counts: his Short Treatise of the
English Stage, published in 1664 as a preface to his play
Love's Kingdom, has been described as "the first truly historical
view of English drama"[20]; his Idea of His Highness Oliver (1659)
is an early example of the epic style that reached its artistic
peak in—ironically—Dryden's MacFlecknoe and Absalom and
Achitophel[21]; and his Heroick Portraits (1660) marks him as
an early conveyor of French court culture into England.

Flecknoe's characters do not represent any new trends in
the genre; but they are probably the last ones to offer
genuine attempts at humor. He was an assiduous writer of

[20] Alfred Harbage, Cavalier Drama, p. 47, note 45.

[21] Ruth Nevo, The Dial of Virtue, pp. 93-95. Flecknoe's
literary career is thoroughly discussed in Paul H. Doney,
"The Life and Works of Richard Flecknoe," unpublished Harvard
dissertation, 1928. Doney's discussion of Flecknoe's characters consists mainly of classification under subject headings
and of extended quotation. He largely ignores the more interesting
aspects of Flecknoe's literary ideas, and his strictures on
Flecknoe's "vulgarity" are often arbitrary and irrelevant.

characters, many of which appear in his three different collections in revised versions, some characters telescoped into others. His idea of the character changed during his career, becoming briefer and more concise in phrasing--closer, in fact, to the character of the Overburian collection, except for the general leveling of metaphoric wit that occurred in the intervening years.

Flecknoe's first characters appeared in 1653 in Miscellania; but there are only four here, two of which were reprinted in other collections. The first of his real character books is Enigmaticall Characters, All Taken to the Life, from severall Persons, Humours, and Dispositions, appearing in 1658, and containing sixty-nine characters. Regarding Flecknoe's choice of subjects, there is nothing to occasion any surprise; he repeats to a large extent the approach of the character-writers of the earlier part of the century. Several characters describe an ethical type, such as the suspicious person, the valiant man, a proud one, and a wicked person. Other characters, as one might expect, deal with occupations; there are characters of a chambermaid, physician, nobleman's chaplain, Dutch waggoner, and a governess. And as a reminder that Flecknoe was a lay priest, there are characters of a Fifth-Monarchyman and a Jansenist.

The great majority of the characters are descriptions of types that abound in court society. Decorousness is praised and deviation from rational standards of proper social behavior is condemned. Flecknoe is utterly incapable of expressing the moral truths of humanistic tradition. He owes his allegiance, not to the traditionally expansive interests of the older character, but to the restricted, court-dominated concerns of French culture. Flecknoe is the sedulous ape of court fashion; his criticisms arise from the inability of the individual to conform successfully to accepted patterns of conversation and comportment. He illustrates quite accurately the observation of Douglas Bush on the change that overtook the character in the century: "The essay and the character alike embodied ideals of rational, civilized behaviour and culture. These ideals were a traditional and international inheritance, yet in England they continued to be nourished by a vigorous and heterogeneous individualism. In contemporary France the same ideals and the same literary forms suffered from the dominance of a standardized and overcivilized minority."[22]

The critical basis of Flecknoe's characters is found in his character "Of Raillerie." Ruth Nevo's comment--although concerned with Flecknoe's "Scarronesque" poem _Diarium_ . . . (1657)--is pertinent here. She points out that Flecknoe "is one of the earliest, if not the first, to notice, however sketchily, the nature and origin of the raillery of his time. And he uses, significantly the two terms which were to become crucial in the debate--Railing vs. Raillery--which accompanied the emergence of the new satire during the remainder of the century and well on into the following era."[23] Flecknoe carried

---

[22] _English Literature in the Earlier Seventeenth Century 1600-1660_ (Oxford, 1962), p. 219.

[23] _The Dial of Virtue_, p. 203.

this interest into his character book of 1658. "There is as much difference, " he begins, "betwixt <u>Raillerie</u> and <u>Satyrs</u>, <u>Jesting</u> and <u>Jeering</u>, etc. as betwixt <u>gallantry</u> and <u>clownishnesse</u>; or betwixt a <u>gentle Accost</u> and <u>rude Assault</u>." The author's satiric stance, then, signifies his position in polite society. To succumb to the "<u>rude Assault</u>" is to jeopardize one's standing among courtly circles. Flecknoe defines <u>raillery</u> more specifically: "It being a gentle exercise of wit and witty harmlesse <u>calumny</u>, speaks ill of you by contraries; and the reverse or tother side of complement, as far beneath as that above reality. There's nothing in it of abusive, and only as much in it of handsome invective and reproach as may well be owned without a blush. . . ." Flecknoe firmly bases his theory of raillery upon climatic differences. The inhabitants of northern countries are naturally subject to choler. They are not, therefore, particularly amenable to raillery as a means of social criticism. For raillery, one must look elsewhere: "In fine, tis a plant grows more naturally in your <u>Southern</u> Regions, and seldome farther North than <u>Paris</u> yet: Whence whilest the <u>French</u> would have transplanted it with their others fashions into <u>England</u>, like those who first brought in <u>Tobacco</u>, they had but the Curses of the common People for their pains. . . ."

No wonder that Flecknoe's wit is often so tepid and uninviting in his characters. His satiric theory prevents him from donning "hair-cloth" and "home spun-stuff." Thus his characters are drawn with the purpose in mind that even the most reprehensible social type is to be treated gently, lightly spiced with the "poignant sauce of wit." Even the fanatic Fifth-Monarchy man is let off easily, a far cry from the treatment reserved for such an irrational subject in the pamphlet characters. He is no longer in league with the devil; he is simply unmannerly, for "he so hates a <u>Gentleman</u>, as he can't endure <u>God</u> should be served like one." His error is simply a matter of poor breeding. If he were fitted out with the proper conversational garments, he would undoubtedly be well on the road to spiritual recovery.

Flecknoe's penchant for the character form continued for many years. There were fifteen characters in his <u>Heroick Portraits</u> of 1660. Twenty-two new characters were added in <u>Rich. Flecknoe's Aenigmatical Characters. Being Rather a new Work, then new Impression of the old</u> in 1665. Contrary to the claim in the title, 56 of the 78 characters are revised versions--in varying degree--of characters published in 1653, 1660, and 1658--which supplied 46 of them.

The next addition to Flecknoe's cabinet of characters was in 1666. This work, <u>A Farrago Of several Pieces</u>, adds six more, three of which were reprinted in the 1673 collection. In the 1673 work, entitled <u>A Collection Of the choicest Epigrams and Characters</u>, eighteen more were given.

Flecknoe was very frugal with his literary materials. He liked to refurbish his older characters with additional comments and print them in subsequent editions. His character "On a Dutch Frow" appears in three editions--1660, 1665, and 1673.

"Of a Dull Countrey Gentleman," a character in the collection of 1665, combines material from two characters in the book of 1658--"Of a Dull-fellow" and "Of a hom-bred Country-Gentleman." Many other characters are hybrids, containing some new matter mixed with old. Many characters are pastiches made up of opening lines from an older character, new material added to fill in the middle, and concluding thoughts from the older character.

Flecknoe particularly favored his opening thoughts. The 1673 character "Of an Honest Man" begins: "He is that Verus Israelita, or true Israelite, in whom there is no deceit; and you may as safely take his word, as an others Bond. He says as he thinks, and does as he says, and means well and honestly in every thing."[24] The remainder of the character shows how the true honest man is willing to suffer for his principles, even if others think him a fool. There is no indication from the lines just quoted that they were used in 1665--with some inversion of order and interposition of other words--to characterize "a good honest Catholick." The religious character has really no doctrinal bias that needed to be pruned before being printed as a secular piece. This is not an unusual precaution for a Catholic living in England, but it shows how Flecknoe easily manipulated his materials to suit his public. Flecknoe commented briefly on his literary husbandry in the Postscript to his collection of 1673:

[24] A Collection . . . , sig. H4^r.

> The Idea which I have framed of these Characters, is to spin them out into as fine a Thred as I can, and then weave them into a handsome stuff. . . . Did I not hope to mend them in another Impression, I should be ashamd to let them pass in this. I pass then my Thoughts thorough finer and finer Sieves of first Writing, then Printing, and lastly Reprinting them before I have done with them; and after all, to think to clear them of all their faults, were to think to sweep an Earthen Floor to the last Grain of Dust.[25]

If this appears to be slightly pretentious, it must be said in Flecknoe's favor that his later characters are indeed better than his earlier ones—those printed before 1665. The characters of 1665 and 1673 are much briefer, generally, and more pointed in their emphasis, bearing out his stated purpose in the character "Of these Characters" in 1673: ". . . I study more to contract, than to dilate; and like that Giant with his Iron Bed, cut off all that are too long, without Racking out those that are too short for it, to gain the double advantage by it, That those who like them not, may be glad they are no longer; and those who do, may be sorry they are so short."[26] Flecknoe's early work in the character form tended towards the discursive and rambling. Although he could not really eliminate this tendency—it is really the dominant cast of his mind and personality—the brevity of his later characters required a concomitant tightening of phrasing and limitation of description to pertinent characteristics.

As an example, the beginning of the character "Of your Ladies Coronel" from the 1658 collection is here quoted, followed by the 1665 version, "Of one who falsely styles himself Collonel."

---

[25] A Collection . . . , sig. I2^v.

[26] A Collection . . . , sig. A3^r.

> Not to be Souldier, he was made Coronel at first, and to scape fighting, has remaind so ever since; whence he's a superlative without a positive, or like a Hovell all rouff without foundation; you may call him souldier yet in extraordinary, as they do Courtiers who ordinarily have nothing to do at Court, no more than he in the Feild ere since he brought the name of Coronel to Town, as some did formerly to the suburbs that of Lieutenant or Captain.[27]
>
> Not to be Souldier he was made Collonel at first, and to 'scape fighting, has continued so ever since; whence he is a Superlative without a Positive; or like a Hovel, all Roof, without a Foundation. He drunk formerly when he shu'd be fighting, and now talks onely of fighting in his drink; whence his Sword can so little boast of its Blood, as all its Gentility lies in the Hilt and Belt; and it derives its Honour more from the Scabbard then the Blade.[28]

The later version incorporates elements from other parts of the 1658 version in addition to the nearly identical opening. But the 1665 character is tighter and more epigrammatic, hence better equipped to achieve the traditional wit of the character as it was practiced earlier in the century.

Some of Flecknoe's interests have already been indicated--his concern with decorum of behavior and satiric treatment. An important aspect of this emphasis on social conduct is the ability to converse. Several of Flecknoe's characters deal with the theory of conversational matter and technique. The character "Of a Lady of excellent Conversation" links the ability to converse fluently with the quality of mind responsible for it: ". . . she is all that is delightfull in Conversation; her matter not stale and studied, but resent and occasionall; not stiff, but ductile and pliable to the

---

[27] Enigmaticall Characters . . . , F7^v.

[28] Rich. Flecknoe's Aenigmatical Characters, D7^r.

company; high not soaring, familiar not low, profound not obscure; and the more sublime the more intelligble and conspicuous. Her Words not too scanty, nor too wide, but just fitted to her matter, not intricately involving, but clearly unfolding and explicating the notions of her minde."[29]

The high-spirited man is "more singular than proud, and though he knows his degrees of persons, know himself so well withall, as he will converse with no subject but on equall terms, counts none greater that has a lesser minde than he. . . ."[30] The dull-fellow, on the other hand, "is the mute of the company, and only plays a part in the Dumb Shew; or if he say any thing like a pump, he labours for it, and presently his spirits sink down again, and leave him dry."[31] And the character "Of one that is the foyle of good Conversation" concerns one whose "matter is some stale Common-places, like cold meat grown nauseous with often repetition; or else some new whimsies of his own, like French quelques choses, with no substance at all in them: his words or low, and creeping . . . or so affectedly high and ramping, as if Eloquence stalkt and went on stilts. . . ."[32]

---

[29] Enigmaticall Characters . . . (1658), sig. B1^r.

[30] Enigmaticall Characters . . . , sig. I7^v.

[31] Enigmaticall Characters . . . , sig. H2^v.

[32] Enigmaticall Characters . . . , sig. B2^v.

The real significance of Flecknoe's stress on fresh, fluent conversational matter is that it can largely be subsumed under the rubric "Wit." Wit--as it is defined by implication in Flecknoe's characters--is really a matter of success in the salon. And the witty person "is the Sparkling Liquor of the company, others but Dregs and Lees, and the life and spirit of it, that else would be dull and dead. He is never dry nor pumping, but always full and flowing with conceit; and when he meets with one who can but uphold aside as at Shuttlecock, you would be delighted to see how handsomely they keep it up."[33] As a means of stimulating this fluency, "Wine," says Flecknoe, "is a good Whetstone of Wit." Flecknoe's strenuous efforts at revision can be interpreted as attempts to fulfill his definition of wit as the "Point of the Spirit." Wit, Flecknoe states, "is no solid food of life, but an excellent sawce or seasoning, if it be not unseasonably used. . . ."[34] The food imagery is no incidental allusion; it represents Flecknoe's whole attitude toward life and art-- a pleasant banquet table replete with pleasant dainties. As he says of his characters: ". . . tis a garden, not journey, or a feast, where by reason of the subjects variety, he is never cloyed, but at each Character, as at a new service, falls too with fresh Appetite."[35]

[33] A Collection . . . (1673), sig. H2^v.

[34] A Collection . . . , sig. H2^r.

[35] Enigmaticall Characters . . . (1658), sig. H2^r.

Associated with Flecknoe's Restoration interest in conversation and behavior is a concern for the mental state of his subjects. They circulate in polite society, they engage in repartee, yet they are subject to considerable breaches of decorum and sociable conduct. Like the "modern censurers" of Flecknoe's character, they are "Clowns of Automicks, who see the motion of the Dials hand without, but not the Wheels and Resorts by which it is moved within."[36]

Ignorant of their inner motivations, these characters act without design or purpose. The woman in "Of a changeable Disposition," perpetually restless, cannot adjust to more rational norms: "Her thoughts and imaginations differ from others, as Grotesque figures do from natural; and from Grotesque, in that these have some design in them, but they have none. . . ."[37] The "suspitious Person" is always "explicating others words and actions still as Hereticks do scripture in the dark and mystick sense, when the litterall is clear and manifest enough. . . ."[38] The disturbed woman in "Of one who troubles her self with every thing" possesses a mind which "seems onely an Hospital of sickly thoughts;

---

[36] A Collection . . . (1673), B1^r.

[37] Rich. Flecknoe's Aenigmatical Characters (1665), sigs. F4^v-5^r.

[38] Enigmaticall Characters . . . (1658), sig. C7^r.

being so thronged with them, there's hardly room for any healthy one. . . ."[39] Also unhealthy is the "low spirited man," who "contracts and shrinks up himself at every little touch, and looks on him; and you daunt him, and strike his eye inward strait; and his words congeale in his mouth through fear, and want breath still to finish a period. . . ."[40]

Flecknoe's analysis of his subjects' psychological behavior is not totally weighted on the side of rationality. Surprisingly, he accepts the possibility of a beneficial--or at least entertaining--irrationality. His character "Of a Running Head" gives the picture of a man whose thoughts "are like a swarm of Bees buzzing up and down his head, without Consistance, Coherence, and Consequence. . . . His head is a Leaking Fountain, and would be wholly dry, but for the continual currant of his Running Thoughts. . . ." But when his disjointed thoughts are placed on paper, "you may see they have more of Democrates than Heraclitus in them, that they more laugh than cry, are more merry than sad; And finally, make sport with the World, not for any ill will, but for its good, and with those in it, for their amendment, not their shame. A pattern all of which, you have in these Characters."[41] And the pattern of Flecknoe as given in his characters is that of a man humorously oblivious to life's profundities, content

[39] Enigmaticall Characters . . . , sig. D1^r.

[40] Enigmaticall Characters . . . , sig. K1^r.

[41] A Collection . . . (1673), sig. A3^v.

to sketch the superficial niceties of Restoration society with a fundamentally unquestioning--though pleasantly observant--sensibility.

Flecknoe's best characters are probably those that do not arise from the efforts of a parvenu priest to render polite society in flatteringly unctious tones. In his off-guard moments, when he draws less formal vignettes of a school boy, a mendicant Irish priest, and a miserable old gentlewoman, he reveals a talent for amiable, unaffected observation of human experience. Flecknoe's divinity student, "having got a few scraps of Latine together, is made Priest; when like a ragged Colt, he changes his Coat for a Cassock, so old and thread-bare, as t'has neither lining nor outside, and you wo'd doubt ever t'were new or no."[42] The miserable old gentlewoman is pictured in her house, "sitting purring in the Chimney-corner like a melancholly Cat, mumping like an old Ape when she saluteth you; and when shee'de Regale you indeed, sends for a bottle of Sack from her Closet (as everlasting as the Widdows cruch of Oyle) has served this twelve months all strangers that come to house, together with a Box of mermelate so dry, as the flyes have given 't over long since, in dispaire of extracting any more sweetnesse out of it."[43] And Flecknoe's fledgling school boy, who "has nothing so ready, as his Hat at his fingers ends; which he twirls about

---

[42] Rich. Flecknoe's Aenigmatical Characters (1665), sig. F3^r-

[43] Enigmaticall Characters . . . (165?), sig. F6^r.

in mighty agony; when he is out and knows not what to say, and if you question him, he looks another way, as if he sought an Answer in the Seeling, or the Floore, and scraps you just such a leg in answering you, as <u>Jack</u> oth' clock-house going (about to strike). . . ."[44]

Here, clearly, is Flecknoe's real talent at work. There is a whimsical, sympathetic realism in these characters that one can search for futilely in much Restoration literature. Like Abraham Cowley, who spent most of his literary energy in writing a turgid epic poem and declamatory love poetry when his real bent was for the graceful, personal essay, Flecknoe was drawn into genres for which he was artistically ill-prepared. Marvell's burlesque description of his dinner engagement with Flecknoe, who, after eating, drew from his breast pocket ten quire of paper filled with his poetry, is believable as well as hilarious. But if Flecknoe was surely the cause of wit in others, he was also--as several of his characters show--himself a source of wit.

To move from a discussion of Richard Flecknoe to Samuel Butler is to require an intellectual leap of impressive distance. It is an astonishing fact of literary history that two such diverse authors were both drawn to the character form years after it had ceased to be viable. Butler condemned the ideals of polite society that moved Flecknoe to write fervid panegyrics. Flecknoe took an obvious delight in the pleasures

---

[44] <u>Enigmaticall Characters</u> . . . , sig. F8^v.

of food, wine, and gay repartee; Butler was a disillusioned rationalist, one of the first to experience genuine Tory gloom. Any discussion of Butler's characters is bound to be a cursory and fragmented one, for he used the character form as a container of great plasticity which could hold all his deepest and ripest judgments of Restoration society. His characters move from a consideration of the man to a discourse on the implicit principles--social, religious, political, or artistic--that motivate him. Hence a discussion of the characters must begin with some comment on the ideas that inform them.[45]

Butler's view of the world was inherently critical. His creativity was not the result of any positive assumptions about the nature of man or the universe that he wished to foster on his contemporaries as did Bacon and Milton. The essence of Butler's thought is a polemical, corrective drive to strip mankind of its vast accretion of errors and blunders, particularly in light of their acceleration of growth since the period of the Revolution. The longest section of his "Miscellaneous Observations and Reflections on Various Subjects" is called "Contradictions," in which Butler ranges across all subjects, attacking the inconsistencies that abound in human endeavors.

[45] Discussions of Butler's thought are amply provided in Dan Gibson, Jr., "Samuel Butler," _Seventeenth Century Studies_, ed. R. Shafer (Princeton, 1933), pp. 279-335; Edward Ames Richards, _Hudibras in the Burlesque Tradition_ (New York, 1937), pp. 3-23; and in Ricardo Quintana, "Samuel Butler: A Restoration Figure in a Modern Light," _ELH_, XVIII (1951), 7-31.

Butler's principles were strongly conservative; he constantly urged the return of man to those first moments of pristine simplicity when truth was open and unadorned: "And though truth be the difficultst thing in the world to be acquainted with, yet when it is once known, it is the playnest, and most easy to be dealt with; that is always constant to it self, and has no variations to be allow'd for, nor alterations from its originall Simplicity, and therefore is the more to be undermin'd by falshood that never deals fairly and openly in the Affayres of the world, but has change of faces and every one proof against all impression."[46] Butler saw the truth counterfeited everywhere around him, in politics, science, religion, and literature. The virtuosi with their precious speculations on nature's laws; the Quakers with their intense individualism of the spirit; the Hobbesian politician with his ruthless absolutism; the poet Benlowes with his strange configurations of wit--all were rejected by the pragmatic, tradition-conscious satirist. As the spectres of irrationality proliferated, so the manuscript notebooks of Butler swelled with random jottings and--especially-- prose characters.

The character was the natural form for Butler's approach to life and art. To a man so conscious of the shortcomings of human constructs, the character offered an ideal combination of an indeterminate formal structure and a satiric approach already

---

[46] _Characters_ _and_ _Passages_ _from_ _Note-Books_, ed. A. R. Waller, (Cambridge, 1908), p.293. Hereafter referred to as _Characters_.

determined by a poet of like sensibility--John Cleveland. Cleveland's work, although more vituperative than Butler's, exhibits the same rhetorical thrust and grotesquerie, the same concentration of invective into the satiric image. Butler had the more penetrating intelligence of the two, and his satiric work is at once broader in intellectual range and less attached to the economic realities of the time--such as property and class status--than Cleveland's. Butler inherited Cleveland's effective use of "Clashing tearms," but gave it greater significance by applying it to the vast number of subjects satirized in the characters, which form, in effect, a huge catalog of fools and charlatans, a veritable anatomy of folly. Although one encounters in the characters the figures of Prynne, Hobbes, and Benlowes--as one also finds in Hudibras the thrusts at William Lilly, Oliver Cromwell, and Samuel Luke embedded in the allegorical narrative--the characters are never used as a means for venting mere personal frustration or prejudice. The character form gave Butler the same possibility for achieving impersonality in his satire as did the Mènippean framework in Hudibras.

The difficult stylistic task facing Cleveland and Butler--indeed all satirists--was unintentionally stated by an anonymous author of a commendatory poem in Richard Whitlock's Zootomia, Or, Observations on the Present Manners of the English (1654):

> Thy Characters so circumstance each sin,
> As 't not Describ'd, but had Embowell'd bin,
> The Knife, joyn'd with the Pencil, glories here:
> As thou both Limner, and Dissector were.[47]

---

[47] Sig. A4r.

The author of these lines chose from Whitlock's medley of essays, characters, psychological and physiological speculations, and storehouse of quotations from Charron, Montaigne, Lipsius, and Seneca, the character as an effective instrument of moral correction. In the conventional use of medical terminology to define Whitlock's technique,[48] the author also states the double task of the satirist: he is both limner and dissector; that is, he creates by synthesizing even as he destroys by analyzing. The mediator in this paradoxical situation is the author's choice of satiric technique—how he manages to combine the knife and the brush. In Butler's characters the mediating device is the similitude. This is the technique he uses to render his satiric victim helpless and ridiculous. He had already employed it with devastating effectiveness in Hudibras, Parts I and II, published respectively in 1663 and 1664. The characters, written after 1667, continued and expanded Butler's interest in distorted analogy.

No other collection of characters has undergone such vagaries in its presentation to the public. None of Butler's characters was printed, of course, until R. Thyer edited the Genuine Remains in Verse and Prose of Mr. Samuel Butler in 1759. To the one hundred and twenty-one of Thyer's edition were added sixty-six from the British Museum Add. MSS. 32626 in A. R. Waller's edition for the Cambridge English Classics series. Two more characters were added to Butler's canon from his commonplace book, analyzed in 1944 by Miss Norma E. Bentley

---

[48] See Mary Claire Randolph, "The Medical Concept in English Renaissance Satiric Theory," Studies in Philology, XXXVIII (1941), 125-157.

in an unpublished Syracuse University dissertation.[49] And in 1948 eight more characters came to light, having been published in the London Magazine of 1825-26 and then completely forgotten for over a century.[50] It is doubtful that more characters will be added to the present total of one hundred and ninety-seven.

The characters repeat the subject matter of the earlier collections of characters, as one might expect considering their vast bulk. Plotting them on a line of relative particularity, they range from the extremely personal--"A Duke of Bucks"--to a description of the mechanic, professional, and clerical types, and of the traditional ethical types of the older characters-- "A Proud Man," "A Debauched Man," and "A Malicious Man." There is a conspicuous absence of ideal types. Butler's marked distrust of rhetoric and panegyric and his temperamental pessimism would militate against the inclusion of types that seemed so worthy of praise to John Earle. In length the characters range from the short squib to the lengthy, digressive investigations of "A Modern Politician," "An Hypocritical Nonconformist," A

---

[49] The "Character of a Schoolmaster" and "Character of a lawyer" are printed in the appendix of Miss Bentley's dissertation, "Hudibras Butler." Cited by Ricardo Quintana, "Samuel Butler: A Restoration Figure in a Modern Light," ELH, XVIII (1951), 25, n.71.

[50] Josephine Bauer, "Some Verse Fragments and Prose Characters by Samuel Butler Not Included in the Complete Works," Modern Philology, XLV (1948), 160-168. The characters printed by Miss Bauer are "A Self-Conceited Man," "A Bawd," "An Ambitious," "A Vapourer," "A Morose Man," "A Railer," "A Drunkard," and "A Master of Arts." Twelve of the twenty characters printed in the London Magazine were reprinted in Waller's ed. Miss Bauer conjectures that the remaining eight were somehow lost while in the possession of the magazine.

Small Poet," and "An Hermetic Philosopher." The characters can also be classified stylistically: the lucid exposition of "A Modern Politician" contrasts with the rhapsodic structure of burlesque analogies in "A Huffing Courtier."

Probably the best rationale of Butler's stylistic approach was given by the author himself. In one of his "Miscellaneous Observations" he states:

> . . . wit by a certaine slight of the Minde, deliver's things otherwise then they are in Nature, by rendring them greater or lesse then they really are (which is cal'd Hyperbole) or by putting them into some other condition then Nature ever did (as when the Performances of Sensible, and Rationall Beings are apply'd to Senseles and Inanimate things, with which the writings of Poets abound) But when it imploys those things which it borrows of Falshood, to the Benefit and advantage of Truth, as in Allegories, Fables, and Apologues, it is of excellent use, as making a Deeper impression into the mindes of Men then if the same Truths were plainely deliver'd.[51]

To the benefit and advantage of truth--this is the standard that must be adhered to if the use of falsehood is to be justified. Speaking elsewhere, of the Fifth-Monarchy man's irrationality, Butler states that "so near of Kin are all fantastic Illusions, . . . you may discern the same Lineaments in them all."[52] The moral, utilitarian aims of the satirist determine the value of his illusions. If the aims are rational, the satirist will reflect that rationality, eschewing the affected and the obscure in his use of language. Butler's own definition of satire in

---

[51] *Characters*, p.336.

[52] *Characters*, p.46.

the section "Unclassified Notes on Various Subjects" is cast
in the form of an allegory: "A Satyr is a kinde of Knight
Errant that goe's upon Adventures, to Relieve the Distressed
Damsel Virtue, and Redeeme Honor out of Inchanted Castles,
And opprest Truth, and Reason out of the Captivity of Gyants
or Magitians: and though his meaning be very honest, yet some
believe he is no wiser then those wandring Heros used to be,
though his Performances and Atchievments be ever so Renownd
and Heroicall."[53]

That the author of <u>Hudibras</u> should find such a similitude
a natural mould for his thought is not surprising. But what
is surprising is the frequency of use to which Butler puts this
analogy. Paul B. Anderson has remarked that Butler "was
extremely frugal in using and re-using carefully husbanded
materials." His mind "was a veritable warehouse of well-arranged
burlesque properties."[54] Thus the imagery of the Knight Errant
is employed to ridicule the "opinionater," who "is bound by
his Order to defend the weak and distressed, and deliver
enchanted Paradoxes, that are bewitched, and held by Magicians
and Conjurers in invisible Castles."[55] The "Hermetic
philosopher" reveres the Rosicrucians, who "are a Kind of

---

[53] <u>Characters</u>, p.469.

[54] "Anonymous Critic of Milton: Richard Leigh ? Or Samuel Butler?" <u>Studies in Philology</u>, XLIV (1947), 510.

[55] <u>Characters</u>, p.137.

Philosophers Errant, that wander up and down upon Adventures, and have an enchanted Castle, invisible to all but themselves. . . ."[56] The image is appropriate and convenient, possessing a clear traditional association and an unmistakable referential base. As in all Butler's burlesque imagery, there is no ambiguity of meaning, no possible room for differing interpretations. Undoubtedly Butler, an avowed critic of Hobbesian philosophy, was aware of this passage in Hobbes's Leviathan of 1651: "The ecclesiastics have their cathedral churches, which . . . have the power to make those towns . . . seats of empire. The fairies also have their enchanted castles, and certain gigantic ghosts, that domineer over the regions round about them."[57] But Butler read widely and gleaned material from other sources--such as previous writers of characters. There is imagery from Cleveland in "The Henpect Man"[58] and "A Curious Man."[59] Brathwait's "A Gamester Is a Merchant-venturer" attracted Butler, whose character of "A Gamester" begins "Is a merchant adventurer, that trades in the bottom of a dice-box."[60]

[56] Characters, p.100.

[57] Cited from the edition of Michael Oakeshott (Oxford, 1946) by Samuel I. Mintz, The Hunting of Leviathan (Cambridge, 1962), p.36.

[58] Characters, p.47.

[59] Characters, p.67.

[60] Characters, p.225.

Although Butler was repelled by Hobbes's ruthless political theory, in one respect his characters reflect Hobbes's view of truth. "The truth which reason yields for Hobbes," states S. I. Mintz, "is the truth about words, not things; it is a hard truth to find because words are such notorious snares; their meanings shift according to the 'nature, disposition, and interest of the speaker,' or else they are used metaphorically 'in other sense than they are ordained for. . . .'"[61] A frequent cause of Butler's agitation toward his subjects is their irrational distortion of language, their manipulating of words to fit their own desires and interests. His criticism is best put forth in the character of "A Small Poet," where Edward Benlowes, author of Theophila, a grotesque poem that "represents metaphysical religious poetry in excelsis and in extremis,"[62] is thoroughly drummed by Butler's burlesque wit. But in many other characters as well, the subjects are castigated for their misuse of language. The lawyer, of course, refines the subtle meanings of words until they are reduced to nonsense; the "quibbler" "rings the Changes upon Words, and is so expert, that he can tell at first Sight, how many Variations any Number of Words will bear."[63] The pedant uses words "merely for their own

---

[61] The Hunting of Leviathan, p.25.

[62] Douglas Bush, English Literature in the Earlier Seventeenth Century 1600-1660, p.158.

[63] Characters, p.90.

Sakes, . . . without any Regard of Interest, as they are useful and serviceable to Things. . . ."[64] And the "affected man" "loves the Sound of Words better than the Sense" and "breaks" words "to his own Fancy."[65] In this respect Butler would seem to be one of the virtuosi himself, for they too wished to see words used more closely related to things. Butler, however, was aware of the pitfalls of language, even regarding those who would appoint themselves its watchdogs: "The Historian of Gresham Colledge, Indevors to Cry down Oratory and Declamation, while He uses nothing else."[66]

Language is important to Butler, for it is man's rational use of language that makes him man. When he misuses language by distorting it or mining it for fantastic subtleties, he loses his reason. "Men without Reason," Butler states in his "Miscellaneous Observations," "are much worse than Beasts, Because they want the end of their Creation, and fall short of that which give's them their Being. . . ."[67] Thus, humanity in Butler's characters is reduced to a jostling mob of animal forms, metamorphosing, like the "Huffing Courtier," from a butterfly, to a horse, a chicken, sheep's fleece, and

[64] Characters, p.136.
[65] Characters, p.143.
[66] Characters, p.424.
[67] Characters, p.339.

an Indian monster. "This intelligible World," says Butler, "is a Kind of <u>Terra incognita</u>, a <u>Psittacorum Regio</u>, of which Men talk what they do not understand."[68] This prideful ignorance is a corrosive force. If man talks long enough like a parrot, he becomes a parrot. Butler's figure of the cuckold is not just another recipient of horn-mad jokes; he loses his humanity by <u>becoming</u> a horn: "The Poets say, the Gate of Sleep is made of Horn, and certainly his is so; for he dreams of nothing else sleeping or waking. Thus he apprehends himself, upon Suspicion, for a Cuckold, is cast by his own Confession; and, as he that believed he had pist a Mouse, because he found one drowned in his Chamber-Pot, he interprets every Thing in favour of his Horns, until he becomes really a Cuckold in his Heart."[69] There is an earnest seriousness underlying Butler's grotesque playfulness that takes his imagery out of the class of humorous comment usually mandated by the character. The characters are appropriately placed in the volume in which they are presented as part of Butler's complete works--in the beginning of the volume, supported at the rear by the "Miscellaneous Observations." The two forms--characters and random thoughts--are really to be treated as one, for they give together a fuller picture of Butler's art than they would if treated as distinct works. The characters are to be viewed as reflections of Butler's

[68] <u>Characters</u>, p.100.
[69] <u>Characters</u>, p.150.

pessimism fleshed out with startling analogies; the miscellaneous thoughts as formless matter to be licked into shape by Butler's mimetic sensibility. The characters take their intellectual base from the miscellaneous thoughts, which, in turn, are inchoate characters.

Butler's work was an impressive addition to the genre--even if its presence in manuscript form prevented it from exercising much of an influence. It is doubtful that it could have had much of an effect even if it were published, for the character had really ceased to be an active genre. Readers of Butler after 1759 did not prefer the character to the moral treatise or the personal essay. In the future age of successful Whig mercantilism, the Butlerian character, with its dark implications about the nature of man, could only be pitied for its unfortunate bad spirits.

After Samuel Butler's death in 1600, the character became more the real province of the verse satirist, who pruned its burlesque wit to fit the neater demands of the heroic couplet. Some of the characters occasioned by the Papist scare have already been mentioned. But the tone of the later characters is decidedly more temperate and less questioning than earlier works, with their tendency toward the philippic. The new tendency is toward effusive praise of the subject's economic standing and patriotic faith, as in The Character and Qualifications of an Honest Loyal Merchant (1686)[70] and The

---

[70] Reprinted in Gwendolen Murphy's A Cabinet of Characters, pp. 326-331.

Character of a Williamite (1690). The latter, a response to a tepidly satiric piece, The Character of a Jacobite (1690), illustrates an unpromising environment for the satiric character. The tone is proper and didactic: "... 'tis easier to scratch than to remove what itches, or to make a Wound than cure it. Thus proportionably, Satyr has a much larger Field than Panegyrick, and the ill nature of the World generally gives more Scope in Dispraise than Commendation."[71] In this character the comfortably bourgeois world of Sir Roger de Coverley is not far from realization: "He thinks a good dish of meat looks full as well at his own Table in the Country, as at a City Tavern. After Dinner he drinks King Williams Health heartily."[72] The Character of the Beaux (1696) took a further step towards the manner of Addison and Steele by narrating the typical day of the fashion-plate, from his rising, to his jaunt to the coffee-house.[73]

The new spirit of toleration reached its humane heights in the Marquess of Halifax's The Character of a Trimmer (1688). Its stately dignity and restrained tone, its epigrammatic polish and generalized statement mark it as more of an eighteenth-century political essay than pamphlet character. Halifax, unlike the earlier pamphleteers, would include rather than exclude.

[71] Sig. A2^r.
[72] Sig. B1^r.
[73] Reprinted in Murphy, pp. 335-339.

Even the Popish dissenters--those who could be spiritually reclaimed--have a place in the Trimmer's ship of state. Men's feelings, once wrapped up in internecine religious struggles, must now be fixed on the glory of England:

> Our Trimmer is far from Idolatry in other things, in one thing only he cometh near it, his Country is in some degree his Idol; he doth not Worship the Sun, because 'tis not peculiar to us, it rambles about the World, and is less kind to us than others; but for the Earth of England, tho perhaps inferior to that of many places abroad, to him there is Divinity in it, and he would rather dye, than see a spire of English Grass trampled down by a Foreign Trespasser. . . .[74]

The stage is set for the genial exemplar of those qualities that best represent the English spirit--Sir Roger de Coverley. And the stylistic form to contain the new ethos of sceptical, rational individualism is the Montaignean essay. The character focused attention on others--usually their most unattractive features; the essay drew the reader into the mind of the author. "He let his Mind have its full Flight," said Halifax of Montaigne, "and sheweth by a generous kind of Negligence that he did not Write for Praise, but to give to the World a true Picture of himself and of Mankind. He scorned affected Periods, or to please the mistaken Reader with an empty Chime of Words. He hath no Affectation to set himself out, and dependeth wholly upon the Natural Force of what is his own, and the Excellent Application of what he

---

[74] *The Complete Works of George Savile, First Marquess of Halifax*, ed. Walter Raleigh (Oxford, 1912), p. 97.

borroweth."⁷⁵ When emphasis is placed on the natural force of what is one's own, the character has outlived its usefulness as a literary genre.

⁷⁵ "*A Letter sent by his Lordship to Charles Cotton, Esq.; upon his New Translation and Dedication of Montaigne's Essays*," Works, pp.185-186.

Introduction to the Text

The only edition of Richard Brathwait's <u>Whimzies</u>: <u>Or,A New Cast of Characters</u> appeared in 1631. It comprises twenty-four characters with an additional four characters in a separately-titled section called <u>A Cater-Character, throwne out of a Boxe By an Experienc'd Gamester</u>. The title page reads:

> Whimzies: | OR, | A NEW | CAST OF | CHARAC- | TERS. ‖
> <u>Nova, non nota delectant</u>. ‖ [ornament] | LONDON, |
> Printed by <u>F. K.</u> and are | to be sold by <u>Ambrose Rithir-</u> |
> <u>don</u> at the signe of the Bulls- | head in <u>Pauls</u> Church- |
> yard. 1631.

The section title on sig. K8^r reads:

> A | CATER- | CHARACTER, | throwne out of a | <u>Boxe</u> | By an
> Experienc'd | Gamester. ‖ --<u>Ova prognatus ab uno</u>. ‖ I. <u>An</u>
> <u>Apparator</u>. | 2. <u>A Painter</u>. | <u>3. A Pedler</u>. | 4. <u>A Piper</u>. ‖
> LONDON | Imprinted by <u>F. K.</u> and | are to be sold by <u>R. B.</u> |
> 1631.

The Bodleian copy and one of the three Harvard copies have a variant title page:

> <u>WHIMZIES</u>: | [. . . as in description above to "LONDON"] |
> Imprinted by <u>F. K.</u> and | are to be sold by <u>R. B.</u> | 1631.

Some copies have a variant section title:

> [Title as in description above to "sold by"] |A. R. | 1631.

The copy-text for this edition is the Huntington Library copy in a xerographic reproduction. It has been collated with the copy in the Arents Collection of the New York Public Library. All variants in the two copies are noted in the list of textual changes.

Collation: 12° [A]4, A3-12, B-L12, M9, 143 leaves, with pagination 1 (A11)-211 (K7) and 1 (K10)-34 (M2^V). [A]1 title, 1^V blank; [A]2-2^V blank; A3-8 "The Epistle Dedicatorie," to "Sir Alexander Radcliffe," signed "Clitus-Alexandrinus"; A8^V blank; A9 "To the equall Reader"; A10^V blank; A11-K7 text of <u>Whimzies</u>; K7^V blank; K8 section title; K8^V blank; K9 Dedication to Sir Alexander Radcliffe; K9^V blank; K10-M2^V text of <u>Cater-Character</u>; M3 Verses to the author; M3^V blank; M4-6 Verses "Upon the Birth-day of his Sonne John"; M6^V blank; M7-8 "An Alphabeticall Table of the Characters"; M8^V blank; M9 "Upon the <u>Errata's</u>"; M9^V blank.

The following census of known copies of <u>Whimzies</u> includes those that will appear in the revised edition of the Pollard and Redgrave <u>Short-Title Catalogue</u>:

1. British Museum (press mark 1076. b.7)
2. Bodleian Library (press mark 8°. I.29. Art.)
3. Worcester College, Oxford (imperfect)
4. St. John's College, Cambridge
5. John Rylands Library, Manchester
6. Henry C. Folger Library, Washington, D. C.
7. Chapin Library of Williams College, Williamstown, Mass.
8. Harvard University Library
9. Harvard University Library (with imprint "<u>F</u>. <u>K</u>., . . . sold by <u>R</u>. <u>B</u>. 1631.")

10. Harvard University Library--formerly in the collection of W. A. White
11. Morgan Library, New York, New York
12. New York Public Library, Arents Collection--formerly in the collection-ef John L. Clawson
13. Huntington Library, San Marino, California

This edition of Brathwait's *Whimzies* preserves the spelling, pointing, and capitalization of the copy-text. In accordance with modern practice "i" has been changed to "j," "v" to "u," and modern "s" has been used throughout. The use of "y" for modern "j" has been retained, particularly since the order and pronunciation of the characters require the distinction. All abbreviations have been expanded, except the ampersand when it appears in a Latin quotation. The "misplaced" apostrophe in plurals has been retained, as in "memento's" and "corranto's." The auxiliary verb "ha's," incorrectly conceived as a contraction of "haves," is also retained. Words that are now always divided, such as "as well" and "as much," and are printed in *Whimzies* as one word, appear in their modern form; conversely, a word printed in the copy-text as two words when it is today normally joined has also been silently changed. A few changes have been made in the original pointing for the sake of clarity. Corrections given in the list of *errata* have been silently incorporated in the text, except where the correction itself was in error. Variant readings from the Arents copy have been designated in the list of textual changes by a capital "A." Although separately titled and numbered, the characters in the <u>Cater-Character</u> have been numbered consecutively as part of <u>Whimzies</u>; thus, the character of "An Apparator" is numbered 25., following the last character of <u>Whimzies</u>, 24. "A Zealous Brother."

The racy idiom of expression and the broad range of allusions in <u>Whimzies</u> have made necessary a large number of explanatory notes--nearly seven hundred. The main intent has been to elucidate briefly all words and allusions which even the scholarly reader might find puzzling. Whenever deemed relevant, quotations from contemporary authors have been provided. For the characters that treat rather specialized areas of seventeenth-century life--almanacs, corantos, and apparitors, for example--introductory notes are supplied.

Superscript numbers in the text refer to the annotation following the text. Textual changes are referred to by page and line numbers.

Richard Brathwait's **Whimzies: Or, A New Cast of Characters** (1631)

1.	An Almanack-maker	148	15.	A Post-master	201
2.	A Ballad-monger	151	16.	A Quest-man	205
3.	A Corranto-coiner	154	17.	A Ruffian	209
4.	A Decoy	159	18.	A Sayler	213
5.	An Exchange-man	163	19.	A Traveller	218
6.	A Forrester	166	20.	An Undersheriffe	223
7.	A Gamester	170	21.	A Wine-soaker	227
8.	An Hospitall-man	174	22.	A Xantippean	230
9.	A Jayler	178	23.	A Yealous Neighbour	235
10.	A Keeper	182	24.	A Zealous Brother	240
11.	A Launderer	186	25.	An Apparator	245
12.	A Metall-man	190	26.	A Painter	249
13.	A Neuter	193	27.	A Pedler	253
14.	An Ostler	194	28.	A Piper	257

RICHARD BRATHWAIT,

WHIMZIES: OR, A NEW CAST OF CHARACTERS (1631)

1. An Almanack-maker

Is an annuall Author, no lesse constant in his Method then matter; enlarging his yeerely Edition with a figure or cipher.[1] He cites as familiarly, as if they were his familiars,[2] Euclid, Ptolemie, Ticho-Brache, etc.[3] But beleeve it, many have spoke of Robin Hood, that never shot in his bow.[4] Hee scrapes acquaintance[5] of a fortunate gentleman, one Euphumemismus,[6] whom he erroneously takes for brother of that feigned knight Parismus;[7] whose name hee interprets to bee, Boni ominis captatio,[8] whereof he himselfe for his part, was never capable. Horizons, Hemispheares, Horoscopes, Apogaeum's, Hypogaeum's, Perigaeum's, Astrolabes, Cycles, Eipcycles[9] are his usuall dialect; yet I am perswaded they may bee something to eate, for ought he knowes. His frequent repetition of Mazzaroth, Arcturus, Orion, and the Pleiades, proclaime him highly versed in the astrologicall observations of Job,[10] whom he resembles in a Paralell line of Poverty, rather than patience. Hee ha's the true situation and just proportion of the principall Angles or houses of the Heaven or Firmament: yet can hardly pay house rent for his owne.[11] Forty shillings[12] in his yeerely pension upon every impression:[13] but his vailes[14] are meaner, unlesse he have the Art for stolen goods to cast a figure:[15] wherein, trust me, hee ha's a prety smattering. He walks in the Clouds, and prates as familiarly of the influence of the Moone, as if hee had beene the man that was in her. Hee would make you beleeve hee had a smacke of Poetry, by the verses which hee fixeth above every moneth, but doe not credit him, hee is guiltlesse of that art: onely some stolen shreads he hath raked out from the kennell[16] of other Authors, which most pedantically hee assumes to himselfe, and makes an additament[17] to his Labours. Whole Summer nights long hee lyes on his backe, as if hee were melldew'd[18] or Planet-strucke,[19] gazing on the starrie gallerie: and would make you believe that hee knew the names and markes of all the oxen that draw Charles waine.[20] Hee talkes much of the 12. Signes, yet I am confident, that one might perswade him that the Cardinals hat, or Sarazens head[21] were one of them. He keeps a terrible quarter[22] with his Jacobs staffe,[23] which he conjectures was first found at Jacobs Well;[24] as his erring Erra pater[25] informes him: for other Cabals[26] hee disclaimes them. The Memorable work of conveying the New River from Ware to London,[27] was the issue of his braine, if you may believe him: yea, he will tell you, the state is much engaged to his notions. He ha's some small scruple of Physitian in him, and can most Empyrically discourse of the state of your Body:[28] but had he store of Patients, hee would slaughter more than a Pestilence. He ha's a little judgement in your Chrisis:[29] and which is best season for Phlebotomie:[30] yet hee knowes not, whether Phlebotomie bee a man or a woman. Not a highway man in Europe can direct you better in the Roade: all which he ha's by inspiration,[31] for he scarce ever travail'd out of smoke o'th

Citie. He ha's excellent observations for planting, plowing,
setting, sowing, with other experimentall rules[32] of husbandrie,
yet never was Master of a Plough in all his time. Certaine
(but most uncertaine) generall Notions hee ha's of the seasons
of weathers, which hee expresseth in such strange and unbaptized
language, as like the Delphian sword, it may cut either way.[33]
About four a clock at night (saith he) which may as soone fall
out at foure a clocke i'th morning for ought he know's, there
will fall some mizling,[34] drizling drops, with some whistling;
rustling windes, etc. all which he findes out of the depth of
Art. He professeth some skill in palmistry; wherein trust me,
the Gipsies do farre out-strippe him: poring on the table of
your hand, hee fetcheth a deepe sigh, thinking of his owne
unfurnish'd Table at home, than which none can bee barer. And
examining the lines of your Table, he alwayes findes his owne
to be most ominous. Hee shewes himselfe deeply read in
antiquitie, by the artlesse draught of his threed-bare
Chronologie;[35] and imps[36] his illiterate worke, for want of
better stuffe, with a trite discourse of weights and measures:
most ponderously dividing them into Troy and Averdepois: where
hee findes his owne gold still[37] too light by many graines for
either scale. His Cage (or Studie if you please) is hung about
with Moath-eaten Mappes, Orbes, Globes, Perspectives;[38] with
which hee can worke wonders. His shelves for want of authors,
are subtilly inter-woven with Spiders Caules, which hee makes
the stupid vulgar beleeve, are pure Elixirs extracted from the
influence of the Moone. It is the height of his ambition to
aspire to the credit of a Blanke Almanack;[39] upon which

election hee holds himselfe a Classicke Author.[40] If famous, he seldome dies; for some inferiour Artist will assume to himselfe his name. But if he die, an other Phoenix-like, will bee forthwith raked out of his ashes. His death makes him in this infinitely happy; It is not bitter to him in respect of his substance: And in this onely hee expresseth himselfe a Scholer; He dyes poore. In a word, this may be his comfort, he leaves his kindred in a settled and composed peace: for they neede not fall by the eares together for his goods. That which he long discoursed of but understood not (I meane his Clymactericall yeare[41]) ha's now attach'd him: And so ends his perpetuall Almanack.[42]

2. A Ballad-monger

Is the ignominious nickname of a penurious poet of whom he partakes in nothing but in povertie. His straine (in my opinion) would sort best with a funerall Elegie, for hee writes most pittifully. Hee ha's a singular gift of imagination, for hee can descant on a mans execution long before his confession. Nor comes his Invention farre short of his Imagination; for want of truer relations, for a neede he can finde you out a Sussex Dragon,[1] some Sea or Inland monster, drawne out by some Shoelane man[2] in a Gorgon-like feature, to enforce more horror in the beholder. Hee ha's an excellent facultie in this; Hee ha's one tune in store that will indifferently serve for any ditty.[3] Hee is your onely man in request for Christmas Carols. His workes are lasting-pasted monuments upon the insides of

Country Alehouses, where they may sojourne without expence of
a farthing: which makes their thirstie Author crie out in this
manner, if he have so much Latin: <u>Quod licuit chartis</u>, <u>non licet
ire mihi</u>.[4]

    He <u>stands</u> much upon <u>Stanza's</u>, which halt and hobble as [5]
lamely as that one legg'd <u>Cantor</u> that sings them: It would doe
a mans heart good to see how twinne-like <u>hee</u> and his <u>songman</u>
couple. Wits of equal size, though more holding <u>vailes</u> befall
the <u>voyce</u>.[5] Now you shall see them (if both their stockes
aspire to that strength) droppe into some blinde Alehouse, [10]
where these two naked <u>Virginians</u>[6] will call for a great potte,
a toast, and a pipe. Where you may imagine the <u>first</u> and <u>last</u>
to be only called for out of an humour; but the <u>midst</u> out of
meere necessitie, to allay hunger. Yet to see how they will hug,
hooke, and shrugge over these <u>materials</u> in a Chimney corner [15]
(O <u>Polyhymnia</u>[7]) it would make the <u>Muses</u> wonder! But now they
are parted: and <u>Stentor</u> ha's fitted his <u>Batillus</u>[8] with a
Subject: wheron hee vowes to bestow better lines than ever
stucke in the <u>Garland of good will</u>.[9] By this time with botches
and old ends,[10] this <u>Ballad-Bard</u> ha's expressed the Quintessence [20]
of his <u>Genius</u>, extracted from the muddie spirit of Bottle-Ale
and froth. But all is one for that; his <u>Trinkilo</u>[11] must have
it, if he will come to his <u>price</u>, yet before hee have it, it
must suffer the <u>Presse</u>.[12] By this, <u>Nick Ballad</u> ha's got him a
Quarterne[13] of this new Impression; with which hee mounts [25]
<u>Holborne</u>[14] as merry as a <u>Carter</u>; and takes his <u>stand</u> against
some eminent <u>Bay-window</u>; where he vents his stuffe. Hee needs
not dance attendance; for in a trice you shall see him guarded

with a <u>Janizarie</u> of <u>Costermongers</u>,[15] and <u>Countrey</u> <u>Gooselings</u>: while his <u>Nipps</u>, <u>Ints</u>, <u>Bungs</u> and <u>Prinado's</u>,[16] of whom he holds in fee,[17] oft-times prevent[18] the <u>Lawyer</u>, by diving too deepe into his <u>Clients</u> pocket; while hee gives too deepe attention to this wonderfull Ballad. But stale Ballad-newes, like stale fish, when it beginnes to smell of the Panyer,[19] are not for queasie stomacks. You must therefore imagine, that by this time they are cashier'd[20] the Citie and must now ride <u>poast</u> for the Countrey: where they are no lesse admir'd than a Gyant in a pageant:[21] till at last they grow so common there too, as every poore Milk maid can chant and chirpe it under her Cow; which she useth as an harmlesse charme to make her let downe her milke. How therefore you must suppose our facetious <u>Ballad-monger</u>, as one nectar-infused[22] with some poetical Liquor, re-ascending the horse-hoof'd mount, and with a cuppe of sixe (for his <u>token-pledge</u>[23] will bee taken for no more) hee presum's to represent unto the world a new conceite,[24] intitled; <u>A proper new Ballad, to the tune of Bragadeery round</u>.[25] Which his <u>Chanteleere</u> sings with varietie of ayres (having as you may suppose, an instrumentall <u>Polyphon</u>[26] in the cranie of his nose.) How he counterfeits a naturall <u>Base</u>, then a perpetuall <u>Treble</u>, and ends with a <u>Counter-tenure</u>.[27] You shall heare him feigne an artfull straine through the Nose, purposely to insinuate into the attention of the purer <u>brother-hood</u>:[28] But all in vaine; They blush at the <u>abomination</u> of this knave, and demurely passing by him, call him the <u>lost childe</u>. Now, for his Author, you must not take him for one of those pregnant criticke Suburbane wits,[29] who make worke for the fidlers of the Citie. For those are more

knaves, than fooles, but these quite contrary. In those you
shall finde salt, sense, and verse; but in these none of all
three. What then is to bee expected from so sterile a
Pernassian,[30] where impudence is his best conductor, Ignorance
his best Instructor, and Indigence his best Proctor?[31] Shall
we then close with him thus? Hee is constant in nothing but
in his Clothes. He never casts his slough[32] but against[33]
Bartholomew Faire:[34] where hee may casually endanger[35] the
purchase of a cast suite:[36] Else, trust me, hee is no shifter.[37]
In a word, get his poore corpes a sheete to shrowd them in at
his dying, they get more than his Muse could ever make worth
while hee was living.

3. A Corranto-coiner

Is a State-Newes-monger; and his owne Genius is his
intelligencer.[1] His Mint[2] goes weekely, and he coines monie
by it. Howsoever, the more intelligent merchants doe jeere
him, the vulgar doe admire him, holding his Novels oracular.
And these are usually sent for Tokens[3] or intermissive Curtsies
betwixt City and Countrey. Hee holds most constantly one forme
or method of discourse. He retaines some militarie words of
art, which hee shootes at randome; no matter where they hitt,
they cannot wound any. He ever leaves some passages doubtfull,
as if they were some more intimate secrecies of state, clozing
his sentence abruptly,--With heereafter you shall heare more.
Which words, I conceive, he onely useth as baites, to make the
appetite of the Reader more eager in his next weeks pursuit for

a more satisfying labour. Some generall-erring relations he
pickes up, as Crummes or fragments, from a frequented
Ordinarie:[4] Of which shreads he shapes a Cote to fit any
credulous foole that will weare it. You shall never observe
him make any reply in places of publike concourse; hee ingenuously acknowledges himselfe to bee more bounden to the
happinesse of a retentive memory, than eyther ability of
tongue, or pregnancy of conceite. Hee carryes his Table-booke[5]
still[6] about with him, but dares not pull it out publikely: yet
no sooner is the Table drawne, than he turnes Notarie;[7] by which
meanes hee recovers the charge of his ordinarie. Paules is his
Walke in Winter;[8] Moorfields in Sommer.[9] Where the whole
discipline, designes, projects, and exploits of the States,
Netherlands, Poland, Switzer, Crim chan[10] and all, are within
the Compasse of one Quadrangle walke most judiciously and
punctually discovered. But long he must not walke, lest hee make
his Newespresse stand. Thanks to his good invention, he can collect much out of a very little: no matter though more experienc'd
judgements disprove him; hee is Anonymos, and that wil secure
him. To make his reports more credible (or which he and his
Stationer onely aymes at) more vendible, in the relation of
every occurrent: he renders you the day of the Moneth; and to
approve himselfe a Scholler, he annexeth these Latine parcells,
or parcell-gilt[11] sentences, veteri Stylo, novo Stylo.[12]
Palisado's, Parapets, Counterscarfes, Forts, Fortresses, Rampiers,[13]
Bulwark's are his usual dialect. Hee writes as if he would doe
some mischiefe; yet the charge of his shot is but paper. Hee
will sometimes start in his sleepe, as one affrighted with

visions; which I can impute to no other cause but to the terrible skirmishes which he discours'd of, in the day time. He ha's now tyed himselfe Apprentice to the trade of __minting__: and must __weekly__ performe his taske, or (beside the losse which accrues to himselfe) he disappoints a number of no __small fooles__, whose discourse, discipline, and discretion is drill'd from his __State service__. These you shall know by their Mondai's morning Question, a little before Exchange time;[14] __Stationer have you any newes__. Which they no sooner purchase than peruse; and early by next morning (lest their Country friend should bee deprived of the benefit of so rich a prize) they freely vent[15] the substance of it, with some illustrations, if their understanding can furnish them that way. He would make you beleeve that hee were knowne to some forraine intelligence, but I hold him the wisest man that hath the least faith to beleeve him. For his __relations__ he stands resolute, whether they become approved or evinced for untruths; which if they bee, hee ha's contracted with his face never to blush for the matter. Hee holds especiall concurrence with two philosophicall sects, though hee bee ignorant of the Tenets of either: in the collection of his observations he is __Peripateticall__, for hee walkes circularly: in the digestion of his relations he is __Stoicall__, and sits regularly. Hee ha's an Alphabeticall Table of all the chiefe Commanders, Generals, Leaders, provinciall Townes, Rivers, Ports, Creekes, with other fitting materials to furnish his imaginary building. Whisperings, muttrings, and bare suppositions are sufficient grounds for the authoritie of his relations. It is strange to see with what greedinesse this ayrie __Chameleon__[16]

being all lungs and winde, will swallow a receite of Newes,[17]
as if it were physicall: yea, with what frontlesse[18] insinuation he will scrue himselfe into the acquaintance of some
knowing Intelligencers,[19] who trying the Cask by his hollow
sound, do familiarly gull him. I am of opinion, were all his
voluminous centuries of fabulous relations compiled, they would
vye in number with the Iliads of many forerunning ages. You
shall many times finde in his Gazetta's, Pasquils[20] and
Corranto's miserable distractions; here a City taken by force,
long before it bee besieged; there a Countrey laid waste before
ever the enemie entered. He many times tortures his Reader
with impertinencies: yet are these the tolerablest passages
throughout all his discourse. He is the very Landskip[21] of
our age. He is all ayre; his eare alwayes open to all reports;
which how incredible soever, must passe for currant, and find
vent, purposely to get him currant money,[22] and delude the
vulgar. Yet our best comfort is, his Chymera's live not long;
a weeke is the longest in the Citie, and after their arrivall,
little longer in the Countrey. Which past, they melt like
Butter, or match a pipe and so Burne.[23] But indeede, most
commonly it is the height of their ambition, to aspire to the
imployment of stopping mustard-pots, or wrapping up pepper,
pouder, staves-aker,[24] etc. which done, they expire. Now for
his habit, Wapping and Longlane[25] will give him his Character.
Hee honours nothing with a more indeered observance, nor hugges
ought with more intimacie than antiquitie, which hee expresseth
even in his Cloathes. I have knowne some love fish best that
smell'd of the panyer; and the like humour reignes in him, for

hee loves that apparell best that ha's a taste of the Broker.²⁶
Some have held him for a Scholler, but trust mee such are in a
palpable errour, for hee never understood so much Latine, as to
construe Gallobelgicus.²⁷ For his Librarie, (his owne continuations excepted) it consists of very few or no Bookes: he holds
himselfe highly engaged to his invention, if it can purchase
him victuals, for Authors hee never converseth with them, unlesse they walke in Paules. For his discourse it is ordinarie:
yet hee will make you a terrible repetition of desperate Commanders, unheard of exployts; intermixing withall his owne
personall service. But this is not in all companies: for his
experience hath sufficiently inform'd him in this principle:
That as nothing workes more on the simple than things strange
and incredibly rare; so nothing discovers his weaknesse more
among the knowing and judicious, than to insist by way of discourse, on reports above conceite. Amongst these therefore, hee
is mute as a fish. But now imagine his Lampe (if he be worth
one) to be neerely burnt out; his inventing Genius, wearied
and surfoote with raunging over so many unknowne Regions; and
himselfe wasted with the fruitlesse expence of much paper,
resigning his place of weekly Collections to an other: whom in
hope of some little share, hee ha's to his Stationer recommended,
while he lives either poorely respected, or dyes miserably suspended. The rest I end with his owne cloze; next weeke you shall
heare more.

4. A Decoy

Is a brave metall'd <u>Blade</u>, as apt to <u>take</u> as to <u>give</u>. His morning preparative is, <u>What sconce shall we build</u>? Though he never bare <u>office</u> in the <u>Ward</u> where he lives, he ha's the word of a <u>Constable</u>, and can bid <u>stand</u>.[2] He is a witty Hypocrit; for sometimes if occasion serve, he can play the <u>civill Divell</u>, and counterfeite a demure carriage.[3] He will cloze with you in any argument out of a pregnant-present conceite:[4] so as hee would make one beleeve he had the Elements of all Learning: But hold him to it, and he will fall off, as hee doth in his whole course from the practice of goodnesse. To bestead his friend, or rather befriend himselfe, hee will turne true <u>Asian knight</u>,[5] and sweare for you most pragmatically.[6] A more affable or sociable companion the world cannot afford you: for hee will mould himselfe to your humour, be it in the quest of businesse or pleasure; your owne shadow cannot bee more attendant, not more obsequiously observant. His onely desire is but to know where you lodge (and for want of his <u>highroad</u> revenewes[7]) hee will bee your incessant visitant. Having by this wrought on your easie temper, and in your bosome purchased him a friendly harbour: Hee pretends occasions abroad; and complaines his horse is lame, and the base Farrier had done him. This in Civility you cannot chuse but take notice of, especially to so intimate a friend, who ha's so many times vow'd to engage his person for

your honour. By this hee mounts your Palfrey, and makes for the
Countrey; where if he doe not speede himselfe of a fortune by
the way; next friday in Smithfield[8] you shall finde your
Demilance[9] in the Faire. Whom if you should chance to owne,
yet were you never a whit neerer your owne: for your sweete-
bosome friend will not sticke to face you and sweare you out of
him. Nay, hee will taxe you of impudence and countenanc'd by
some of his own Comrades, vow revenge for this undigested[10]
imputation. Now, if your discretion will not bee thus outbrav'd
nor baffelt, hee will shew himselfe true sparke of valour, and
encounter you where you will or dare. But set up this for your
rest, if you adjorne time, you shall as soone meete with your
hoste as him. But these are but petty assayes to other of his
master-peeces. By this hee hath taken upon him the title of a
great Heire; which is seconded by the approvement of his in-
genuous Frye. All Cubs of one Litter, and equally furnished
for a cheating Lecture. This some rich Mercer, Milliner, or
Taylour, or some other necessary appendice of a gentleman is
presently possest of; who become humble Supplicants for his
Custome,[11] and by corrupting the Groome of his Chamber, (who
was corrupt enough already) purposely cheate themselves with
expence of some few Crownes. Along goes our Decoy, as an
imaginarie Heire, well accoutred and attended, towards his
receite of Custome.[12] Where, as one borne to more meanes than
braines, hee behaves himselfe like a very Gandergoose, which
strengthens his credulous Creditors gainefull expectance, hoping
to make an Essex Calfe[13] of him. But his acquaintance begets
a good effect in them, for it ever ends with repentance. But

these are but his civill Citie cheats, for want of employment
abroad. For howsoever his <u>Name</u>, in its owne proper signification seeme to render him, his profession ha's proclaim'd him an
<u>universall Cheate</u>. <u>Publike faires</u> are his <u>revenewes</u>; and there
is nothing which hee keepes better in heart than their time.   5
He ha's his varietie of Led suites:[14] and can (if neede require)
counterfeate the habit of <u>Grazier</u>, <u>Gallant</u>, or <u>Citizen</u> all in
one day. With which habits he playes the cunning Imposter,[15]
and deludes those whose condition hee represents: He had neede
bee one of <u>Volpone's</u> truebred Cubbes[16] that shall smell him out. 10
Private alleyes and by-lanes are his Sanctuaryes in the Citie:
but places of publike frequent in the Countrey. Hee ha's more
<u>Doxes</u> than a Gipsie,[17] which hee makes use of, either for
receiving his purchase, or for informing him of a prey. If at
any time hee shall bee accused or attached by some simple   15
Countrey Officer: hee affronts him with such bigg-swolne words
of <u>points of reputation</u>, <u>gentile</u>, <u>estimation</u>, <u>detraction</u>,
<u>derogation</u>; as holding all these to be severall <u>Titles</u> of his
<u>honour</u>, hee not onely releases him, but <u>most humbly complaining</u>,
invites him to a dinner; lest his too rash attach of a <u>Gentleman</u> 20
<u>of worship</u>, (for so his <u>ignorance</u> holds him) should bring him in
danger. Which simplicitie of his our <u>Decoy</u> observes, and workes
upon it. Hee must have his <u>reputation</u> salv'd with some <u>Unguentum</u>
<u>album</u>,[18] or hee will not sit downe with this disgrace. Which
(to prevent all ensuing harme, taking him bound withall that hee   25
shall stirre up no powerfull <u>friend</u> against him, whereof our
<u>cheate</u> pretends a myriad) this officiall Offal applyes, to cure
the ulcer of his impostum'd[19] reputation; and so they part, a

foole and a foist.[20] You shall finde him now and then betting
with some of his rooking consorts in Bowl-alleyes;[21] where if
a young Novice come, he stands confident of a purchase. You
shall see him presently (yet with a reserved counterfeit
civility) cloze with him. His owne Genius[22] shall not seeme
more intimate. But our young Master still goes by weeping-crosse;[23]
He leaves as few Crummes of Comfort[24] in his Purse, as haire on
his Chinne, or wit in his Pate. It is above the reach of conceite,
to observe him, how understandingly he will converse with a
Countrey Farmer, after hee ha's saluted him at the Salutation
doore. His tale is of a Turfe, his matter a Mattocke, his plea
a Plough. But the Catastrophe is a peece of plate, which he
ever leaves the Country-man in pledge for. To display him by
his garbe, or describe him by his garment, were a taske of some
difficultie; hee sorts[25] and suites himselfe purposely to foole
the world, in such varietie. Sometimes you shall see him neate
and briske, and accoutred bravely: next day, like one at Oddes
with himselfe, nitty and nasty.[26] Which indeed, is his true
naturall garbe, that best becomes him; and may bee best pre-
serv'd in regard of those uncertaine veils[27] which befall him.
Hee may for most part compare with those brave Roman Emperours
for the manner of his death; for hee seldome dyes in his bed.
Hee hopes one day to be advanc'd above the residue of his
fellowes, which I conjecture must either bee on the Pillorie
or the Gallowes: where I leave him.

5. An Exchange-man

Is the peremptorie branch of an Intergatorie; What do ye lacke?[1] He would make you beleeve, that hee will furnish you gratis; but such profuse bounty will not pay Scot and lot;[2] your mony therefore must be your pledge, before you have his trinket. It is a wonder to see what variety of Knick-knacks he ha's in so small a Compasse. His quest of inquiry is, what is most in request: so as, his Shoppe consists as much of fashion as substance; forme as matter. It would make one muse how ever so many Gew-gawes should finde vent[3] in a wise state; And yet the labouring invention of the Braine is ever teeming and producing some eye-tempting Babie[4] or other, to allure the Newfangle passenger. The hurriing of a Coach is as pleasing melody to usher in his expectance, as the last sound before a New-play is to an itching audience. When the Simple goe to market, then the Craftie get mony. By this my Lady with her Diapred[5] traine, having as many poakes[6] as heads, are mounted the staires; and entring now the long Peripatetick gallery;[7] they are encountred with volleyes of more questions, then they know to resolve. Gladly would this Salique traine[8] but all they see, if their revenues would mount to the price. But they must in civill curtsy leave some few Commodities for others. Meane time they buy more then they know how to employ. "That is a prety conceited toy (sayes my Ladies gentlewoman) I will buy it whatsoever it cost me:" which discreete speech

delivered in the hearing of our Exchange-man, it must want no
praise, and consequently no price. Hee will usually demand
the three times value for any commodity; but farre bee it from
me to imagine him to have the Conscence to take it if they
would give it. It is his onely drift without any other policy
to make triall of their judgement: his equall and conscionable
moderation is such (at least hee will pretend so much) as hee
hates to worke on any ones weakenesse, being the expressivest
argument of mercinarie basenesse.[9] But were all that traffick
with him as well-lin'd in pate as purse, wee should finde many
emptie shoppes before the next vacation.[10] By this, a new
troope of ruffling plum'd Myrmidons[11] are arrived; and these
will swoope up all before them; Not so much as a phantastick
tyre,[12] be it never so ougly, shall escape their encounter.
Now out with your lures, baites, and lime-twiggs,[13] my nimble
Didapper.[14] Your harvest is not all the yeare. See how hee
shruggs; and with what downeright reverence hee entertaines
them! If oaths, civill complements, demure lookes have any
hope to prevaile with raw and unexperienc'd credulity, he is in
a notable thriving way: for he ha's set his Partridge already;
there is no doubt of springing them till his Net be spread over
them: By which meanes he ha's a tricke to catch the Old one.[15]
Silence, and you shall heare his project.[16] The Ancient Matron
which strikes the stroake, and directs her young charge in their
merchandize, is by this time as firmely retained by our
Exchange-man, as ever was Lawyer by his Client. What great
matter is it, though it cost him a Muffe, a wrought Wastecoate,
or some curious[17] Border? Hee may pay himselfe in his price:

for they are too generous (so their Directresse approve it) to
stand upon tearmes. Let this suffice; it is a good market,
where all are pleased, and so are these. They joy no lesse in
his Commodity, than hee in their money. Yet are the Savages,
in my opinion, much more to be approved in their Commerce than
these. Indeed they exchange pretious stuffe for trifles: Bevers
and Ermins for knifes, hatchets, kettle-drums and hobby-horses.
But this they doe out of their Superfluity; whereas our nicer
Dames bestow that upon trifles, which might support a needfull
family.[18] But the Age labours of this Epidemicall Error; too
universall therefore is the Crime to admit of Censure. Now you
must suppose that Invention is the Exchange-mans most usefull
Artizan. Therefore, for his better returne, he keepes his
weekely Synodall[19] with his Girdler, Perfumer, Tyre-woman[20]
and Sepmster; who bray[21] their braines in a mortar, to produce
some usefull renew,[22] some gainefull issue for their thriving
Master. Never was poore Jade more troubled with fashions[23]
than these are. By this time, imagine something invented; which,
whilst it is now in his Embrio, receives admittance to his shoppe,
and to take the curious passenger, appeares in his full shape.
He needs not use any Exchange-Rhetoricke to set it forward;
Novelties will vend themselves. A vacation is his vexation; and
a Michaelmas tearme the sole hope of his reparation.[24] Hee ha's
by this time, serv'd all offices in his Ward; and now drawes
homeward. That portion hee had of the World, hee ha's bequeathed
to his Executors, Administrators, and Assignes. The Birds are
flowne;[25] his Customers gone; It is high time to shut up shop.

6. A Forrester

Is a Wood-man; but by all likelyhood hee shall lose that title, if hee live to another age; for there will be little or no Wood left in all his Forrest. Hee proves by his Windfals,[1] it is an ill winde that blowes no man profit.[2] His Common-weale is his Chace,[3] his People Deere. Though his Subjects bee wilde, hee can tame them with a Powder. Though hee make no Porters of them, hee drawes a part of his maintenance from their shoulders. The judgement which is most requisite to a man of his qualitie, consists in singling out a good Deere. Hee is an excellent Marke-man, and will serve your warrant daintily, if you Fee him. Hee weares by his side, what hee would not for a world have fixt on his front:[4] though hee have many times deserv'd it, by playing the Rascall Deere, leaving his owne Doe, breaking over his owne Pale,[5] and ranging in anothers Purlew.[6] But for all that she is impaled,[7] when fitly tappised,[8] she may prove one of Swetnams brood,[9] hee Acteons bird,[10] if Calysto's egge[11] bee rightly hatched. One would take him for the Living signe of Robin Hood with a Forrest bill in his hand. Hee ha's a warren to turne Conie-catcher; where he erects a place of Execution for his vermin. You would thinke him a contemplative man by his solitarie Walkes; and no question but hee might benefit himselfe much that way; but his minde stands not so affected. He weares his Mothers Livery,[12] and domineeres like a petty

king in his owne Liberty.[13] Hee keepes a choyce consort of
Musicians; with which hee is not at so much charge as to the
value of a Lute-string. Amorous and attractive is his colour,
else Semele had never so much affected it in her Juppiter.[14]
His very Habit includes an Embleme.[15] Hee attires himselfe to
the Colour of the Forrest to deceive his game; and our Spirituall
enemy attyres himselfe in the Colour we most affect and least
suspect, to receive his prey.[16] Were he a Scholler, hee might
infinitely improve his knowledge by the Objects which hee dayly
sees. He is as the Antipodes to us;[17] for our Day is his Night,
his Night our Day. Hee is one of Latona's servants;[18] and is
so conversant with her, as hee knowes certainely whether the
Moone be made of greene cheese or no. Hee is a proper man of
his hands; but most couragious when hee is impal'd. Yet if his
friend come for a peece of flesh, he will not talke that Night,
but sleepe as soundly as a Constable. But visit any other his
Chase, hee will ferret them. He can do miracles with his
Linehound;[19] who by his good Education ha's more Sophistry[20]
than his Master. Hee were a brave man, had hee the World as hee
ha's his dogge in a string. For Venison, hee is generally better
provided than the Commander of the game: and give the Blade his
dew, hee is no niggard of his flesh: for hee will cut large
thongs out of anothers leather.[21] If his Game thrive not, the
cause must bee imputed to a murraine[22] or a stormie Winter; but
his generous, if not mercenary bounty, was the occasion rather.
His body proclaimes him apt for any employment, but his breeding
hath accommodated him better for a Pale than a Pike, a Chace
than a Campe. For discourse,[23] expect no such matter at his hands;

A very small quantitie of reason will suffice the Creatures hee
converseth with. A naturall bluntnesse doth best beseeme him;
for Rhetoricke becomes not the Woods. If wee bee companions to
Ostridges, wee shall be sure to savour of the wildernesse. Hee
knowes whether the Poets conceite of Faunes and Sylvanes bee   5
true or no; for they walke in his raunge. At Wakes[24] and Maygames
hee keepes a brave quarter: for our wenches of the greene hold
him a marvellous proper man. For the rest of our Hobbinols,[25]
they retaine such an opinion of his valor, they dare scarcely
say their soules are their owne. For his revenew's, bee they   10
more or lesse, hee makes even worke at every yeeres end. He ha's
no land but Leases;[26] and these will weare out in time. The
parts which most dignifie him, are these; he can hallow, give
a gibbet,[27] wind a horne, cut up a peece of flesh, and laugh
at an ignorant Animal that takes saime between the frontlets.   15
When he is to present some neighbouring Gentleman in his Masters
name, with a side or a fouch[28] hee ha's an excellent art in
improving his venison to the best; and in aggravating the difficulties hee suffered before hee could come to his purpose;
And whereto tends all this, but to binde a greater curtesie   20
upon the receiver, and to purchase a better reward for himselfe?
For memory, hee may vye with Xerxes;[29] he knowes all his wilde
regiment by head. For religion, hee cannot be justly taxed in
his tenets, either of heresie or error; for hee is yet to chuse.
The Lawnd is his Temple, the birds his quirresters.[30] His   25
employment for the winter quarter is a continuate imposture;
laying Springes for Woodcockes, Snites,[31] Quailes, etc. His
condition of all others is most mutable; his Masters Countenance

variable; and his place to many overtures lyable. It were
necessary therefore that hee tooke <u>fat fees</u> while he is in
office; that he may have something to build on in his vacancie
from service. But in this particular he is so well cautioned,
as his predecessors Lecture hath made him completely armed. If
he live till he be old, he incurs the generall fate of an ancient
discarded Servingman; clozing the Evening of his life with
contempt or neglect.[32] Those materials or appendices of his
place, <u>Horne</u>, <u>Lease</u> and <u>Bill</u> he resignes (if not pawn'd already)
to his successour; who keepes a mightly racket the first quarter,
but afterwards falls off, imitating Endymion,[33] his predecessors
steppes, in conniving at his friends, and compounding[34] with his
foes. The greene Livery, that Embleme of frailtie, which hee
wore living, must now bee the Carpet to cover him dying. Out
of all his spacious raunge, he ha's reserved so much ground as
may afford him a Grave. More hee needes not, and to bee de-
barred this, even in humanity he cannot. What rests then, but
that hee rest after his long Walke? While we affixe his owne
Epitaph upon his owne naked monument, to make his memory more
perpetuate; <u>Defessus sum ambulando</u>.[35] Pitty were it then to
disquiet him.

7. A Gamester

Is a Merchant-venturer,[1] for his stocke runnes alwaies
upon hazard.[2] Hee ha's a perpetuall Palsey in his Elbow;
which never leaves shaking till his fortunes bee shaken. Hee
remembers God more in Oaths than Orisons. And if hee pray at
any time, it is not premeditate but extemporall. The summe of
his devotion consists not in the expression or confession of
himselfe like a penitent sinner, but that he may come off at
next meeting a competent[3] winner. But where findes hee any
such in all our Collects?[4] Hee so over-braves[5] and abuseth
the poore dice, that if they were his equalls, they would,
questionlesse, call him to account for't. The Ordinarie is
his Oratorie,[6] where hee preyes upon the Countrey-gull to feede
himselfe. Hee was a great Heire, and entred the world full-
handed; but falling to Game purposely to make him more
compleate, his Long acre hath past the Alienation office,[7]
and made him a stranger to his fathers Mansion-house: And now
hee is fitter for a Gamester than ever hee was; Let fortune doe
her worst, his estate cannot be much worse. In his minority,
he plaid ever upon disadvantage; but Experience hath now sufficiently inform'd him now in his maturity; though his dice
seeme square, he seldome playes so. Advantage is his advancement; wherein if you prevent[8] him and bring him to square, he
is ever seconded with swifter fortune. Sundrie prety passages
and conveiances he ha's in his pockets, sleeves, and other

private places for his little familiars;[9] and these furnish
him at a dead lift.[10] You feare cogging,[11] and to make sure
worke, you bring him a Box; but all this will not serve your
turne; hee ha's a Bee in a Box to sting you. It is his care
to creepe into a good suite of Cloaths; lest the Ordinarie
should barre him by and maine.[12] Which having purchased, by
translating[13] and accomodating it to the fashion most in request, it seemes quarterly new. Hee feedes well, howsoever
hee fare. Hope and feare make his recreation and affliction.
Hee ha's no time to refresh his mind, being equally divided
betwixt hope of gaine, and feare of losse. For his losse of
patience, it is so familiar with him, as hee holds it no losse.
Money is of too deare and tender an estimate to let it slippe
from him, and hee like a Stoicall Stocke[14] to say nothing.
Tullus Hostilius put FEARE and PALENESSE in the number of his
gods: and it is pittie (saith Lactantius) that ever his gods
should goe from him.[15] These two are our Gamsters Furies,
which startle him in midst of his Jubilee. Hee is poore, yet
miserably covetous; Envie, like Ivie, is ever wreathing about
his heart: Others successe is his eye-sore. Hee seldome ha's
time to take ayre, unlesse it be to a Play; where if his pockets
will give leave, you shall see him aspire to a Box: or like the
silent Woman, sit demurely upon the stage.[16] Where, at the end
of every Act, while the encurtain'd Musique sounds,[17] to give
Enter-breath to the Actors, and more grace to their Action,
casting his Cloake carelesly on his left shoulder, hee enters
into some complementall discourse with one of his ordinarie
Gallants. The argument of their learned conference is this;

<u>Where</u> <u>shall</u> <u>we</u> <u>suppe</u>, <u>or</u> <u>how</u> <u>shall</u> <u>we</u> <u>trifle</u> <u>away</u> <u>this</u> <u>night</u>?
<u>Where</u> <u>shall</u> <u>we</u> <u>meete</u> <u>tomorrow</u>; <u>or</u> <u>how</u> <u>bestow</u> <u>our</u> <u>selves</u>? Hee
takes no course how to live, nor knows any way how to thrive
but in this high-bet-path of idlenesse. Any other imployment
were his torment. It were the wisest part to deale with such
lewd and <u>inordinate</u> <u>walkers</u>,[18] time-triflers, standers, sitters
in the wayes of idlenesse, and incendiaries to a Civill state,
as <u>Philip</u> of <u>Macedon</u> dealt with two of his Subjects, in whom
there was little hope of grace, or redemption of time: Hee made
one of them runne out of the Countrey, and the other drive him:
So his people was rid of both.[19] The longer hee lives, more
arguments of his basenesse hee leaves. Whom hee consorts with
he depraves, and those that beleeve him hee deceives. It were
a strange account that hee would make, if he were call'd to't;
since his first initiation in this profession. Surely, hee
would expresse himselfe a second <u>Margites</u>,[20] of whom it is
said, that hee never plowed, nor digged, nor addressed himselfe
to ought all his life long that might tend unto goodnesse,
being wholly unprofitable to the World. To disswade him then
from this habituate Course of perverted Liberty, might seeme a
fruitlesse taske: for <u>cheates</u> must be his <u>revenues</u> or he
perisheth. Howbeit to such as are but <u>freshmen</u>, and are not
thoroughly <u>salted</u> with his rudiments, these Cautions will not
prove altogether uselesse. This <u>complete</u> <u>Gallant</u>, which you
see every way thus accoutred, is master of nothing but what hee
weares; and that in <u>Lavender</u> ere long. Hee is famous in nothing
but in being the last of his house. He is onely used by the

Master of the Ordinarie, as men use Cumminseede, to replenish
their Culverhouse;[21] his employment is the draught of Customers.
Have your eyes about you, if you play with him: for want of a
Launderer hee can set your ruffe neatly by helpe of a glasse
behinde you, or a dammaske pummell[22] to discover your game.   5
This he will do so nimbly, as you shall scarce know who hurt
you. In a word, bee our young Novices affected to play?
Let them remember Plato's golden rule: Parvum est aleam ludere,
& non parvum assuescere: It is no great matter to play at dice,
but it is a great error to make dice their dayes-taske.[23] Let   10
it be their pastime, not their practice. Let them know further,
that Gamesters are but as Rivolets, but the Boxe that maine
Ocean into which they descend. By this time you may suppose our
cunning Gamester to bee now fallen to his very last stake; his
wit in the waine; and his fortune in the ebbe. Hee cannot hold   15
out long, for infamie ha's mark't him for a Cheat; and the more
generous professants have by this discarded him for a Bum-card.[24]
Hee is out of Credit with the Ordinarie; and entertain'd with
a scornefull looke by his owne familiars. Hee resolves therefore to turne penitentiarie,[25] now when he ha's nought else to   20
doe. Suppose him then walking like a second Malevolo[28] with a
dejected eye, a broad-brim'd hat or'e-pentising his discontented
looke, an enwreathed arme like a dispassionate Lover, a weake
yingling spurre guiltlesse of gold, with a winter suite, which
must of necessitie suite him all Summer; till drawing neere   25
some Cookes shop, hee takes occasion to mend his spurre-leather,
purposely to allay his hunger with a comfortable savour. Happy

were hee, if hee who in his time had beene so bountifull to
the Gamesters boxe might now receive any benefit or competent
releef from the Pooremans boxe: but miserie no sooner found
him, than pitty left him: it is high time then for us to leave
him.

8. An Hospitall-man

Is the remaines of a greater work: being all that is left of
a decayed Gentleman, a maimed Souldier, or a discarded
Servingman.[1] Hee is now tasked to that in his age, which hee
was little acquainted with in his youth. Hee must now betake
himselfe to prayer and devotion; remember the Founder, Benefactors, Head and members of that famous foundation: all which
he performes with as much zeale, as an Actor after the end of
a Play, when hee prayes for his Majestie, the Lords of his most
honourable privie Councell, and all that love the King. He ha's
scarce fully ended his Orisons, till hee lookes backe at the
Buttry hatch,[2] to see whether it bee open or no. The sorrow
hee conceives for his sinnes ha's made him drie: The Proselyte
therefore had neede of some refreshment. His gowne and retyred
walkes would argue him a Scholler: but it is not the hood that
makes the Monke;[3] hee can bee no such man unlesse hee have it
by inspiration. But admit he were, hee is at the best but a
lame Scholler. A great part of a long winter night is past over
by him and the rest of his devout Circumcellions[4] in discoursing
of what they have beene and seene. While sometimes they fall at
variance in the relation and comparison of their actions. But

all their differences are soone rinsed downe in Lambs-wooll.[5]
Which done, with a friendly and brotherly regreete one of
another, as loving members of one societie, they betake them-
selv's to their rest. Before the first Cocke at the longest
awakes our Hospitall-man; for aches and crampes will not suffer
his sleepes to be long: which is a great motive to make his
prayers more frequent. The morning Bell summons him early to
his devotions, whereto, howsoever his inward man stand affected,
his outward is with due reverence addressed. No sooner ha's hee
got repast for his soule, than he prepares releefe for his belly.
Hee cannot endure to chastise it so long as he may cherish it.
Austeritie he can embrace, so it restraine him neither in his
repast nor rest. For other bodily exercises, hee stands indifferent: for hee findes his body unable to use them. To
speake of the condition of his life, hee might conceive an
high measure of Contemplative sweetnesse in it, if the Sunne
of his Soule (too long eclipsed by the interposition of earth)
could clearely apprehend it. It is strange to see with what
tendernesse he embraceth this life, which in all reason should
bee rather by him loathed than loved. His head is a receptacle
of Catarrhs,[6] his eyes Limbecks of fluxes[7] and inflammations,
his brest a Conduit of rhumaticke distillations; the Sciatica
ha's seazed on his hippes, aches and convulsions racke his backe
and reines; in a word, his whole body is a very Magazen of
diseases; and diseases, you know, are the Suburbs of death.
Yet he hopes to put the Hospitall to the charge of another
Livery gowne, and a whole yeers Commons;[8] whence hee seemes to
verifie the proverbe: There is none so desperately old, but

he hopes to live one yeere longer.[9] Yet for all this, hee can
never be heartily merry: being injoyned to a taske, which he
cannot inure himselfe to without irksomnesse or distaste. For
to bring an old Haxter[10] to the exercise of Devotion, is to
bring an old Bird to sing pricksong[11] in a Cage. The rules of
his house hee observes most punctually; but for Clancular[12]
houres of private prayer and devotion, hee absolutely holds them
workes of Supererogation.[13] His Campe is now translated into
a Cloister; yet his zeale as much then as now: for an Hospitall-
fire, and too liberall fare ha's cool'd his fervor. He conceives
as much delight in discoursing at the Gate, as meditating in his
Cell; yet his demure countenance, aged reverence, and ancient
experience promise more fruits to any ones expectance. Hourly
motives and memorialls he ha's of his frailty, and guides he ha's
to waft him to the port of felicitie; wherein it were to be
wished, that as hee is retentive of the one, so he would not bee
unmindefull of the other. There is no Provision hee neede to
take care for, but how to dye, and that he will doe at leasure,
when necessity calls him to't. The world is well changed with
him, if he could make right use on't. In stead of the cold
ground for his pallat, Armes and Alarmes, and volleyes of shot;
he may now lie softly, sleepe sweetly, repose safely, and if hee
looke well to the regiment of his soule, discampe securely.
Feares and Foes he may have within him, but neither Foes nor
Feares without him. Armour he ha's as well as before, and that
more complete: this is spirituall, that corporall. Methinks
it should not grieve him to remember hee was a man in his time.

That condition is the best, which makes him best. Admit he had meanes, yet being a meanes to corrupt his minde, they were better lost than possest. In his Summer Arbour of prosperitie hee was desperately sicke, for hee had no sense of his sinne. Sycophants he had to dandle him in the lappe of securitie, and belull him in his sensuall Lethargie. These tame beasts are gone; These Summer-swallowes flowne; the fuell of his loose-expended houres consumed; the veile which kept him from discovery of himselfe, removed. What remaines now, but that hee alien himselfe from the world, seeing what he had in the world is aliened from him? His soules-tillage is all the husbandry hee neede intend. This neglected, his case is desperate; This respected, all is fortunate. Every day then, as his body is nearer Earth, let his soule bee nearer Heaven. Hee feedes but a languishing-lingring life, while hee lives here: It is but a Tabernacle at the best, so long as he is encloistred;[14] upon his manumission hence, hee is truly enfranchised.[15] While he had meanes, he might leave an estate to his successour; and so much meanes hee ha's now, as will cause some Hospitall-Brother thanke God for his departure. The thirstie Earth gapes not more greedily for his Corpse, than some Beadsman[16] or other doth for his place. He ha's by this got his pasport; hee ha's bid the World adew, by paying Nature her dew: Dry eyes attend him; his gowned Brothers follow him, and bring him to his long home. A short Peale closeth up his funerall pile; more state hee needes not, and lesse hee cannot have.

9. A Jayler

Is a Surly hoast, who entertaines his Guests with harsh language, and hard usage. Hee will neither allow them what is sufficient for them, nor give them Liberty to seeke an other Inne. Hee is the Physitian, and they are his Patients; to whom hee prescribes such a strict diet, that if they would, they cannot surfet. If at any time they grow irregular, hee allayes their distemper with cold iron. Hee receives the first fruits of the Almesbasket, and leaves them the gleanings. He holds nothing more unprofitable to one of his place than pitty, or more dissorting[1] than compassion; so as it little moves him to see his famish'd family in affliction. His Meney[2] cannot bee more impious than he is imperious: hee domineeres bravely; beares himselfe towards his ragged regiment bravingly; and makes himselfe Almner[3] of their poore treasury. Hee is in fee with the Constables of all the Wards to send him Night-walkers[4] to be his Pay-masters. Hee turnes not his key but hee will have his fee of every Inmate. If hee would turne them out, hee deserv'd it better; but hee both stayes and starves them together. If hee provide any cheere for them, it must be Whipping-cheere.[5] His Ornaments are fetters, boults, and mannacks. These are his Bracelets, yingles, and Caparisons: Thus must his enthralled Crickets live ever in an Iron age.[6] Yet according to a proportionable weight in

Iron. Hee so doubles and redoubles his wards,[7] as one would thinke he had some infinite treasure; but hee that should seeke for any such within his precincts, should lose his labour. Hee ha's a rough hoarse voice ever menacing fire and faggot: for hee ha's contracted with tongue never to utter one syllable of comfort: And concludes, that the Jayler in the Acts,[8] was of too milde temper to supply the place of a Jayler. If his Prisoner have revenew's, and desire to breathe the ayre of liberty hee may purchase an artificiall daies[9] freedome and a Keeper to boot, by his bounty. But his Exhibition[10] must be good, otherwise he sleights his quality. For those poore Snakes who feed on reversions,[11] a glimpse through the key-hole, or a light through the Grate, must be all their prospect. He ha's many times troubled and broken sleepes; and starts out a bed, crying, The prison is broken: So incessant are his feares, so impressive his cares. Which to prevent, he redoubles his Wards, reburdens his irons; and if all this will not doe, but that the fury of feare still dogges him: hee fortifies his thoughts against suspition with strength of liquor. Which makes him as insensible of feare, if occasion were offered, as he was before apprehensive of feare, ere any ground of suspition was ministred. Hence it appeares, that nothing amates[12] him so much as feare of a Prisoners escape. For his sinnes, they never so much as breake his sleep, trouble his head, or afflict his minde. When the Sessions[13] draw neere, how officiously obsequious he is to any of his well-lin'd Prisoners? Now hee must worke how to mince his guilt, and inhance his owne gaine.

He ha's already compounded with him for the Summe: the project
must be drained from his braine. Which, if it hit, hee ha's
vow'd to bee drunke that night; but if it faile, purposely to
be reveng'd of himselfe, he will quench his hydropicke[14] thirst
with six shillings beare,[15] and so dye of a male-tympanie.[16]
If any of his more happy Prisoners be admitted to his Clergy,
and by helpe of a compassionate Prompter, hacke out his
Neck-verse,[17] hee ha's a cold iron in store if hee be hot, but
an hot iron if hee be cold. Where there by many Irons in the
fire, some must coole. If his pulse (I meane his purse) bee
hot, his fist may cry fizze, but want his impression: but if
his pulse be cold, the poore beggarly knave must have his
literall expression.[18] Hee heares more ghostly instruction at
the Ordinaries funerall Sermon[19] before an Execution, than all
the yeare after: Yet is his attention as farre distant from that
Sermon as Newgate from Tyburne. And yet say not but hee is a
most constant friend to his convicted Inmates, for hee seldome
ever leaves them till hee see them hang'd. Now some againe will
object that hee is a subtile Macchiavel, and loves to walke in
the Cloudes, because he never resolves those with whom hee deales,
but fils them full of doubts, and in the end ever leaves them in
suspence. But this is a badge of his profession, and consequently
pleades exemption. Doe you heare you New-gate bird?[20] How
sweetely the pilfring Syren sings! Well warbled Chuck. The
Crim Tartar[21] with the bunch of keyes at his belt will requite
thee. Thou knowest hee expects a masters share, or no release.
One Note higher than, as thou hopes for releefe. He ha's

Collectors too with basons to improve his rents: which consist
of vailes and bribes: but hee is more beholden to the later.
It is just contrarie with his Oeconomie and with others; the
greater his theevish family is, the richer is his fare. Hee
can doe sometimes very good offices (if hee please) by dis-   5
covery of Cacus cave.[22] But it is not the publike which hee
must preferre before his particular: annoint him, and he will
come on like an oyl'd glove. Notable intelligence hee receives
dayly from his ancient Inmates: who for the good entertainement
they have already received, and what they may expect heereafter,   10
present him now and then with a remembrance of their love; and
so they may afford it very good cheape, for it cost them nought.
But now what with Surfets, colds, fears, frights, supose him
drawing neare his Goale-delivery. Though hee had about him
Emblemes of mans life dayly; though hee saw continuall Objects   15
of humane misery; though hee encountred with nothing but
Spectacles of infelicity: yet his security imprisoned his
understanding, so as hee made no use of them. Hee is now
roming, hee knowes not whither; and must of necessity grapple
with that which hee scarce ever thought of before this instant   20
of his departure. Death ha's entred one Ward already; No
churlish affront can possibly amate him; no humane power repell
him. Now hee ha's a poore prisoner within him, that suffers
more anguish than ever any sicke Captive did without him. Hee
gropes under his head, and hee findes his keyes gone; he looks   25
inward, and he finds foes many, but friends few or none. Cold
are those comforts which are in him; many those discomforts

which enthrall him. Yet two beame-lines of comfort dart upon
him in this houre of terrour; from him[23] he expects succour
who received the penitent thiefe, and converted the Jayler.

10. A Keeper

Is an equivocall officer; For if by a Keeper you intend
a raunger or forrester, he is a Wild-man, or a Woodman, as wee
have formerly given him his character. If by him you intend a
Jayler, hee is an Iron-monger, whose Iron sides will suffer no
compassion to enter. If an Alehouse-keeper, his house is the
Divels Booth, and himselfe the recetter.[1] If a Keeper of horses
at Livery, he is a knave without a Livery;[2] he will put in your
hand a lame Palfrey, who will lay your honour in the dust. If
a field-keeper, hee is a Night walker, who though he have store
of neare Inmates ever about him, they ever backbite him.[3] Hee
imitates the Bellman[4] in his dogge, but wants his bell. If the
world doe not bely him, hee will sooner share with a Night-
catcher than descry him.[5] If a Doore-keeper a frequent third
day at a taking New play, will make this Collector a Colloquer.[6]
If a Shop keeper, deepe oathes, darke shoppes, base wares,
false weights have already proclaim'd him a civill cunning
Impostor. If a Booke-keeper, he may get him friends, if his
Master bee not all the wiser; and improve his owne meanes by
change of a figure. But leaving these, give me a good
House-keeper, who onely of all these merits a deserving
Character.[7] He preserves that relique of Gentry, the honour of
hospitality, and will rather fall, than it should faile. He

revives the Black Jack,[8] puts beefe in his pot, makes poore
passengers pray for him, his followers to sticke neere him,
his Countrey to honour him, his friends to love him, his
foes to prayse him. Hee wonders how any one should bee so
voyde of pitty as to leave his smoaklesse house in the Countrey,
where he ha's his meanes, to riot in the Citie, and estrange
himselfe to his friends. Hee conceives for what end he was
borne, and keepes his dayes-account to discharge the old
score.[9] Hee affects nothing so much as discreet and well-tem-
pered bounty: he admits no injurious thought to lodge within
him. How it pleaseth him to see a full table! Men to eate his
meate, meate to feede those men! Hee cannot stoope so low, as
to acquaint himselfe with those base and ignoble spirits, who
preferre their owne store before the publike state. It is his
joy to become a Liberal dispencer, and to releeve the needy with
the fattest portion of his Trencher. Competence[10] hee holds the
best fortune; and herein hee strives to confine his owne desires.
The Summe of his aymes tends rather to the releefe of others
want, than his owne weale; yea he holds the releefe of their
want his Supreme weale. The Court seldome takes him, but if it
doe, he is never taken by it.[11] Hee hath set up his rest, that
the place which gave him first being, with meanes to support
that being, shall receive what with conveniencie hee may bestow
while hee lives in it; with some lasting remembrance of his love
when hee departs from it. Hee is generally the pooremans friend,
and will suffer no oppressor to nestle neare him. Neither is
hee altogether so precise[12] as to admit of no pleasure. Wherefore

hee <u>keepes</u> <u>Horses</u>, <u>Hawkes</u>, <u>Hounds</u>, or whatsoever the most free
and generous dispositions usually affect: yet shall not his
<u>recreations</u> so seaze on him, as to fore-slow any usefull Offices
in him. Hee divides his day into distinct houres, his houres
into devout taskes. His affabilitie mixt with sweetnesse of
bounty, his bounty with alacrity, hath so wonne his family, as
no earthly state can promise more felicity. It is like a well-
rigg'd ship; every one knowes their peculiar charge or office:
their love unto their master makes it no eye service. His
<u>Garner</u> is his Countryes <u>Magazin</u>. If a famine threaten that
Coast, his provision must bee brought forth, purposely to bring
downe the Market.[13] His heart bleeds to see a famish'd soule
languish; he will therefore by timely releefe succour him lest
hee perish. Hee sets not his aymes on purchasing: it contents
him well to preserve what his Ancestors left him. Hee makes
even with the <u>World</u>, as hee would with his owne <u>Soule</u>. One
principall care counterpoizeth the rest: yea, the more seriously to addresse himselfe to his onely one, he disvalues all the
rest. Neither is there ought which conferres more true glorie
on these deserving actions, than his disesteeme of worldly
praise or popular applause. Hee shuts his eare when he heares
himselfe approv'd, and rejoyces most within himselfe when his
deservingest actions are least observed. The Begger or
distressed Traveller, hee holds to be his most bounteous
benefactors, rather than he theirs. Hee holds it better to
<u>give</u> than <u>take</u>: Wherefore he acknowledges himselfe their
debtor, who petition his almes in this nature. Knocke at his
gate, and you shall finde it not surly but civilly guarded;

enter his Court, and you shall see the poore and needy
charitably rewarded; Ascend up higher and steppe into his
Hall, and you shall read this posie[14] in Capitall Letters
inscribed; A PILGRIMES SOLACE IS A CHRISTIANS OFFICE. Suppose
Christmas now approaching, the ever-green Ivie trimming and   5
adorning the portalls and partcloses[15] of so frequented a
building; the usuall Carolls, to observe antiquitie, cheerefully sounding; and that which is the complement of his
inferiour comforts, his Neighbours whom he tenders as members
of his owne family, joyne with him in this Consort of mirth and   10
melody. But see! The poore mans comfort is now declining with
the old yeare; which fills their eyes as full of water, as he
is of sicknesse through infirmitie of nature. This Mirror of
hospitality now breathes short; it is to be feared he will
breath his last. He may leave an Heire to inherit his meanes,   15
but never his minde. Well, funerall blacks are now to bee worne
as well inward as outward; his Sonne mournes least, though hee
bee at most cost. It is thought erelong, he will mourne in
Scarlet, for vanitie ha's seaz'd on him already, and got him to
forsake his Countrey, and forsweare Hospitalitie.   20

11. A Launderer

Is a Linnen Barber, and a meere Saturnine; for you shall ever finde her in the Sudds.[1] Used shee Clipping as much as washing, shee were an egregious Counterfeite, and might quickly come within compasse of the Statute.[2] Shee is an Epicene, and of the doubtfull gender: for a Launderer may bee as well a Male as a Female, by course of nature.[3] But for her, there would be no Shifter, with whom quarterly shee becomes a Sharer.[4] Shee is in principall request with Collegiat Underbutlers,[5] Punie Clarkes in Innes of Chancery,[6] with other officers of inferiour qualitie; unlesse higher graduates[7] will deigne to shew her their humility. In Progresse time[8] (being fallen into Contempt) shee followes the Court; and consorts familiarly with the Black-guard.[9] But shee scornes the motion (I meane to be so poorely employed) during the flourishing Spring of her youth: for shee ha's good vailes, besides her standing wages: and now and then gets good bits which neither the Principall nor Seniours know of. Her young Masters, whom shee serves with all diligence, neede no Cocke but her: shee'll come to their Chambers, and wake them early; and if they have the Spirit to rise, may at their pleasure use her help to make them ready. Shee is a notable witty, tatling Titmouse; and can make twentie sleevelesse arrands[10] in hope of a good turne. By her frequent recourse and familiar concourse with professours of

Law, She knowes by this how to put a Case: and amongst her
ignorant Neighbours can argue it when she ha's done. In some
By-Alley is her dwelling generally; where she keepes a quarter,
as if shee were She-Constable of the Ward. If shee demeane
herselfe wisely, and pretend onely a care of preserving her   5
honesty, shee may come in time to some unexpected advancement.
But truth is (as it fares commonly with the easiest and tract-
able natures) she is of that yeelding temper as she cannot
endure to bee long woo'd before shee bee wonne. Her Fort may
be sackt by paper pellets of promises and assumpsits,[11] if shee   10
be credulous; or by silver shot of plates and peeces, if shee
be covetous. Whence it is, that in very short time, the dropping
fruite of his Launderer, becomes like a Medlar; no sooner ripe
than rotten; yea many times rotten before it bee ripe. Now for
the Stocke which should support her trade: a very little will   15
set her up, and farre lesse will bring her downe. She will
finde friends, if her parts be thereafter. Neither shall shee
neede much curiositie in her breeding: onely she must indent[12]
with her brest to bee secret, with her tongue to bee silent, and
with her countenance to bee constant. Shee must not tell what   20
shee sees; dictate on what shee heares; nor blush at what she
enjoyes. Shee must bee modestly seeming strange, where shee
most affects, and relish nothing more than what shee inwardly
rejects. To salve the credit of the Punie Clerk her young-Mas-
ter, she turnes honest woman, and matcheth herselfe to the   25
Houses Botcher.[13] The necessitie of the time is such, as these
hopefull Nuptialls must not stay for a Licence, admit they could
purchase it. Delay breedes danger; and so pregnant the wench

is growne, as shee doubts lest before she be honoured with the
style of <u>Bride</u>, shee become a <u>Mother</u>. But her long experience
in law-quirks hath sufficiently inform'd her; a Childe borne
within marriage is freed from bastardy, and may inherit all
their hereditarie lands, if they had any. She by this ha's
aspir'd to the purchase of a <u>gowne</u> and a <u>felt</u>: so as shee now
wives it, as if shee were <u>Head-Marshals</u> wife of the <u>Ward</u>. She
ha's got a neate guilded book too, to make her Neighbours
conceite her to bee a <u>Scholler</u>: but happy were shee if shee
were as guiltelesse of <u>lightnesse</u> as of <u>learning</u>: for the
Cover, shee may handle it, and upon alledging of a text of
Scripture tosse it, but for the <u>Contents</u>, as she knowes them
not, so she greatly cares not. She now scornes to be so meanly
imployed in her owne person, as she ha's formerly beene; she
ha's got her therefore a brace of <u>Under-Laundresses</u> to supply
her place, performe her charge, and goe through-stitch[14] with
her trade. The sweate is theirs; but the <u>sweete</u> is hers.
These must be accomptants weekely of their <u>commings in</u>; and
returne a just particular of all such vailes, profits, or
emoluments, as usually or accidentally have any way accrued.[15]
Shee now stands upon her pantofles[16] forsooth; and will not wet
her hand, lest shee spoyle the graine of her skinne: Mistris <u>Joan</u>
ha's quite forgot that shee was one <u>Jugge</u>.[17] Yet shee keepes
some <u>ancient records</u> of her former youthfull profession. When
a Horse growes old, he loseth the marke in this mouth: but it
is not so with her, for shee in her age retaines the marke of the
<u>beast</u> in her nose, that is <u>flat</u>.[18] Severall waies she ha's to

advance her inconstant meanes in severall places: If her continuance in <u>Court</u> purchase her the least scruple of esteeme, by petitionarie course she labours her preferment: but her request must not be great, because her repute is but small. Which upon procurement, must suffer many divisions, subdivisions, and subtractions, before she be admitted to a share. If her aboad in the <u>Citie</u>, hath possest her mistresses with an opinion of her secrecy: shee is made an usefull agent that way. Nothing can bee to deare for her: shee becomes a gainefull factor, and though she neither <u>doe</u> nor <u>suffer</u>, yet receives shee with both hands from <u>agent</u> and <u>patient</u>.[19] If her residence in any <u>incorporate</u> societie[20] hath got her esteeme, her age receives for her long service a pencionary recompence: meane time exchange of broomes for old shoes, and other vailes of decayed Linnen raise her a maintenance. But like a <u>Barbers-ball</u>,[21] with much <u>rinsing</u> and <u>rubbing</u> shee now growes quite <u>wash'd</u> away. She dyes neither very rich nor contemptibly poore; neither with much love, nor great hate. So much she hath reserv'd out of all the labours of her life, as will buy some small portion of diet bread, Comfits, and burnt Claret[22] to welcome in her Neighbours now at her departing, of whose cost they never so freely tasted while she was living.

12. A Metall-man

Is nothing lesse than what his name imports. Hee ha's a beetle head, and a leaden heele.[1] The Embleme of him is exprest in the hollow-charnell[2] voyce of that walking Trunkhos'd[3] goblin, any ends of gold or silver?[4] The Arch-artist in this Minerall is the Alchymist; for the rest are all sublunarie unto him, hee onely Mercurie sublimate unto them.[5] His Stoves, Limbecks, and materialls are already provided: his longacres[6] have beene measured out to make his provisions come in. Hee holds himselfe nothing inferiour to Kelley[7] in art, hee onely wisheth but himselfe like fate. Seven yeares are now expired, since his Promethean fire received first light; and yet the Philosophers stone may be in Sysiphus pocket,[8] for ought that hee knowes. There is no Artist that ha's more faith than he, upon lesse grounds. Hee doubts not but before the signe enter Aries,[9] hee shall, like another Jason, purchase a golden fleece.[10] It is the highest imployment wherein hee ingageth his most intimate friends, to furnish him with sufficiency of Brasse, Copper, Pewter, etc. Hee will make the state rich enough, if hee have enough to doe withall. By this, hee thinkes hee sees a corner of the Philosophers Stone, yet hee cannot discerne the colour. Hope of profit bereaves him of sleepe; but the cost of his art deprives him of profit. It is a wonder to observe what rare crotchets[11] and devices hee retains purposely to gull himselfe! What choyce structures he intends to erect out of his pure Elixirs! Yea, so farre deluded is hee with the strength of a transported imagination, as one might easily make him beleeve that the reparation of Pauls[12] was onely reserv'd to be his Master-peece; and that many of our Duke Humfreys knights[13] expected when he should perfect it. The flourishing Citie-walkes of Moorfields,[14] though delightfull, yet not so pretious or beautifull as he will make them. Those sallow-coloured Elmes, must be turned into yellow-Hesperian Plants:[15] where every Bankerupt Merchant may plucke a branch at his pleasure, to refurnish his decayed treasure. O the transcendencie of Art! Hee lookes backe at the house of his Nativitie, and by a probable argument of the Constellation wherein hee was borne, hee gathers that the Crucible of his braine must be the Indies of this State.[16] Not a morning shines upon him, wherein he expects not before the West receive him, but that his hopes shall enrich him, and those many jeering Mountebanks that attend him. Every dayes experience, becomes now a pretious observance: which makes him thinke hee drawes neare the shore; and so he doth, for now the ship of his fortune rides at low water. Yet is he as rich in mountaines of golden conceites[17] and ayrie imaginations as ever hee was: His Speculation[18] in time will make him as rich as a new-shorne-sheepe; but this his wisedom beleeves not. Heyday; what a racket hee keepes? "Elevate that tripode; sublimate that pipkin; Elixate your antimonie; intenerate your Chrysocoll; accelerate our Crucible.[19] Quicke, quicke, the Mint staies for our metall. Let our materials bee infused.[20] Our Art requires your diligence; your diligence ample recompence. How much may one houres remissnesse prejudice this consequent businesse? Frustrate the States expectance? And perpetually estrange the richest discovery that ever age brought forth, from our Successours." Deare Democritus,[21] hold thy sides or they will cracke else! This diving Paracelsian[22] seekes Amalthea, but findes Amalga.[23] His metalls have more Moone than Sunne in them.[24] How hee tyres himselfe in a wilde-goose-chase? As neere he was yesterday as to day, yet poorer today than yesterday. His Art ha's arriv'd her secretest port, attain'd her highest pitch. Which makes him now convert his Speculation into admiration: wondering that this Stone should be so long conceal'd from him. By this time hee encounters with a nimble Quackesalver, who forgeth new trickes to delude him. He encourageth him in his attempt, seconds him with his advice and assistance; purposely to extract out of the decreasing Limbecke of his fortunes a monethly allowance. Hee limits him a time, which expir'd, his hopes are arriv'd: but before the time come, this nimble Doctor is flowne. But what more powerfully prevalent than error? All these rubbes shall not draw him from his byas.[25] Hee will not desist till he see an end of something; and so he may quickly, for his fortunes now lie a bleeding. But now his expence becomes more easie and temperate: for though his device be delicious,[26] yet the ebbe of his fortunes makes him in his disbursements more parcimonious, and in distillations lesse pretious. Before the next Moneth end, his art hath wrought out the end of his state: so as this Alchymist becomes All-A-Mist, and Theogenes-like[27] ends in smoake. A Bill must bee now erected, a Chymical Schedule pasted,

where his hopefull <u>Utensils</u> were lately reared; and if any
metall'd <u>Sparke</u> will spend some Crownes in the same <u>Science</u>,
the <u>Pupill</u> may have a <u>Tutor</u>: whose judgement and pretious
experiments hee may use for board-wages. Now will any one
buy a kettle, a Caldron, or a Limbeck? How much is the <u>State</u>   5
deceiv'd in this <u>greatmans</u> masterpeece? How his hopes are
thawed? His fortunes distilled? And his aymes miserably
cloz'd? How this threede-bare Philosopher[28] shruggs, shifts,
and shuffles for a cuppe of sixe,[29] whose thirsty desires were
once for <u>aurum potabile</u>?[30] Few or none compassionate his 10
infelicitie, save onely the <u>Metall-men</u> of <u>Lothburie</u>,[31] who
expected for their grosser metalls ready vent by meanes of
his philosophy. His sumptuous fires are now extinguished, the
oyle of his lifes lampe consumed, his hopes into impossibilities
resolved, and hee in his last Scene on earth, to earth returned. 15

13. <u>A Neuter</u>

Is an <u>Hedgehog</u>; Who hath two holes or portals in his
siege;[1] one toward the <u>South</u>, another toward the <u>North</u>. Now
when the <u>Southern</u> wind blowes, hee stoppes up that hole, and
turnes him <u>Northward</u>: Againe, when the <u>Northerne</u> Winde blowes, 20
hee stoppes up that hole likewise, and turnes him <u>Southward</u>.[2]
Such an <u>Urchin</u>[3] is this <u>Neuter</u>, who will suite himselfe with
the habit of any profession for lucre. <u>Gregorie Nazianzen</u>
called <u>Julian</u> the <u>Apostata</u> a <u>Chameleon</u>;[4] for hee could change
himselfe into all shapes and colors. Such a <u>Chameleon</u> is the 25
luke-warme <u>Laodicean</u>.[5] What aboundance of <u>zeale</u> hee will

pretend among the <u>zealous</u>? What <u>indiferency</u> among our
<u>Timists</u>?[6] How <u>hot</u> he is in <u>palat</u>, but how <u>cold</u> at <u>heart</u>? Hee
ha's procur'd a <u>dispensation</u> with his <u>Conscience</u>, that hee may
the warilier and wiselier run with the tyde. Hee holds him a
simple Christian that will professe publikely, what hee holds
to bee <u>Orthodoxall</u> privately. It is his Art to put the
wrongside outward; and to dazle the eye of the World with
faire showes, and golden shadowes. What Cringes[7] he will make
to a <u>rising favorite</u>? How he will mould him to his temper? And
scrue himselfe into his knowledge in servilest manner? His owne
shadow cannot bee more inseparably attendant, nor more officiously[8] observant. It is the bent of his studies to dive
into his disposition; and then to apply fuell of his owne
provision to feede it. He desires to be nothing lesse than
what hee seemes: for hee feares by wearing himselfe too familiarly in the world, hee might in short time weare himselfe out.
A formall Morall zeale calls him to the Church; where hee ha's
one <u>Pharisaicall</u>[9] eye to looke up, and an other <u>Publican</u>[10] eye
to looke downe. For the Notes which he gathers, they are either
worldly-politicall, or none at all. He will resolve of nothing
definitely without some <u>reservation</u>; but of all others, what
<u>religion</u> he will bee of, must be his last <u>resolution</u>. Hee
were a wiseman that could catch him in any <u>Tenet</u> that hee holds.
Hee admires the <u>discipline</u> of our <u>Church</u>; but is not fully
resolved as yet to be a <u>member</u> of her. He grounds his <u>faith</u> on
what the <u>bravest</u>,[11] not on what the <u>best</u> hold. Preferment is
a tender object to his eye; he affects nought with more fervor;
receives nought with more honor; forgoes nought with more dis-

pleasure. "A <u>Conscience</u> (saith he) I professe; but yet I would not have it so nicely scrupulous, as to reject opportunitie of profit; that conscience is too regular, that makes her master a beggar; He is too Stoicall that is wholly for his <u>Cell</u>, and nothing for the <u>World</u>." Thus hee labours to take off the fire-edge[12] from his <u>Conscience</u>, and to coole it; to the end hee may be lesse limited or restrained by it. By which meanes, hee beginnes to bee more secure; since <u>libertie</u> of <u>Conscience</u> tooke from him all grounds of a religious feare. Propose now the way, so it direct him to profit, which hee will not tread with delight. One minutes Taske in the <u>Schoole</u> of <u>vertue</u> tastes of more strictnesse, than <u>Iliads</u> of yeeres in the <u>Temple</u> of <u>Mammon</u>. Hee ha's now taken a course with his <u>Conscience</u> for quietnesse sake, never to call it to an Evening account; that might trouble his sleepe, and distemper his next dayes projects. He hath enough to doe, that hath to doe with the World. Diviner Contemplations might hinder his practice that way. Whatsoever therefore he professeth himselfe to be, he hath made a covenant with his heart to cleave to the world, as the <u>Remora</u>[13] to the ship: Hee ha's conceived such infinite sweetnesse in it, as he can relish nothing but what savours of it. These <u>Rules</u> therefore are those <u>Memorials</u> which informe him in this thriving course of godlesse policie: and which hee holds as <u>Maximes</u> in each societie. "He will seeme to love the <u>Church</u>, but live by <u>sacriledge</u>. Honour his <u>Lord</u>, but creepe cunningly into his <u>Lordships</u>. Hold the <u>middle path</u> betwixt <u>Baal</u> and <u>Bethel</u>.[14] Heare much, and observe it, speake little that may be observed; and lastly remaine in such <u>suspence</u> in matters of <u>religion</u>, as to bee as farre from resolving at the

day of his death, as the houre of his entering." Excellent
conclusions, drain'd from a dangerous sconce, but a farre more
dangerous soule. What will this Puffin[15] come to in time?
Long ha's hee walk'd in the Clouds; and hung his conscience in
even a ballance betwixt Atheisme and Religion as one graine   5
would cast him. How serious an Instrument of Justice he will
shew himselfe towards Recusants,[16] upon Proclamation touching
th' execution of Penall Statutes?[17] Againe, how remisse and
conniving, if hee perceive no such thing intended? It is a
singular argument of his wisedome not to fish in troubled   10
waters, nor swin against the streame. Hee makes that use of
religion, which men make of upright shoes; to weare them with
an indifferencie on either foot. Upon perusall of antient
Martyrologies[18] (but seldome is he so well employ'd) he wonders
at mens constancie, how they could finde in their heart, by   15
insisting on scruples, to deprive themselves of life and
liberty. The paines of compiling so large a volume might have
beene sav'd, had all those constant professors beene possessed
of his spirit. Thus hath he liv'd to deceive all the World,
and himselfe the most. For hee, who tendered the welfare of   20
no friend; nor relyed on any vertuous ground; nor reserv'd one
poore minute to meditate of the Supreme good; nor valued ought
worthy esteeme, but what the world brought forth; nor ever
entered into consideration of his owne estate; nor accounted
otherwise of religion, than as a Cloake; nor of Christianitie,   25
than as a dreame; nor of the whole practice of Pietie,[19] than
of humane policie. Behold how his friends discard him; hypocrisie

arraignes him; his long belull'd Conscience awakes him; Atheisme
condemnes him; and his desperate contempt of veritie hopelesly
torments him! See how this grand Polititian[20] hath deluded
himselfe! How this counterfeite picture, who was neither
masculine nor feminine Christian, but a Neuter, hath catcht
himselfe in his owne error! His discourse of Heaven, was as of
a matter of complement; his treatie[21] of Earth, as of his choicest
continent. But now his mouth is filled with gravell; and that
which once cheer'd him, hath now choakt him. To his outward
friends hee walk't in a mist, but to his inward hee could not;
by the former as hee was discarded, so by the latter is hee
discovered. Long time hee dispenc'd with Conscience: who now
hath vow'd no longer forbearance.

14. An Ostler

Is a bottleman; not a Barber in Europe can set a better
edge on his razor, than hee can set on horses teeth, to save
his provender.[1] The proverbe is; The masters eye feedes his
horse; but the Ostlers starves him.[2] Now, if you desire to
have your Palfrey make quicke dispatch of his provender, make
your Ostler his Supervisor, and by nimble conveyance he will
quickly make an empty Manger. What a rubbing and scrubbing
hee will make in hope of a small reward at cloze of a reckoning? What humble Obeysance may you expect at his hand, when
he prostrates himselfe in such low service to the heeles of
your Horse? Thus labours he by currying your beast, to curry

favour with your selfe. Hee ha's no <u>Litterature</u>,[3] though hee
trade something <u>neare</u> it. Hee profits out of <u>measure</u>; his
<u>Ostrie</u> must not betide to Winchester.[4] If Oates seeme deare,
hee will tell you how much their price quickned at every
<u>quarter</u> last Market day: and hee ha's one close at his elbow
that will second him. Hee will justifie it, that no <u>Hoast</u> on
all the <u>Road</u> got his hay so sweetly or seasonably as his Master.
Though there bee <u>Ostlers</u> of all Countreys, yet generally are
they <u>Northerne</u> men; and those you shall finde the <u>simplest</u>, but
<u>diligent'st</u>, and consequently the <u>honestest</u>; for <u>industry</u> and
<u>simplicitie</u> are antidotes against <u>knavery</u>. But it is twenty to
one, hee will be as neere your <u>Countreyman</u> as hee can informe
himselfe, purposely to procure your better respect, and purchase
the larger reward. Hee will tell you, if hee find you <u>credulous</u>,
that your horse hurts at <u>Withers</u>,[5] or hee is <u>hoofe-bound</u>;[6] but
referre all unto him, and you shall bee sure to pay both <u>Sadler</u>
and <u>Farrier</u> for nothing. Hee can direct you to a pot of the
nappiest[7] Ale in all the streete, and conduct you too, so the
<u>Tapster</u> know not. Hee ha's sundry <u>petty-officers</u>, as <u>Under-
Ostlers</u>, <u>Litter-strowers</u>, <u>Boot-catchers</u>, to whom little accrues
after his deductions. He professeth some skill in horses, and
knowes how to cure divers maladies with Oyle or Oates;[8] but hee
will never cure so many as he ha's diseas'd, nor fat so many as
he has starv'd. To a bare stranger that promiseth but small
profit to the <u>Stable</u>, hee will be as peremptorie as a <u>Beadle</u>.[9]
He will feed his horse with delayes and demurres, and cause him
stay greater guests leasure. But how officious the <u>Snake</u> will

bee, where hee smels benefit? He speakes in his <u>Ostrie</u> (the
chiefe seate of his <u>Hypparchie</u>[10]) like a <u>Frog</u> in a <u>Well</u>, or a
<u>Cricket</u> in a <u>Wall</u>. When Guests horses stand at <u>Livery</u>, he
sleepes very little, fearing lest they should eate too much;
but at <u>bottle</u>, hee is more secure; howsoever, he ha's a dainty
<u>Dentifrice</u> that will charme them.[11] Hee is a constant <u>stable</u>
man; and herein onely commendable; <u>constancy</u> in respect of his
<u>place</u>; and <u>humilitie</u> in respect of his <u>person</u>, makes him both
<u>knowne</u> and <u>knavish</u>. He ha's a notable glib <u>veine</u> in vaine
discourse: No Countrey can you name, but it is in his <u>verge</u>;[12]
his long acquaintance with people of all conditions and Countries, is become so <u>Mathematically</u> usefull unto him, as he ha's
the <u>Geographicall</u> <u>Mappe</u> of the whole Continent (so farre as
this Iland extends) in his illiterate <u>pericranium</u>; which he
vents by way of description, upon every occasion; and this he
makes his weekely Stable-Lecture.[13] He is at very little charge
with his <u>Laundresse</u> but for his false shirt and night-cap; which
he weares as Ornaments to his profession, and in them acts his
daily penance: for it is his use to encounter your Palfry in a
<u>shirt</u> of <u>male</u>, be he <u>male</u> or <u>female</u>. If he rise to any prefer-
ment, he may say, <u>Gramercy</u> <u>horse</u>; yet wil he hardly confesse so
much. He aspires sometimes to <u>Tapster</u>, holding it the more
beneficiall place; but howsoever, better for him, for hee may
now drinke of free cost. Long-Winter nights watching, and early
rising (for hee must bee either the Guests Cocke, or they his)
have much foreslow'd his diligence: for now hee will endure a
call or two before hee rise. But this is no fault of his, but

the diversitie of his occasions: for his desire is naturally to
rise early, and to be officious[14] to his guests before they bee
stirring, in giving their horses provender, which they may dispatch in a trice, before ever their Masters come out of their
chambers. When hee finds convenient time and leasure, hee will
tosse a pot sociably with his Neighbour. But none are so
familiar with him as the Smith and Sadler, whom hee is bound to
present (upon some private composition) to any Gentleman or
other, that shall have occasion to use them. If hee may make
so much bold with you, hee will send his commends sweetned with
a Nutmeg, by you to the Ostler of your next Inne; and this begets
reciprocall courtesies betwixt them, with titles too, which they
are wholly guiltlesse of; as honest Boy; true Blade, etc. But
these stiles are but given them by their fellow Ostlers, whose
desertlesse commendations exact as much at their hands. If
hee but indifferently honest (as I would have no superlative
degrees of honesty in that profession) hee improves the benefit
of the Inne above comparison: All desire to harbour where there
is an honest Ostler. Which opinion once purchased, hee retaines
for ever; and by it strengthens him with his Masters favour.
Hee begins now to bee a Landed man by meanes of his honesty and
usury. If hee have the grace to stay the good houre, hee may
succeed his Master, and by matching with his Mistresse rise to
Inne-keeper. But this is very rare, for hee is not by halfe so
neate a Youth as the Chamberlaine. Long and sore did hee labour
in the Spring of his youth, before hee came to reape any crop in
the Autumne of his age. Hee is now growne resty.[15] Profit is
an alluring baite, but it cannot make him doe that which hee

did. Now hee loves to snort under the Manger, and sleepe out
his time before his departure: yet he cannot endure that any
should succeed him in his place, though hee cannot supply it
himself. Well, suppose him now drawing on to his last Quarter;
some graspes or gripes of mortality hee feeles, which makes
him conclude in his owne Element; <u>Grasse</u> and <u>Hay</u>, <u>we</u> <u>are</u> <u>all</u>
<u>mortall</u>. Hee could for all this, finde in his heart to live
one yeare longer; to compare his last yeares vailes[16] and this
together; and perchance, redeeme his arrerages too with better
measure. But his <u>Ostrie</u> is shut up; the <u>Guests</u> gone; their
<u>reckoning</u> paid; onely a poore <u>Guest</u> of his owne stayes yet in
her <u>Inne</u> and ha's not discharged. But now I see the <u>Inne</u>
dissolved; the <u>Signe</u> of her <u>being</u> fallen to <u>Earth</u>, and defaced;
and his <u>Inmate</u> lodged where the great <u>Inne-keeper</u> ha's appointed.

15. A <u>Post-master</u>

Is a <u>Chequerman</u>: who though hee gallop never so fast, yet
can hee hardly with his <u>post</u> overtake his <u>pay</u>; for that is
alwaies <u>before</u> <u>hand</u> with him.[1] The first question he askes you
(for else he ha's none materiall) <u>Where</u> <u>is</u> <u>your</u> <u>Commission</u>?
Though you know the <u>length</u> of his <u>stage</u>, and <u>price</u> of his <u>miles</u>,[2]
yet his <u>Post-boy</u> hath horses of all prices: to whom if you bee
not liberally minded, looke for no other but to bee lamely
mounted. One would verily thinke that hee had some <u>charme</u> in
the blast of his <u>horne</u>, for he makes Passengers leave their
<u>high-road</u> and give way in the midst of winter, to foundred
Hackneys inevitable danger. Hee rides as securely as if hee

were in fee with High-way men, before whom hee may whistle as
merrily as an emptie Traveller, without least feare of encounter.
Our Night is his artificiall day,[3] as hee makes it. There is
nothing that gives so terrible a report in his eare as a packet
of Letters, for that postes away at free cost. To save weight
hee seldome rides with a band, unlesse it be upon affaires of
highest consequence, and then this hopefull sprig holds it no
small honour to pride himselfe in the weare of an halter.[4]
Hee is generally more peremptorie than other guides; for you
may have them as you two can agree; and they will usually abate
of their demands; but two pence half pennie a mile is his price,
and hee will not abate a denere[5] of it through out all his
stage. Hee will discourse withyou most cursorily, touching
what hee heares of matters of state; and to gaine him more
esteeme in the opinion of the ignorant, will not sticke to bely
his knowledge. Hee is valiant, not by naturall instinct, but
by vertue of his Commission, which authorizeth him to take way
of his betters. Hee can returne a surly answer, or resolve a
waggish question, and this is wit enough for one of his
profession. He is familiarly vers'd with oaths of all natures;
and these hee blusters out as frequently, as if they were his
naturall Rhetorick. Hee quarters out his life into foure
Cantons, Eating, drinking, sleeping and riding; but the second
and last are two principall ones. Hee trusseth up your
Portmantua[6] with all diligence and alacrity, to purchase your
good opinion, but most of all in hope of your bounty. His
vayles are meerely voluntaries, which (so prevalent is custome)
hee as constantly expects, as if they were his stage-hire:

your liberality makes his register your name; enroule you among
his Benefactors; and take notice of you upon your returne: yet
must you continue your munificence, or former Bounties will dive
deepe into the Lethe[7] of forgetfulnesse. He will bee your
servile servant so long as hee tastes of your benevolence; your
pampered Jade[8] shall not bee foundered[9] of all foure, your
palfrey loosely saddled, or budget[10] carelesly trussed. Besides,
to expresse a kind of morall remembrance of curtsies received,
like a gratefull Gnat, he will recommend your bounty to his
succeeding Post-boy, who will accurately furnish you with a
dreaming Dromedary, to accelerate your journey. Hee rides
altogether upon spurre, and no lesse is requisite for his dull
supporter; who is as familiarly acquainted with a Canterbury,[11]
as hee who makes Chaucer his Author, is with his Tale; and who
by sore experience and spur-gall'd[12] diligence is growne well-
neare as intelligble as his Master, in the distance of his
stage; further than which it is impossible to hale him. Hee
rides most commonly with one spurre; and to him that is so in-
quisitive, as hee will demand the reason of it, hee can readily
shape him this waggish answer; Hee holds two superfluous, for
if the one side of his Jade goe forward, hee thinkes hee will
not leave the other behind. Hee becomes in short time an
excellent Farrier; which knowledge he attaines out of his owne
proper but bitter experience: for his Stable is a very shop of
all diseases; Glanders, Yellowes, Fashions, Maladers, Curbs,
Scratches, Staggers, Strangles, Ringbones, Windgalls, Navel-
galls, Bogspavings,[13] with a Myriad more of practicall
contingents become his familiar acquaintance. On these hee

daily practiseth, but rarely cureth. A Packe of Dogs he usually
keepes, which hee feedes with the provision of his owne <u>Stable</u>:
For hee that us'd to <u>carry one</u>, in short space becomes <u>Carrion</u>.
He holds shooes uselesse implements, for hee seldome rides a
<u>bootlesse</u>[14] errand. And now drawing neare the end of his <u>stage</u>,   5
he is neither much <u>wiser</u> nor <u>richer</u>, then when hee first entred
the world. His <u>life</u> as it properly resembles a <u>post</u>, (for it
cannot have relation to an apter comparison) is now very nearely
runne out a breath. And yet observe the miserable condition of
this <u>Horse-fly</u>! Though hee never gained farther experience in   10
the whole course of his life than the <u>practise</u> of some curelesse
<u>cures</u>, the <u>distance</u> of his owne <u>stage</u>, to give a <u>windy</u> <u>summons</u>
with his <u>horne</u>, and to hoise a pot of ale at the doore, yet
nothing is so bitter to him as the remembrance of his dissolution.
His <u>life</u> was a <u>Labor</u>, his <u>age</u> a <u>Pilgrimage</u>, his <u>service servitude</u>.   15
No rest, no repose, poor repast tasted hee on earth: yet preferres
hee this Labour before a quiet and reposed <u>harbour</u>. Many yeares
ha's hee spent to small purpose; his hours are uselesse; his
endeavours fruitlesse; and now after such a <u>quotidian feaver</u>[15]
of an <u>Hecticke</u>[16] <u>labour</u>, being fallen from his horse, and out   20
of request (by a <u>writ</u> of <u>ease</u>[17]) with that science he becomes
wormes provender: for his <u>Legacies</u>, they are to bee discharged
out of arrerages from the <u>Exchequer</u>.

16. A Quest-man

Is a man of account for this yere: yet of no such honour in New-Troy,[1] as he was in Old-Rome.[2] He never goes without his Notebooke, which, if hee have so much Latine, he calls his VADE MECUM. Wherein he ha's the names of all the head-men, middle-size-men, and lowmen, within his whole Ward. And this is all the method which is required in his Common-place book.[3] He is a sworne man; which Oath serves an Injunction upon his Conscience to be honest. Howsoever, hee must bee brought to accompt for it. The day of his Election[4] is not more ready for him, than he for it. Hee assumes upon him a parcell of ill-beseeming gravitie; strokes his beard, as if it were the Dew-lap[5] of his conceite; fetcheth an impertinent hemme, purposely to pump for more wit; and concludes with a set punctual gesture, laying his soape-besmeared hand upon his reverend brest: God make me an honest man. Whence he most ingenuously implyes, that hee is not as yet made that man hee should be: but much may be done in time. Hee keepes an especiall Register of all such inmates as nestle within his Ward: whose povertie must be squeezd to ease the richer; yet sleighted with neglect for their labour. These hee visits quarterly, which visitation they (poore Gnats) may properly tearme a plague; which in time they recover of, for it leaves not a token.[6] Some treasure he hath under his hand, which

hee must returne; hee can convert very little to his owne use,
nor defeate the Parish of any house rent: for hee ha's as wise
men as himselfe in the Ward, who now in his lifetime are made
his Supervisors, to looke to his fingers, that the pretended
gravitie or reverence of his person authorize him not to abuse
his place. This makes many more unwilling to be so dignified;
because much labour but small profit is to accrue it. Yet his
wifes Pew in the Church is a mighty motive: for by this meanes
shee becomes exalted according to the dignitie of his office,
which with a most supercilious zeale she accepts; and doubts
not but some of her neighbours will envie it. This place hath
not put on more reverence in him, than state on her. Eye but
her postures, and you will confesse it. Her eye is wandring,
wooing observance. Her foote most gingerly paced, for more
state-reservance. Her tongue too civically mincing, for vulgar
attention. Meane time, this Questman her husband, the better
to enable him for his place, becomes frequently versed in sundry
ancient Presidents.[7] He casts his eye behinde him, to see what
was done before him: and hee smiles at the simplicitie of his
preceeding Officers; and turning to himselfe, most Sagely
concludes: These wanted thy sconce, Boy. He is now admitted
(by reason of the reverence of his haires) to the Learned
Counsell of the Ward. Where he shoots his bolt with the fore-
most. Some Orders or Parochiall constitutions, hee ha's beene
long studying, which he purposeth the next Revestrie day[8] to
present to the rest of his worshipfull Brethren, to the end
they may bee put in speedy execution. But like good purposes,
(the more is the pitty) they seldome take. After Evening prayer

time, he descends immediately into the <u>low Gallery</u>, which
he with the rest of the <u>wise</u> <u>masters</u> make their <u>Consistorie</u>.
Where (like good Parishioners, studious of the publike good)
they treat of all such abuses as are crept into the body of
their <u>Ward</u>. While their <u>censures</u> become as different, as   5
their <u>persons</u>; their <u>voyces</u> as their <u>places</u>. One shewes
himselfe a <u>Paracelsian</u>,[9] and hee professeth the cure of these
maladies by <u>mineralls</u> and <u>incisions</u>; another a <u>Dioscoridan</u>,[10]
and he holds them more curable by <u>leniments</u>, <u>emplasters</u>, and
<u>unctions</u>; the third a meere <u>Mountebanke Florentine</u>,[11] who   10
wraps up his <u>receits</u> in a remnant of Rhetoricall bombast,[12]
but never returnes one healthfull patient. So long, and as
fruitlesse as long, debate they the cause and cure of these
enormities, till an aged nod or two dissolve their Councell:
and summon them to a new parley upon expence of halfe pints   15
a peece. Where they fall in, till some argument, whereof they
are ignorant, make them fall out. All which time our <u>Questman</u>
scornes to bee silent; as one desirous rather to speake
to no purpose, than not to speake at all. Some quaint words
hath he got, which he understands not; and these he useth   20
upon all occasions. Neither are they more ignorantly delivered
by him, than they are pittifully admired by them. It is a
strange thing to observe how much hee is improved since the
last yeere: Neither is it possible to dive into the reason
of it. For either is there some admirable secret facultie   25
concealed from the judgement of man, in the Lining of a furr'd
gowne, or else it is to bee wondred at, whence this late-bred

sufficiencie of his should proceede. But in this surely hee shewes himselfe most wise, in that hee communicates not his knowledge to any but the ignorant: for it is that makes his judgement passe for current. But his yeere is now upon expiration; and his <u>Account</u> drawing to his preparation. Where <u>Honestie</u> and <u>Sufficiencie</u> meete, there cannot chuse but bee a good <u>account</u>. And in him neither can bee wanting; for his <u>beard</u> shewes the one, and his <u>place</u> proves the other. Hee cannot now shew himselfe so shallow nor appeare so silly,[13] but hee will retaine the opinion of a deepe-head-peece: For hee is now one of the <u>Seniours</u>. A very small portion of understanding, and lesse of wit, will serve him to spinne out the remainder of his time. For a <u>Cipher</u> in some place stands in more account, than a <u>figure</u> doth in another. What rests now, but that he rest, since his rents are collected, his account perfected, himselfe discharged, and another <u>pew-fellow</u>, equall to him both for <u>worth</u> and <u>wit</u>, by generall <u>vote</u> and <u>voice</u> elected?

17. A Ruffian

Is a roring Dam without a Ruffe.[1] None more valiant than
hee in tongue, lesse resolute in heart. He ha's vow'd to bee
ill-condition'd in all Companies; and to presse a quarrell
rather than misse it. A white-liver'd[2] Souldier and a Gallant
is the fittest patient hee can practise on. One would thinke
his very language would fall at ods with itselfe, and out-brave
the Speaker. He ha's a dangerous[3] eye, not to strike (for so
I meane not) but to move ones patience to strike him. For a
kinde of uncivile contempt doth alwayes attend his looke, as
base provoking language accompanies his tongue. Hee hath
ranked himselfe with a troppe of shallow uncivile Shallops,[4]
like himselfe: whose chiefest valour consists in braves,[5]
scru'd faces, desperate mouchato's,[6] new-minted Oaths; all
which moulded together, make a terrible quarter in an Ordinarie.
He weares more metall on his heele, than in his purse. He
triumphs damnably on some stolne favour, bee it lighter than
a feather, and threatens mischiefe to him that will not pledge
her. But it falls out many times, that he is bastinado'd[7] out
of this humour. You shall best distinguish him by a nastie
neglectfull carriage, accoutred with disdaine and contempt, so
as his very countenance is a Letter of Challenge to the beholder.
Those which know him, rather jeere him, than feare him: for they
experimentally know,[8] that a Pigmey would beat him. And with

such (for as much as his shoulders have felt their censure)
hee keepes a faire and civile quarter. His Soveraignty is
showne highest at May-games, Wakes, Summerings, and Rush-
bearings:[9] where it is twentie to one but hee becomes
beneficiall[10] before he part, to the Lord of the Mannour,[11]
by meanes of a bloody nose or a broken pate. Hee will now
and then for want of a better Subject to practise on, squabble
with the <u>Minstrell</u>, and most heroically break his <u>Drone</u>, because the <u>Drone</u> cannot rore out his tune.[12] The wenches, poore
soules, shake in their skinnes, fearing a mischiefe: and in-
treat their <u>sweethearts</u> to give him faire language. All is out
a square[13] while hee is there. But these are but his rurall
pageants. Hee will intrude most frontlesly[14] into any Company;
and advance himselfe with the highest at an <u>Ordinarie</u>; yet
many times hee eates farre more than hee can defray; yea, now
and then hee <u>receives</u> where hee should <u>disburse</u>; a kicke, I
meane, from some surly <u>Naprie</u> groome,[15] which serves in full
discharge of his Commons. Never crept fardell[16] of worser
qualities into more choyce and select companies. But these
hee cannot consort with long. For their Purses are too strong-
string'd, their hearts too well-temper'd, their hands too
truly-metal'd to veile[17] to his basenesse. He must be discarded, and with disgrace, if he haste not. Suppose him then
with his <u>restie</u>[18] <u>regiment</u> dropping out of a three-pennie
<u>Ordinarie</u>:[19] where the last mans Cloake is sure to bee seaz'd
on for all the reckoning. But when the <u>Cooke</u> eyes it more
precisely, and considers how irreparably it is aged, hee will

not take it in full satisfaction of his hungry Commons,[20]
without some other pawne: which for feare of Clubbes,[21] they
submissively condescend to: by disroabing one of their
Complices, who may best spare it, of an ancient Buff-jerkin;[22]
whose lapps you may imagine, by long use, so beliquor'd and
belarded, as they have oyle enough to frie themselves without
any other material. Yet they cannot pocket up this indignitie
with patience: wherefore they vow to be revenged, which for
most part, is as basely clozed. Next night therefore, these
nittie Haxters[23] intend with strong hand to breake his glass
window's, or at dead-time of night to pull downe his Signe:
and so ends their faire quarrel.[24] To a play they wil hazard
money: where after the second Act, when the Doore is weakly
guarded, they will make forcible entrie; a knock with a Cudgell
is the worst; whereat through they grumble, they rest pacified
upon their admittance. Forthwith, by violent assault and
assent, they aspire to the two-pennie roome;[25] where being
furnished with Tinder, Match, and a portion of decayed
Barmoodas,[26] they smoake it most terribly, applaud a prophane
jeast unmeasurably, and in the end grow distastefully rude to
all the Companie. At the Conclusion of all, they single out
their dainty Doxes,[27] to cloze up a fruitlesse day with a
sinnefull evening. Whereto (truth is) they repaire, rather
for releefe then to releeve: yea, their house of sin becomes
oftimes their house of Correction: for when they will not pay
for what they call for, Lais and her Laundry[28] will returne
them their payment by assistance of such familiar Inmates, as
she will make bold to call for. But suppose now this Tyndarian

Tribe[29] dispersed, out of all civile societies discarded, and
with no better entertainment than contempt, wheresoever received.
Our Ruffian ha's left his Mates, and they him. Povertie ha's
now seaz'd on him; for his braine, it is as barren of a shift,
as his backe guiltlesse of a shirt. Those Iron tooles of his,
with which hee affrighted his Scar-crowes, hang now in Longlane[30] for a signe of the Sword and Buckler.[31] His slasht
Suite, like Labels or tart-papers[32] hang peece meale, estrang'd
both from substance and colour. His yingling spurre hath lost
his voyce, his head his locke; yea, his decayed Lungs the puffe
of a Rorer. The wall now must bee no Subject of quarrell; nor
his distended Mouchato a Spectacle of terrour. The extreamest
effects of hunger, have taken him off from standing upon points
of honour. He would gladly encounter with death if hee durst:
But there was such distance betwixt him and the rememberance
of it, during the whole progresse of his unfruitfull life, as
now it startles him to entertaine the least thought of death.
Yet may this bee one of his inferiour comforts, hee leaves
nothing behind him, that may be termed properly his owne, that
is worth enjoying. In a word, he cannot be so wearie of the
World, as it was long since of him. Never was Creature lesse
usefull or more unfruitfull; Let it content him, that hee hath
prevented that contempt by dying, which hee should have incurred
dayly by living.

18. A _Sayler_

Is an _Otter_; an _Amphibium_[1] that lives both on Land and Water. Hee shewes himselfe above Hatches in shape like a male _Meere-maid_, visible to the halfe body. Hee stands at his _meerestone_,[2] and holds out his hand to you, as if he craved your acquaintance: where, though hee tell you that hee is your _first man_, doe not beleeve him: for his founder _Zabulon_[3] was long after _Adam_. Hee never shewes himselfe nimbler, nor contests with his _fellowes_ with more active vigour, than in _shooting_ the _Bridge_ at a Low water. Hee will hazard a life in a whirlewind without _feare_, rather than lose the benefit of his _Fare_. The bredth of an inch-boord is betwixt him and drowning, yet hee sweares and drinks as deepely, as if hee were a fathom from it. His familiarity with death and danger, hath armed him with a kind of dissolute security against any encounter. The Sea cannot rore more abroad, than hee within, fire him but with liquor. Hee is as watchfull as a _Crane_ in a storme, and as secure as a _Dormouse_ in a calme.[4] In a tempest you shall heare him pray, but so amethodically, as it argues that hee is seldome vers'd in that _practice_. Feare is the principall motive of his devotion; yet I am perswaded, for forme sake, he shewes more than hee feeles. Hee loves to fish in troubled waters,[5] have an Oare in every mans boate,[6] and to breake the tenth Commandement in the conclusion of his lukewarme

prayer; <u>Hey</u>, <u>for</u> <u>a</u> <u>rich</u> <u>prize</u>. Hee lives in a tottring state,
and he fits himselfe to it. Hee is as constant as the <u>Moone</u>
in his resolves. So hee can have <u>Sea-roome</u>, no coast holds it
selfe to bee of more firme Land. If hee play the <u>Sea-sharke</u>,
and advance his fortunes by a precious prize: yet to spare his
Executors that labour, hee intends a course to leave them a
few ends of gold or silver. Hee must feede his **valour** with the
liquid <u>spirit</u> of some piercing <u>Elixer</u>: and thus hee ducks and
dives out his time like a true <u>Didapper</u>. Hee makes small or
no choice of his pallet; he can sleepe as well on a Sacke of
Pumice as a pillow of downe. He was never acquainted much
with civilitie: The Sea ha's taught him other Rhetoricke.
Compassionate himselfe hee could never much, and much lesse
another. He ha's condition'd with the <u>Sea</u> not to make him
sicke: and it is the best of his conceite to jeere at a queasie
stomacke. Hee is more <u>active</u> than <u>contemplative</u>, unlesse hee
turne <u>Astronomer</u>, and that is only in cases of extremity. He
is most constant to his shirt, and other his seldome-wash'd
linnen. He ha's been so long acquainted with the surges of the
Sea, as too long a calme distempers him. He cannot speake low,
the Sea talkes so loud. His advice is seldome taken in navall
affaires; though his hand be strong, his head-peece is stupid.
He is used therefore as a necessary instrument of action: for
hee can spinne up a rope like a <u>Spider</u>, and downe againe like
a <u>lightning</u>. The <u>rope</u> is his roade, and the <u>top-mast</u> his
<u>Beacon</u>. One would think his body were wounded, for hee weares
<u>pitch</u> <u>cloath</u> upon it: but that is invulnerable, unlesse a

bullet casually finde out a Loope-hole, and that quite ripps
up his Saile-cloath. He partakes much of the Chameleon, when
hee is mounted the top-mast: where the ayre is his Diet-bread.
His visage is an unchangeable varnish; neither can winde pierce
it, nor Sunne parch it. He ever takes worse rest when he goes
to bed most sober. Hee will domineere furiously in the height
of his Potation, but hee is quickly cudgell'd out of that
humour by the Master of the house of Correction. Hee ha's
coasted many Countreys, arrived sundry havens, sojourned in
flourishing Cities, and conversed with various sorts of people:
yet call him to account, and you shal find him the unfruitfull'st
Navigatour that ere you conversed with. Deepe drinkers have
ever shallow memories: He can remember nothing more precisely,
than the great vessel at Heidelberg;[7] affaires of state are
above his sconce. It is his best Arithmetick to remember his
months pay: and if necessitie urge him not, hee would scarcely
thinke on that either. What a starveling hee is in a frosty
morning with his Sea-frocke, which seemes as if it were shrunke
from him, and growne too short, but it wil be long enough ere
hee get another? His Signe is alwayes in Aquarius, unlesse hee
bee in his pots, and then it is in Aries.[8] Hee is of a
Phlegmatick[9] watry constitution; very little Sanguine,[10] unlesse
it bee in a Seafight; wherein, though he expect no honour, he
expresseth some dying sparkes of valour, in hope to become
sharer in a pyraticall treasure. Hee hath an invincible
stomack, which Ostridge-like could well-neare digest iron.[11]
He is very seldome subject to surfet, or shorten the dayes of

his <u>watry</u> Pilgrimage with excesse: unlesse it fall out upon
rifling of Wines, that he endanger his <u>Top-saile</u> with an
<u>over-charge</u>. He is many times so long on Sea, as hee forgets
his friends by Land. Associats hee ha's and those so constantly
cleaving, as one voyce commands all. <u>Stares</u> cannot bee more
faithfull in their society, than these <u>Hanskins</u>[12] in their
fraternity. They will brave it valiantly, when they are
ranked together, and relate their adventures with wonderfull
terror. Yet these relations ever halt through want of Learning,
which defect abridgeth the story of their deserving. Necessary
instruments they are, and Agents of maine importance in that
<u>Hydrarchy</u>[13] wherein they live; for the walles of their state
could not subsist without them: but least usefull they are to
themselves, and most needfull of others supportance. They
taste of all <u>waters</u> and all <u>weathers</u>: onely the gale of
prosperitie seldome breathes on their <u>sailes</u>: neither care
they much for any such Companion. They sleepe without feare
of loosing what they enjoy; and in enjoying little, they share
in the lesse burden of cares. Yet it is much to bee wondred
at, that our <u>Sayler</u> should have such frequent occasion to erect
his eye upward, and retaine such servile dejected thoughts inward. He converseth with the Starres, observes their motions,
and by them directs his Compasse. Singular notions derives hee
from them, meane time hee is blind to <u>Him</u> that made them. He
sliceth the depths, and is ignorant of <u>Him</u> that confines them;
he cutteth the surging swelling waves, and thinks not of <u>Him</u>
that restraines them; he coasteth by the shelfes, and forgets

<u>Him</u> that secures him. True is that Maxime; <u>Custome takes away the apprehension of passion</u>.¹⁴ In the infancy of his Profession, there appeared not a billow before his eyes, which convey'd not a feare unto his heart. Numerous perils ha's hee now passed, hourely objects of approaching danger are presented, yet these as well as those equally sleighted. Death he ha's seene in so many shapes, as it can cannot amate him, appeare it never so terrible unto him. Yet needs must that Enemy affright him against whom hee comes, for whom hee was never provided before hee came. Well; suppose him now drawing towards the <u>Port</u>, where all <u>mortalitie</u> must land. Hee ha's tugg'd long enough upon the <u>Maine</u>, he must now gather up his vessels within the <u>haven</u>. He ha's drawne in his <u>sayles</u>, and taken adew of the Sea: unlesse she shew him so much kindnesse, as to receive him into her briny bosome, and intombe him dying, whom she entertained living: which courtesie if she tender him, the wormes are deceived by him, for hee goes not the way of all flesh, but the way of all fish, whose fry feedes on him, as their forefathers fed him.

19. A Traveller

Is a Journeyman; but can never bee freeman,[1] till hee bee endenized in his owne Countrey. Hee is troubled with a perpetuall migrim;[2] at Sea hee wisheth to bee on Land, and on Land at Sea. Hee makes his life a right Pilgrimage, for hee findes no place to abide in, but only to sojourne in: so as the wandring Jew[3] may bee his Embleme. The whole World is his Inne, where savage beasts as well as reasonable men are his Inmates. Hee converseth with all Nations, and partakes of their natures: wherein generally, vice becomes a more attractive object than vertue. Whence it is, that hee oftner improves his knowledge, than his life; his language, than carriage. Hee takes a survey of this universe, in the sites of Cities, Countries, and Provinces; and observes what seemes most remarkeable; meane time hee observes himselfe so sleightly, as one can hardly distinguish the substance from the shadow. Now hee is for lanching into the deepe; to visit forraine states; wherein, to accommodate himselfe all the better for this giddy age wherein hee lives, hee culls out some humorous Observance or other from every Countrey, to make his fruitlesse freight more valued, himselfe more admired, and his returne more accepted. He will usually lose himselfe in a dilated discourse of his Travaile: and if his memory bee not all the better, impe[4] his relations with tedious repetitions, impertinent diversions, yea, now and then with absurd

contradictions. The principall Subject of his discourse
trencheth upon[5] rare and unseene Monuments, which hee decketh
with such a varnish and variety of art, and expresseth in such
lively Colours, as one would constantly beleeve his relations
to bee farre truer than they are. Cities hee deblazons as if
he were their Herald:[6] styling Constantinople the storehouse
of Greece; Paris the regall of France; Venice the eye of Italy;
Florence the Seat of Beauty; Rome the Lady Citty with her
imprese: ORBIS IN URBE.[7] In which, as in all things els, he
is meerely titular. He can mould himselfe to all conditions,
fashions and religions. But in all these three hee returnes
for most part, far worse than before he went forth. In the
first he ha's learn'd to be loose and lascivious; in the
second, phantastically humorous; in the third, strangely
superstitious. Some things hee observes worth remembring, if
hee liv'd in an other age: but like an understanding Timist,[8]
hee holds no concurrence with that fashion, which agrees not
with the humour of his Nation. Having now chang'd his ayre, and
with continuance, his haire, but not one of his conditions; he
reviewes his owne Countrey with a kind of disdainefull loathing,
as if there were nothing in it worthy loving. He disvalues our
rarities, disesteemes our beauties, jeeres at our complement,
slights our entertainment, and clozeth up his unseasoned distaste with an interjection of admiration: O the rare objects
that I have seene in my dayes! Then hee runnes on in a meere
verball circuit of affected discourse, which the ignorant onely
admire, and weaker than women affect. Meane time, hee intro-
duceth some conceits of his owne, as fashions in request: Which

hee seconds with high approvement, being his owne Master-piece.
And that hee might represent in himselfe this patterne of
perfection, and move others to imitate his postures: you may
suppose him walking, like one made up in Wainescot;[9] not an
irregular haire about him, nor an unset looke to attend him,
nor an uncomposed cringe[10] to accoutre him. With what contempt
he re-salutes a common Congie?[11] And as if it were derogation,
to a man of his place, not to observe his distance, in a spit,
ducke or nod, as well as pace, hee will rectifie that error too,
to make those Consorts with whom hee deignes to converse, or
communicate himselfe, every way accomplished as himselfe. Hee
holds the state much ingag'd to his observances: so highly hath
vaine-glory wrought with him as it hath brought him to idolatrize
himselfe. Now, should hee cast up his accompts, and collect the
benefit and revenew of his Travailes, with the expence of his
time and treasures; hee would finde his decrements[12] great, his
increments small: his receits come farre short of his disbursements. Hee is exquisite, indeed, in that which this age calls
complement. Hee is all for your Servants Servant, and titles of
lowest observance. Hee overcomes his Mistresses stomach with
this overlarded protest; "He lives not but by her, nor desires
to live but for her; hee plants his love in an equall diameter
betweene Bellona and Minerva,[13] reason and courage;" yet is hee
no lesse barraine of the one, than coole in the other. Or else,
hee marrieth with his instrument his voyce, matched with an
Italian Canto,[14] and ayr'd with more Crochets,[15] than hee ha's
pence in his Budget.[16] This is the vintage[17] of his Pilgrimage.

He hath traced this <u>Theatre</u> of earth,[18] and made himselfe the
<u>Embleme</u> of what hee is; much hath hee seene, with many hath
hee convers'd, and a full view hath hee taken of this <u>inferiour</u>
<u>globe</u>. Diversity of soiles, variety of fruits, multiplicity
of creatures have his eyes enjoyed, yet rest not satisfied;
through many Coasts and Countreyes hath hee <u>travelled</u>,yet his
experience in those peoples natures little improved; In sundry
Citties hath he sojorned, yet from their knowledge now
estranged. <u>Merchants</u> of unvalued fortunes hath hee seene
<u>splitted</u>, while <u>their factors</u>[19] sported; <u>ruin'd</u> while they
<u>rioted</u>. <u>Curtizans</u> hee hath observed, their sumptuous state,
the fuell of their maintenance, and how their Comick Scenes
ever clozed with tragick Catastrophees. <u>Forraine favorites</u>
hath hee marked, their projects, designes, events: What faire
flourishes their first admittance to their Princes presence
shewed; how soone those fading blossoms of vading[20] glory were
nipped. Stately and sumptuous <u>statues</u> of victorious Champions
hath hee eyed, their inscriptions perused, and trampled upon
those scattred ashes (the remaines of a greater worke) which
sometimes were with the breath of fame enlivened. Thus <u>great</u>
<u>stones</u> are become <u>great mens</u> covers. No distinction betwixt
the Noble and Ignoble, save onely that the higher <u>Peere</u> is
crushed with the heavier <u>pile</u>. High and goodly <u>structures</u>
brought to rubbish, and flourishing <u>states</u> to ruine, hath hee
noted. And now drawing towards his owne native soile; hee
admireth nothing more, than to see <u>hospitality</u> so much honoured
abroad, and so contemptible at home. Great houses without

Householders', promising Harbours without Harbour. This he
observes for the greatest <u>Eye-sore</u> to the way-bet <u>Traveller</u>;
the grievous'st <u>blemish</u> to a prosperous <u>State</u>. He goes to the
gate and knocks, but the <u>Court</u> ha's swallow'd up the hall;
this <u>complete Peregrine</u> may sooner breake his <u>necke</u> than his
<u>fast</u>; which makes him cry out most passionately, forth of a
sensible compassion of his owne necessity: <u>O the Rendevou's
of Hospitality which I have seene</u>! But by this time, his
<u>Cariere</u> through the world hath made him wearie. He ha's a
great desire for the benefit of his Countrey (as hee pretends)
to communicate these leane scraps of his starved <u>Travailes</u> to
the world. Publish'd hee would have them (according to the
<u>Erata's</u> of his life): in <u>folio</u>: but so indigested[21] are his
collections, and so illaborate[22] his style, as the <u>Stationer</u>
shunnes them like a <u>Noli me tangere</u>,[23] fearing their <u>sale</u>.
Well; though the <u>World</u> will not receive them; long winter-nights
and his Neighbours credulous eares shall entertaine them. Where
having told his <u>tale</u>, hee hopes out of the wide <u>Circumference</u>
of his <u>Travailes</u>, to find so much ground as will afford him
a grave.

20. An Undersheriffe[1]

Is a master of fence; and by deputation, the Countenance[2] of the County wherein hee lives. The Kings Letters he opens as familiarly as if they were but neighbourly commends: and brings more unwelcome salutes from the Prince, to his Subject, than he hath thanks for. Waifes and straies hee impounds in his pocket: for Felons goods, hee compounds for them at his owne rate: all which hee doth by vertue of his Office, if there bee any vertue extant in it. A terrible pudder[3] hee keepes with his repledges[4] and distresses:[5] the State could hardly subsist without such a grave Censor. Hee professeth more execution than judgement. A great portion of his discretion is incorporated in his White staffe: which is as terrible to a yealous[6] debter, as deaths head to an Usurer.[7] If hee attemper his Office with the balme of connivence, it bindes an ample recompence. Next to whetting ones knife at the Counter-gate,[8] I hold it the desperatest assay[9] to affront him. If you would gratifie him, a better turne you cannot doe him, than by turning Informer at the Sheriffs turne.[10] Where, presentments of decayed wayes, Buts,[11] Blood-sheds, with other enormities, are no lesse beneficiall to the publike state in their redresse, than to his private stocke upon the distresse.[12] Notable cunning Terriers hee hath besides, of all sorts and sizes; some to rouse and raise his game; Others

of lighter temper to have it in hot pursuit: the last sort on
whom hee principally relyes, being stronger and stiffer, to
cloze and grapple with his prey, and bring it downe. Thus hee
shewes himselfe every way more active than contemplative. Hee
is of an excellent memory: for if you cannot remember your debts
your selfe, hee will put you in mind of them. His head is many
times full of Proclamations, which, hee cannot rest, till he
vent. Hee would make a strange Secretarie,[13] for hee will not
sticke to cry at the Crosse,[14] what hee heares. Hee tenders
all serviceable observance to his Superiours, a kind of slight
acquaintance to his equalls, but a disdainfull contempt to his
inferiours. By helpe of some Law-presidents, he retaines the
elements of that profession, which hee makes singular use of:
though hee bee no sworne Atturney, hee can accept gratuities in
lieu of fees; and by meanes of his inbred ingenuity, alter the
propriety of them.[15] Hee is much conversant in the Statutes:
imploying a great part of his time in an usefull exposition, or
rather inversion of them. He would gladly bring in profit, and
keepe himselfe within compasse of statute. This is the highest
pitch of knowledge, which his vocation calls him to: and this
hee hopes conference and experience in time will bring him to.
Authority is his sole Subterfuge in all his extremities: which
(by abusing his Author) many times leaves him in his own hand.[16]
In the Subject of wrongs;[17] he is oftner active than passive.
None can justly lay an aspersion on him, which hee hath not some
underhand Depute to take to. It is his constant Tenet; So long
as the root holds untainted, the inferiour sprigs and siens[18] may

bee supported: but when it growes shaken, the branches must needs
suffer. So long as hee holds up his head, his <u>Nits</u> may finde
harbour: but squeaze him, and they are starv'd for ever. Hee
yearely improves his <u>place</u> by some usefull <u>project</u> or other,
which hee leaves as a Memoriall of his love, and argument of his
wit to all succeeding Professors in that <u>Craft</u>. He never serv'd
as <u>Apprentice</u> to <u>Plasterer</u> or <u>Mason,</u> and yet hee knowes the
<u>craft</u> of <u>dawbing;</u>[19] and hee will lay it on before hee suffer
disgrace. <u>Crimes</u> require <u>Curtaines</u>; <u>Spiders</u> their <u>cauls</u>.
Places of Office must be <u>unctuous</u> if <u>vicious</u>. But service is
no <u>inheritance</u>; lest therefore in processe of time, either hee
should grow wearie of his place, or his place of him; like a
provident <u>Pismire</u>,[20] hee beginnes now in his <u>Summer</u>, to store
up against <u>winter</u>. <u>Fines</u> and <u>amerciaments</u>[21] must inhaunce his
<u>rents</u> and <u>hereditaments</u>:[22] for which he contracts now and then
with the <u>Clerke</u> of the <u>Market</u>,[23] whom he palpably guls, and
consequently proves; <u>All</u> <u>Clerkes</u> <u>are</u> <u>not</u> <u>the</u> <u>wisest</u> <u>men</u>.[24]
Such a parcell of ground buts neer him, and is an <u>eye-sore</u> to
him: gladly would he have it, though the owner have neither mind
nor neede to sell it. His braines must plot for this purchase;
and his witty <u>Genius</u>, after long plodding, hath found a way to
supple him. <u>Contempts</u>, which this simple <u>Snake</u> never dream'd
of, must be forthwith levied. No interplea[25] nor demurre[26]
will serve; he must timely prevent[27] the occasion, and remove
the <u>ground</u> (which is the <u>ground-work</u> of his disquiet) from him
and his heires for ever, by accepting a low price to purchase
his owne peace, and make the <u>Undersheriffe</u> his friend. Of two

extreams the lesse is to be chosen; thus scrues he himselfe into
every convenient bargaine. By this time, so important are his
affaires at home, as they estrange him from employments abroad.
His nimble ferrets must now become Pioners[28] for their Master;
who coupes[29] them, lest they should grow too fat to endure
labour. Suppose him then, who was once a man in his time, and
an experienc'd professant; One, who had beene acquainted with
most writs except holy writ; served Precepts many, but observed
few; retired like a Cricket to his Oven-mouth: where he warmes
himselfe well without, having cold comfort to warme him within.
During the whole progresse of his time hee was for gathering,
the residue of his dayes hee bestowes in disposing. Hopefull
Cubbs he hath to conferre his hopelesse state on. No matter;
their Earth-resolving fathers fines make them fine; his
amerciaments cause them dive deepe into the Mercers booke. Now
the Webbe of his fading fortunes interwoven with the injurious
warp of dishonest practices, is to be divided peece-meale into
shredds and parcells. So much hee allots to his sonne and
heire, who meanes to be the very first and last of his house;
so much to his second; so much to his third: with competent[30]
portions, to better his daughters proportions. Meane time,
(see the fatall overture of this wisemans providence!) He is
called to an accompt before his time, (yet all in due time)
for arrerages to the High-sheriffe his Master, and abuse of his
place. His whole estate will hardly repay the stake. Hee
would gladly come off faire, and I cannot blame him: But his
Pinnace road still at Harbour till now: an unexpected tempest

hath assailed him: And he must make speedy restitution for all
his pillage. Hee could dispense well enough with Conscience,
and gaine by the Contract: but the misery of it is, hee findes
himselfe now at last a prisoner and in bonds to the Sheriffe;
whereby hee stands bound to keepe him harmelesse (but well had
it beene for his Countrey if he had prov'd so:) which securitie
is the argument of his Tragedie. It were not amisse that hee
altered his Will, and (though much against his will) made his
Master his sole Executor. It must bee so: Thus by prolling[31]
to get all, hee ha's fool'd himselfe out of all: Onely, hee
may goe with more peace to Earth, since hee ha's made so cleare
account on Earth. It were a sinne to disquiet him, since hee
carries his Quietus est[32] with him.

21. A Wine-soaker

Is an ingenious Engine, that runs on Wheeles.[1] If one
of the wits, he is merry Cricket, or a muddy Criticke; a
wittie waggish Braine-worme,[2] and can solely hug a pot, as
if it were his darling. He is mighty valiant, for he dare
be drunke; And desperate if hee bee challenged, for his
weapons are pot-guns.[3] By this time hee hath called the
Drawers rogues, with much facilitie, yet (as hee is a true
Northerne Blade) joyes in their felicitie. And now, for it
growes late, he hath had his Evening lecture, and trenching
home, supported by his friendly Impressor, makes every foote
an Indenture.[4] Hee calls the Scavingers[5] wife familiarly

whoore, though she be as honest as one of an higher Station.
Casually, through the misery of a long-neckt spurre hee falls
(if the Cellar doore be open[6]) and unsealing his eyes, seeing
the consorts of iniquitie, clinging close to a pot in the
nooke of a Chimney, hee vowes himselfe thrice blest to have   5
fallen into so sweete and sociable a Company. By this, hee
falls further; whence a Pedanticall Translator starts up, and
askes him; What sayes the Prophet? And he answers; He bade me
goe seeke my fathers Asses, and having found them to returne
againe. After him struts up a most Thrasonicall Thraskite,[7]   10
and askes him; What saith the Calydonian Poet: And hee answers,
That the braying of an Asse in the bottom of a Cellar, to an
illiterate gull is a delicate humor. He loves sometimes to take
the ayre, and taste what strong broth the Countrey affords.
Where this Malt-worme encounters with a portion of frontineacke,[8] 15
which sackes his Capitall, makes his tongue cant broken English,
his supporters to faile in their postures, and enterfeare
dangerously. By this time his cause is heard, and now this
val-dunke growne rampant-drunke,[9] would fight if hee knew how,
and make his sally out a doore if hee could finde it. Yet he   20
will out, there is no remedie, and stalke homeward, though it
be late, towards the Citie. Where in the way, if he unhappily
fall into a Gravell-pit, hee taxeth the Citie for her government, for leaving her Cellar doores so wide open at that time
a night. Yet on hee trucks, if he can mount the pit, where   25
indenturing along in some blinde-Alley, hee terribly affrights
the Passenger if hee meete any: For hee coasts here and there,

as if it were Saint Anthonies fire,[10] or some ignis fatuus,[11] whereas, his cresset-flaming[12] nose is the sole incendiary of these Chymera's. Hee ha's a mightie desire to squabble with the Watch; but the inarticulate motion of his tongue makes those illiterate Rug-gownes[13] thinke hee speakes Heathen Greeke. So as their compassion to a stranger, which they gather by his strange language, moves them to commiserate his case; This gets him a Lanthorne and a conducter; but for his lodging, he is nere a whit the nearer, for he ha's quite forgot his plantation. Thus then like Hyppocrates twinnes[14] walke these two coupled together, but secure from danger, for a watchmans Lanthorne is a Drunkards Supersedeas.[15] Gladly would this frozen Centinell returne to his charge, and leave his luggage: but hee clings to him like the barke to the tree; hee calls this goat-bearded Groome his Amaryllis,[16] and hee will love her eternally. At last his Amaryllis (this officer I mean) perswades him for want of a bed to take a nappe on a bench till the morning: but he ha's so much wit as to scorne advice, preferring this walke in his Gallery (for so hee tearmes it) before the repose in his pallet. It is a wonder with what extravagancies hee entertaines his conducter: who admires his learning, if he were himselfe. By this, the blinde Lanthorne growes surfoot, sleepie, and thirstie; along therefore with his zanie (like a night-roving Lazarello[17]) hee accoasts a Taphouse boldly, thumps stoutly, and by vertue of his authoritie, enters couragiously. Halfe a dozen quencheth the Officious Salamanders thirst,[18] and bringeth this wandring planet to his rest; where hee is left to the Tapsters care, or Drawers

cure; For the charge it is his, if his coyne will answere:
howsoever, a good pawne never sham'd his master. In a word,
hee is in the Evening, what you shall not finde him in the
Morning. Hee takes leave of the Drawer, with a solemne salute
as if he were dying; and so he is, for hee droopes and droppes   5
downe dead at the end of a reckoning.

22. A Xantippean

Is a Scold in English.[1] The wheele of her tongue goes
with a perpetuall motion: yet she spits more than she speakes:
and never spits but in spite. Shee is never lesse at ease,   10
than when she is quiet; nor better pleased, than when the whole
family is displeased. Shee makes every place where shee comes,
an Enclosure, and rayles it about at her owne proper charge.[2]
She is never at quiet but when she is at rest, nor at rest,
but when she is sleeping, nor then neither; for purposely she   15
awakes the house with a terrible fit of snoring. A Burre
about the Moone is not halfe so certaine a presage of a tempest,
as her Brow is of a storme. Laurell, hauthorne, and Seale-skinne
are held preservatives against thunder; but no receite[3] can bee
found so soveraigne[4] as to still her clamour. She makes such   20
a pattring with her lips, as if she were possest; and so shee
is, with the spirit of contention. She is wormewood in bed,[5]
and a Chafing-dish at boord. Shee cannot possibly take cold,
for shee is ever in a heat. Shee holds no infirmitie worse then
to be tongue-tyde. She loves a good bit[6] but hates a bridle.   25
It is a wonder shee fell not fowle with the Priest, when shee

was married. Many times since hath she cursed him, but hee
feares no worse. Methinks I see the creeping Snaile her
husband, blesse him, as if there were Lightning, when hee comes
in her presence. Shee ha's either quite forgot his name, or
else shee likes it not, which makes her re-baptise him with
names of her owne. Shee accoasts him with such fresh but
furious encounters, as he sneakes away from her like a Truant
from his Master. Hee is never more homely used than at home:
so as to comfort his cold stomach, and encourage him all the
better against his next encounter, he hath challeng'd a pot of
Ale to enter lists with him in a single combat. The challenge
is entertained, the field pitched, the weapons provided. Where,
though the pot lose more blood, yet the Challenger gets the
foile. Home hee would goe, if he could goe, but he must first
learne to stand before hee goe: and so by holds till hee crawll
home. Meane time, suppose him now drawing out his Indentures[7]
at length; observing his recoyles and retreits, and spending
halfe the night and more in his short journey. Moone-light he
needes not, for hee hath a nose in graine to guide him, which,
were his eyes matches, would quickly fire him. But see the
strength of imagination! While his crazie vessell is rowling
homeward, a sudden panicke feare suggests to his phantasie
ever working, the apparition of a spirit now approaching. Betwixt two wayes, perplexed with two mindes, he stands amazed;
feare bids him retire, and desire bids him go on. And so
strange hath his resolution wrought with him, as he intends
not onely to goe on his way, but to expostulate the case with

this imaginarie Hoblin[8] that bids him stay; and thus hee encounters it, having first blessed him, to make him more successive in the conquest of it: If thou beest a good spirit, thou wilt doe mee no harme, such is my affiance;[9] and if the Divell himselfe, thou hast no reason to doe mee harme, for I married thy sister, and claime thy alliance. But this Spirit in a sheete, is presently transform'd into some sheepe, so as his feare (if he had so much apprehension left him) is to reflect more on his Spirit at home, than this in the way: for this was but seemingly visible, whereas that he goes to, will prove personally sensible. Hee findes her asleepe, but muttering words of revenge: which upon her awaking (and long may it bee first) shee makes shew of, by grinding her teeth, beating her fist, and other outward tokens, fully to execute. All this while, hee sleeps soundly without rocking, till an unseasonable correction awake him. Now the Waspe is raised; the hornet roused. Sure hee is to bee caperclawed;[10] Cap a pe,[11] he hath no sence for it. He must beare it off with head and shoulders, and arme himselfe with patience, against all encounters. Every looke she darts is a lash to scourge him; Every Word she speaks is a wound to gall him. Non vox hominem sonat, O Dea certe![12] Happy were hee, if the World were rid of him, or hee of her. Gladly would hee reclaime her without shame, or disclaime in her his share: But as shee hates ever to admit of the former, so he despaires of the happines to partake of the later. Sundry distracted thoughts doe perplexe him; sometimes hee thinkes verily, that this ill-agrement betwixt

them, proceds either from some ceremonie in his marriage
neglected, or some circumstance or other omitted, or that
the banes of matrimonie were not dewly published, or sure in
some point or other they were not rightly married. So as,
gladly would hee (if the orders of the Church would permit it)
bee <u>remarried</u>, to trie for once a conclusion, if hee could
prevent his former disquiet, by an old marriage new solemnized:
but his <u>Pastor</u> smellt his drift, and will by no meanes condescend to so irregular a motion: fearing (by all likelyhood)
that when hee commes to the giving of <u>this woman to this man</u>,
he will not take her but leave her in his owne hand. But his
indifference little troubles her: her onely feare is, that shee
cannot picke quarrels enough to baste him: which afflicts her
above comparison. If any one reprove her for it, shee twitts
them with ignorance, replying, she knowes better than they what
is good for him; and she seconds her assertion with naturall
reading.[13] "If cudgelling be useful to the <u>Walnut tree</u>, to make
it fruitfull, a little correction seasoned with discretion,
cannot do amisse to make her <u>husband</u> more dutifull."[14] This
causeth him to resolve some times of more violent conclusions:
for hee thinkes with himselfe, how desperate sore must have
desperate cures. He vowes therefore, to bring her in all disgrace to the <u>Cucking-stoole</u>;[15] and shee **vowes** againe, to bring
him with all contempt to the <u>stoole</u> of <u>repentance</u>.[16] Thus,
tread he never so softly, this worme will turne againe. There
is no humour (so strangely is she humorous) can affect her; no
conceit, how pregnant or present soever, delight her; no company,

how affable or sociable soever, content her. Shee is apt to
interpret what shee heares, evermore to the worst sense. More
captious than capable of offence. Impatient of any ones prayse.
Attentive to the report of their disgrace. Onely strong in will,
which shee counterpoizeth with want of worth. All her neighbours   5
blesse them from her: wishing this <u>quotidian fever</u> of her tongue
cur'd with a <u>razor</u>. She hath liv'd to a faire houre; for where-
soe're she comes, shee may have the roome her selfe. She needes
neither contend nor contest for priority of place, nor precedencie
at table, nor opinion in argument; her selfe serves for a whole   10
messe, for her <u>Gossips</u> have left her. Well for all this, there is
a meagre, rawbon'd <u>shrimpe</u>, that dare and will accoast her. He
is not one of many words, though she be. But his <u>will</u> is his
<u>law</u>; which none can <u>oppose</u>, much lesse prevent, with <u>price</u>,
<u>prayer</u>, <u>power</u>, or <u>policie</u>. Her unpeaceable <u>tongue</u> must now bee   15
bound to good behaviour; a lasting silence must charme it. This
her Neighbours heare, that shee is laid <u>speechlesse</u> (which
assures them she cannot live long): to her therefore they repaire,
to performe the last office of Christian charitie, and commend
her (with all their hearts) to Earth, implying how weary they   20
were of her company. Her funerall solemnity is the first day
of her husbands <u>Jubile</u>:[17] for all the wrongs she did him on
Earth, she ha's made him sufficient amends now by her death.
Howbeit, <u>hee</u>, on whom by generall suffrage of the Gods, the
golden <u>Tripode</u> was first bestowed, and to whom our <u>Zantippe</u> was   25
espoused,[18] held that currish opinion of <u>Timon</u> fit to bee ex-
ploded; who wish'd all Women <u>suspended</u>, blessing all such fruit

trees, as were so plentifully stored:[19] to whose milder
judgement I appeale; clozing with the Poet.

>Curst bee the Tree which Timon blest,
>Curst be his hatefull vowes,
>Women were made in Bowers to hugge, 5
>And not to hang on Bowes.[20]

23. A Yealous[1] Neighbour

Is an Eave-dropper. He would make an excellent Ratcatcher,
for hee is creeping and sneaking in every corner. Though hee
have no argument whereon to ground his credulous suspicion, his 10
imagination suggests to him variety of matter, which serves for
fewell to feede his distemper. The signe with him is ever in
Aries,[2] as hee is strongly conceited. The next yeare hee will
bee a high-flyer, for hee is this yeare a Brancher.[3] Hee dare
not for an empire goe a hunting, lest his dogges take him for 15
Acteon,[4] and so worry him. His blood is fouley infected, which
annoyes him desperately with the yellowes.[5] The Bird Galgulus[6]
hath first ey'd him, which makes him labour of an incurable
Jaundise. Hee would pawne his estate for those two rings of
Giges[7] and Hans Carvile,[8] but the latter hee holds fitter for 20
his purpose, though the former might make him an invisible
Cuckold. Hee lookes with a meagre complexion, which discovers
his inward infection. Hee feeles not a pimple in his forehead,
which publisheth not his fate. Sometimes hee will expostulate
his wrongs himselfe, and say; Well; what remedy? I am neither 25
the first nor last; Patience shall be my plaister. Meane time,

hee is as patient as a Waspe or an Hornet. Hee will scarce
credit his owne eyes, when he sees nothing but actions of
modesty: all which he imagins meere deceptions of sight;
purposely to gull his ignorance, and guild sinne with a Saintly
holinesse. He heares all that neighbour neare him, or resort
unto him, say, They never saw Children liker their father; and
yet (replies he) not one of them al is like an other. He is
a little Puritanically affected, yet private conventicles[9]
hee affects[10] not. Hee feedes his humour more with shadowes
than substance. Travaile hee would to the next market towne,
in hope of profit; but hee turnes backe before hee come halfe
way there, to take her napping to his owne discredit. Hee is
sometimes resolved to proclaime his shame, but hee feares by
that meanes, hee shall increase his shame, and adde to the
number of her acquaintance. How like a sillie man hee lookes
in the presence of his wife and a proper attendant? What a
dejected eye hee casts upon himselfe, and yealous he is of this
strangers Count'nance? He feeles whether his eares go not
through his Night-cappe; and if his forehead beginne not to
burgen. Hee bids his Apprentice looke to his foreman, and
acquaint him with what hee heares or sees. Hee calls the
Shoomaker impudent knave, for pulling on his wives shooe; and
offering to beate him, wisheth it were his Last: and that, as
hee is ever working his owne ends, he may have a speedy end.
Hee exclaimes grievously against her Body-maker, and inverting
his name, calles him directly Baud-maker: he vowes to strip
his Corporation starke naked, and lash him with Whalebone. Hee

buyes his wives gownes ready made, fearing (belike) some <u>false
measure</u> from the <u>Tayler</u>. In her presence he fetcheth a deepe
sigh, semi-brev'd[11] in these words: <u>Well; shee might bee
honest, if shee had so much grace; I have been held a proper
man in my time.</u> You shall find him by whole houres together
<u>eave-dropping</u> under his <u>Lettice</u>,[12] or peeping through a a Key-
hole, purposely to take her napping. Never man tooke more
paines to adde fresh fuell to his affliction. Hee could wish
with all his hart, that it were enacted by the whole house of
Parliament for <u>fornication</u> to bee <u>Felony</u>. He hath solemnely
vow'd, never to take journey when either the Signe is in <u>Aries</u>,
<u>Taurus</u>, or <u>Capricorne</u>.[13] When the <u>Lion</u> banished all <u>horne-beasts</u>
his <u>Court</u>, it was impossible for me (saith he) to turne <u>Courtier</u>.
Hee had some smattering in the Elements of all Learning, but
hee ha's forgot all, and now like a <u>Truant</u> must turne back to
his <u>Horne-booke</u>. Thus he trifles out his time in the discovery
of his owne shame. He hunts all the day long from chamber to
chamber: and lest <u>Locks</u> or <u>boults</u> might become a <u>Supersedeas</u>[14]
to keep <u>open-house</u> to give more ayre to his Larder, though he
suffer pillage for his labour. He hath lately created a new
Officer, who every evening cryes, <u>Hang out your Lanthorne and
Candlelight maids</u>;[15] The Night is darke, and the entrie long;
timely preventions is the life of policy. With his wife sleeping and waking he keepes <u>diapason</u>;[16] he wakes till shee sleepe,
lest she should give him the slip. His sleepes are short and
troubled: and when hee awakes, the first thing hee does, is
seeking whether shee bee there or no. Hee lookes sometimes as

if hee were affrighted; but it is his owne **spirit** that haunts him: yet were his wife all **spirit** and no **substance**, he should be lesse affrighted. Hee dare not for a world looke himselfe i'th glasse, lest he should eye his owne **deformity**. He holds that a wife may make her husband one of the strangest **Monsters** in **Europe**. He wisheth he could sustaine nature without sleep, that he might take fuller view of his wives **night-works**. Hee is never lesse drunke with this distemper, than when he is distempered with liquor: and then hee gives best opportunitie, but sees it not. He hath but lately stept into an **office**, and that one of the lowest in all his **Ward**, yet hee verily thinks that the whole **Ward** holds him for one of the **headmen** of their **Parish**. Store of **Bisket**, **Wafers** and **Careawayes** hee bestowes at his Childs Christning, yet are his **cares** nothing lessned; he is perswaded, that he may eate his part of this Babe, and never breake his fast. Hee presents himselfe for a **Gentleman-Usher**[17] to his wife, when her humour is for taking the ayre: before whom he walkes most pedantically stoicall, yet with a reflecting eye, lest some **fiend** should steale away his **Proserpina**.[18] In a word, his **yealous** minde, and his two suspicious eyes are the **Hesperides**, his **Wife** the **golden grove**; whose fruit is so mellow, as he feares it will **fall** before the time. It is in vaine to apply any receites to cure his malady; no **Unicornes horne** can possibly helpe this poisonous infection. Suspition once grounded, and by continuance hardned, can scarcely by force of any argument bee removed. For all this, howsoever it fare with him touching his **reall** estate, it thrives well with him in his **personall**;

for hee ha's store of Cornucopia. He is by this time as weary
of the world, as his wife is of him. He would gladly leave it,
but there is something hee so dotingly loves in it, as he cannot find in his heart to forgoe it, unlesse along with him he
might carry it. He knowes how to dispose of his goods, but not   5
of all his moveables. He doubts another must possesse, what
hee enjoyed with so much care: and jeere at his follies, whilest
his Successour supplies his place. Hee would articulate[19] with
his wife, if hee had so much hope in her constancy; or opinion
of his owne deserts, to expect from her so much loyalty;   10
clozing his short-liv'd words with these passionate interbreaths;
Nay surely, I shall bee soone forgotten. Her protests cannot
remove from his this conceite; it were to no purpose therefore
for her to promise what hee neither will beleeve, no shee
intends to performe. His eyes now begin to shroud themselves   15
in their lodges. He hath by this disposed of all things that
are in his power, even to that vessell of frailtie, his earth-
reverting body, which (according to his mind) is to be buried
in some Cell, Roach,[20] or Vault, and in no open place, lest
Passengers (belike) might stumble on his grave. Meate for   20
his funerall pye is shred, some few ceremoniall teares on his
funerall pile are shed; but the wormes are scarce entred his
shroud, his corpse-flowers not fully dead, till this Yealous
Earth-worme is forgot, and another more amorous, but lesse
yealous, mounted his bed.   25

24. A Zealous Brother

Is a sure stake to his Sister; Hee sets forth in an
Amsterdam print[1] his faith and workes in two severall tomes,
and in two different volumes; the first in folio, the latter
in Decimo Sexto.[2] Hee is an Antipos[3] to all Church government; When shee feasts hee fasts; when shee fasts, hee feasts;
Good-Fryday is his Shrove-Tuesday;[4] Hee commends this notable
carnall caveat to his family; Eate flesh upon dayes prohibited,
it is good against Popery: He buyes a Blank Almanack,[5] to set
downe his conventicle houres. Breach of promise with the un-
sanctified, hee holds an indifferent error, but with his Sister
is is piacular.[6] There is nothing so farre out of tune in his
eare as Church-musicke. He keeps a terrible quarter in his
sinnefull Synodalls,[7] and denounceth an heavie woe upon all
Wakes, Summerings, and Rush-bearings: preferring that Act,
whereby Pipers were made rogues by Act of Parliament, before
any in all the Acts and Monuments.[8] His Band is a Diminitive,
but his choler a Superlative,[9] if hee bee provok't. Hee is so
possest with inspiration, as he holds it a distrusting of the
Spirit to use premeditation. No spirit can affright him so
much in any shape, as in the habit of a Sirpe-cloath.[10] Hee
ever takes the Crosse on his left hand, to avoid superstition.
Hee ha's bountifull Benefactours, from whom hee receives
weekely Presents; and they know his mind: "Halfe Sacrifices
are abhominable"; This faithfull Family is his Monopoly; hee

ha's ingross'd them to himselfe; hee feedes on them, while
hee feedes them.[11] His frequent preaching leaves him no time
to pray in; He can stand better than he can kneele. Hee loves
mixt societies, and hee takes this from the Arke, where there
was a Male and Female of every kind. Hee avoucheth, that
learned Lilie most orthodoxally proved the undoubted necessity
of matrimony in the presbytery, in his declination of hic &
hac sacerdos.[12] Hee holds his Mother tongue[13] to be the
Originall tongue; and in that only he is constant, for he
hath none to change it with all. Hee wonders how Babel should
have such a confused variety of tongues, and hee understand but
one. He never reades any Author, lest hee should bee held for
an Apocryphall Pastor.[14] One would take him for an incessant
Student by his pale visage and enfeebled body; but the bent of
his studies intends more the practick than Theorick. Hee is
seldome or never constant to those Tenets he holds: which prov-
ing for most part scarce Orthodoxall, doe usually convent him:[15]
which makes him grow in great request with the purely-ignorant.
Hee holds all Bonds bearing date at Lammasse, Michaelmasse,
Candlemasse, or any Masse whatsoever, to be frustrate and of
no effect; but by changing masse into tide,[16] they become of
full force and vertue. Mattins and Vespers hee holds two
dangerous words; hee loves not to heare of them. He maintaines
equality in Presbytery; but if the necessity of time be such,
as a Superintendent bee requisite, his zealous followers hold
none fitter to supply that place than himselfe. For the
decision of al doubts, difficulties, and differences hee makes

a private _family_ to his revestry.[17] Whatsoever tends to the doctrine of _mortification_, hee holds for _Romish_: _abstinence_ therefore he avoucheth to be an _error_ newly crept into the Church; but if you put this _Intergatorie_ to him, in what time it crept, this weakly-read _Deponent_[18] knoweth not. No season through all the yeere accounts hee more subject to _abhominations_ than _Bartholomew_ faire: Their _Drums_, _Hobbihorses_, _Rattles_, _Babies_, _Jewtrumps_,[19] nay _Pigs_ and all are wholly _Judaicall_. The very _Booths_ are _Brothells_ of iniquity, and distinguished by the stampe the _Beast_.[20] Yet under favour, hee will authorize his _Sister_ to eate of that uncleane and irruminating[21] beast, a _Pig_, provided, that this _Pig_ bee fat, and that _himselfe_ or some other _zealous_ _Brother_ accompanie her: and all this is held for authentick and canonicall. Though hee seeme all _spirit_, yet during his beeing in this Tabernacle of clay, he holds it fitting to have a little relish of the _flesh_. He preferres the union of _bodies_ before the union of _minds_; and he holds no unity worse than church-conformity. Hee conceives more inveterate hate towards the Church of _Rome_, than the temple of _Mecha_: and could finde with all his heart rather to embrace the traditions of the _latter_, than submit to the discipline of the _former_. His _devotion_ consists rather in elevation of the eye, than bending of the knee. In his extemporall Sermons hee is a _sonne_ of _thunder_, denouncing terror, but seldome hope of favour to the _dejected_ _sinner_. This desperate doctrine hee continues, and holds them till night, and then leaves them _Children_ _of_ _darkenesse_. Hee thumps a pulpit pittifully, as if hee were

angry; but if hee be, it is with those onely that come short
in their oblations. He baptizeth his Children with Scripture-
names; wherein onely hee shewes the depth of his reading. Yet
in these hee mistakes miserably, for want of Etymology; taking
AMAN for AMON, DIANA for DINA.²² He holds one probable Tenet
constantly; "That there are no walking Spirits on earth"; and
yet he finds a terrible one at home: which all his Divinity
cannot conjure. This hath made him sometimes, to have a months
mind to go for Virginia, to save soules: till hee right wisely
considered, how the enterprise was full of perill, and that hee
wanted materialls to defray the charge of his Travell. Of all
Sects of Philosophers, he cannot endure to heare of the
Academicks;²³ for he never came amongst them. Of all metals,
hee hates Latin:²⁴ for hee hath heard how it was sometimes the
Roman tongue;and that cannot chuse but be Schismaticall. He
feares no shot so much as that of the Canon; for it injoynes
him to that which he most hates, Conformity. Hee would beyond
Sea, but his Duck will not swimme over with him: which makes
him peremptorily conclude; Shee is better fed than taught. Hee
was once in election to have beene a Vice-verger²⁵ in Amsterdam,
but he wanted an audible voice. Howsoever, hee is holden a
great Rabbi amongst his Brethren, whose weaknesse hee strengthens
with perillous paradoxes: which when hee comes to explaine, hee
as little understands as his amazed hearers. He was pleased
sometime to make so bold with affaires of State, Church-government,
with otherlike Subjects farre above his verge,²⁶ as a late asthma
ha's taken him, and restrain'd him to a perpetuall silence.²⁷

This makes his illiterate brutes to double their pensions for
his maintenance; and to idolize him the more, because taken
notice of by the State. And now hee is altogether for his privat
Lectures; where he vents such unauthenticke stuffe, as it proves
pregnantly from what spirit it comes. Hee now takes time to
intend controversies, which he secretly commenceth amongst his
owne Familists,[28] against the Communion Book and Book of
common Prayer. Anthems and Versicles[29] he holds papisticall;
sundry other exceptions hee finds no lesse criminall. But
these quarrels become Conventuall,[30] and he must answer them.
In the end, the contemptiblenesse of his person, with the
weakenesse of his fortunes, rid him out a bryers:[31] while now,
after so many altercations in matters of religion, he purposeth
to have some little bartring with the world, before he goes out
of it, lest his poore progeny curse him that ever he came in it.
But truth is, he shewes the necessity of his Mortification in
nothing so much as in want, which onely makes him out of love
with the world, and gives him the true marke of a Scholer.
Some he hath to provide for, if hee knew how: but hee must
leave them, being abjects through poverty, objects of charity;
yet ha's he no great reason to expect that his broode should
partake of those good workes now after his death, which hee
could never endure to heare so much as commended all his life.
By this our Cornelius is become Tacitus, since hee dropt into
his bathing-tubbe, where hee left his haire, and lost his
honour:[32] since which time, he is quite falne off from his
zealous Brethrens favour: for the dampe of his life hath so

darkened the light of his doctrine, as now for want of audience,
hee may save himselfe a labour. Thus rest of friends, fortune,
health and libertie, hee clozeth his Evening Lecture with a
senselesse Lethargie. There is nothing now that troubles him
so much in his sicknesse, as that the Bells shall ring for him   5
after his death.[33] Which to prevent, hee hath taken course
with his Executour to give the Sexton nothing; purposely to put
the Belfrey to silence. Some Mourners hee hath of his owne,
who howle not so much that hee should leave them, as that nothing
is left them.   10

25. An Apparator

Is the usher of a Ghost in a white sheete.[1] He tels you
of that, which hee himselfe seldome or never remembers till,
his end, Summons. He can most pragmatically[2] discourse of the
Subject of pennance, but findes no time to apply the use unto   15
himselfe. Honesty were a maine prejudice to his practise:
which makes him hold that acquaintance of most weight, whose
conversation is most light. Circumspect you must be in your
words, howsoever you expresse your selfe in your works: for
his eare lyes ever open for advantage: which hee will advance   20
in a publike Court, with a frontlesse impudence. His conscience
is a Delphian sword, and will cut both wayes: yet annoint him;
and you berust him, and consequently charme him for being so
glad in the sheath. Hee can tell you of a way how to doe you
good, and it is in his hand, so hee be capable of your gold.   25
He ha's a plaister in store for a debauch't credit; and can

mince a pennance with his familiar acquaintance. Protests he
ha's, and store of them; he will bee your friend, and your fee
shall binde him. He can winke as well as see, and distinguish
of your guilt by your guild. This makes him ever goe partiall-
guilt,[3] holding it an inseparable appendice to his place, to   5
ayme at his owne particular, and by it procure the peccants
peace: His ordinary Dialect is the thundring out of Canons to
the vulgar, whose honest simplicity begets in them wonder:
which thawes and resolves it selfe into admiration, to observe
the fearefull depth of the man. Yet so wise hee is, as one   10
truly conscious of his owne ignorance, hee can cringe low to
a knowing presence, and rellish a submissive reproofe for his
connivence. Hee carries still his Ephemerides[4] about with him,
which he dayly enlargeth with Scandals and defamations. The
best report that comes to his eare, is the ill report of his   15
Neighbour: which he seemes sorry for; meane time out of his
feigned sorrow, he really discovers his neighbours shame. Hee
usually takes more strict notice of Christenings than burials,
and is better vers'd in their filiations, than if he were
Overseer for the Parish. Hee might bee Truth by his true   20
search, for hee lyes lurking in every corner. It were his
breaking for the age to bee vertuous; his vailes are the vices
of the time; which he vowes to ferret, and so turnes Conycatcher.
A pestilent head-peece[5] hee ha's to blow up[6] Suburbane Traders:[7]
with whom hee trucks,[8] if they feare to bee fruitfull: for others, 25
their sterility hath procured them free licence. Hee is the
very scourge of the time, and were the time better he would

scourge himselfe. Revenues are good mens vertues; but his
stocke ha's no such dependance: light weights are his subsistence. An ignorant Curat is his patient; whose purpose
is the subject of his phlebotomie. Bleede hee must, or hee
dyes. The neglect of his cure, is the object of his care; 5
yet cannot this poore Curat doe him a greater injury, than
labour reformation of this malady.^{9} Hee domineers bravely in
his place, as if it were his Chappell of ease:^{10} meane time,
he is as timerous as the hare, lest his clandestine contracts
breede him harme. In a word, he is the safest, that knowes 10
him least; but if knowing, he is securest that knowes him best.
Braves cannot affront, where knowledge hath already arm'd. Let
him appeare then, in what portriature or posture he will, he
cannot dismay where knowing resolution is forwarn'd of his
strength. His Reading is his practise; Nor of all others, 15
needes hee any Choake;^{11} for want of ready pay is the generation of his Subpena. It were great pitty he should want friends,
hee is so obsequiously observant unto his owners: yet those that
are knowne to him most, are affectionately beholden to him
least. He complaines of the iniquitie of the age; but were it 20
better, hee were worse. He ha's a Catalogue of abuses, which
hee makes his morning, meridian, and evening orisons. If he
can be so happy as to adde to their score, it inhanceth his
state: which procures his seldom-thriving Heire an Apparators
place, when he is gone. Long time ha's hee beene an instrument 25
of discovery touching abuses of the Church: yet none informes
of him, whose President^{12} is the worst. Hee ha's so choakt his

accusers with shreads and parcels of broakt <u>Civilian</u> latine,[13] as they are gravell'd, and hee in the opinion of the <u>illiterate</u>, graced. By this, hee ha's perform'd his place with generall approbation: and now hee is to bee <u>Apparator</u> for himselfe. This hee so much the more feares, as he was the more unprovided for it before it came. It were well for him, that he might finde a <u>proxi</u>, to discharge his place: but his conscience summons him to a personall <u>apparance</u>. Bequeath his goods he may, which his <u>Executors</u> enjoy; but the occasion of their joy, is his griefe. Live longer he would, but the world saies he ha's liv'd too long. Experience hath taught him so much, as the ripenesse of his sinne hath raised him to that height, as hee can mount no higher. He must of necessity then leave his place to a <u>Novice</u> to succeede him: while he, poore man, becomes <u>Apparator</u> for himselfe. `His <u>summons</u> are given, his <u>shrowde</u>, the remainder of his conniving fees, prepared; his <u>Sexton</u> stayes at the hole-mouth, and will not bouge a foote, till this old Fox be earthed.

26. A Painter

Is a face-maker; and the worst in all his shop is his owne. He can never hold his hand from the Table,[1] which proves him a true Englishman; for he cannot leave it when it is well. By a speciall priviledge granted to his Art, hee exerciseth Martiall Law, and hangs and drawes within himselfe; wherein hee observes a legall and lineall method in his forme of execution: he drawes first, and hangs afterwards. Sometimes hee will play the egregious flatterer, and bestow more gracefull beauty on your face, than ever nature gave you, and so gull you. He lookes on you as if hee would looke through you, when hee drawes you: yet he shewes you a kinde of Barber-obeisance, being content to stand, while you sit. He is a partiall Artist: he will portray a man of note for nothing; but being obscure, a Cat of Mount[2] shall receive more curtesie from his Pencile, than a nobler Creature. He is not intangled much in law; yet he resorts now and then to Westminster,[3] where hee practiseth upon grave judges, and makes faces, and this hee lives by. Hee will not abate you an haire, if he be exquisite;[4] having none, he will supply the want of that excrement[5] with a curious[6] shadow, and so procure an artfull ornament. He observes small method in the ranking or disposing of his painted creatures: A Lady and a Monkey may stand cheeke by joule one with the other. Nothing so much angers him, as to have dirt thrown on his picture; and yet the

materials of it are of no better temper.[7] Hee sometimes playes
the witty Satyrist, and displayes light Tweakes[8] in loose roabes;[9]
but draw them out with Poakes[10] on their heads, he will not, for
that would darken his Art. Hee ha's an artificiall veile for
all his deformities; and can make the ugliest Hagge unlike her   5
selfe, purposely to make her like her selfe. His judgement consists not in Pulse but Physnomy.[11] There is nothing hee under-
takes, but he ha's some colour for it. He ha's Pomatum[12] and
other rare confections to allay the inflamation of a cinderous
face; and yet a Saint Antonies fire[13] constantly sparkles in his   10
owne. When hee paints a shoulder of mutton, his teeth water,
wishing with all his heart, he could infuse substance into the
picture. Hee can Zeuxes-like, though not like Zeuxes,[14] paint
Grapes, but the fowle that takes them for lively, deserves that
name. He can accommodate his portraiture with a true garb;   15
Hobson the Carrier[15] must have his picture, with his hand in his
bag to designe his Condition. He makes the eye of his feature,
a light gadding creature; for it reflects on every corner. He
miserably abuseth the Nine Worthies,[16] both in their postures,
Palfreys and Caparisons:[17] but prescription pleades excuse   20
beyond exception.[18] The Nine Muses are much misused; The three
Graces[19] ungraciously handled. By all which it appeares, he
assumes to himselfe a Poeticall licence, albeit hee never at-
tained to the freedome of that Company.[20] He holds a Painters
libertie[21] to bee of equall authoritie to the highest professant   25
of Poetry; but his pencile must vaile[22] to their Pen. Ignorance,
which originally hatched this conceit, being retain'd to defend

his cause, replyes; The <u>Painter</u> knowes not what the <u>Muses</u> meane.
Fantasies are his features, and their <u>effigies</u> the <u>Embrio</u> of his
braine. Whence it is, that all those ancient Heroes become his
<u>Proteans</u>.[23] Neither is hee onely familiar with these: for hee
will make no lesse bond in misshaping the Patriarchs, by reserving
one beard in store for a whole Tribe. Hee receives upon trust
some Chronicle stories,[24] both Divine and Humane; which (pre-
supposing him to bee of eminent employment) hee makes use of in
Pageants, Chimney-peeces and Bay-windowes. But if he bee of
no frequent custome, he trudgeth with a trusse of <u>colours</u> on
his back downe to the Countrey; where most humbly complaining,
hee prostrates his Art and industry at the feet of a most vigilant
Church-warden: By whose wisedome if he be entertained, that the
Church may be beautified, and his intolerable Art discovered;
he belards the walles with monstrous false English: for which,
if at any time hee receive reproofe, hee returnes this answer;
<u>He could paint better, but the Countrey will not bee at the
charge of good English</u>. And if you seriously aske him, where
hee had those sentences, he will with no lesse impudence than
prophanenesse tell you, they are <u>foolish conceits of his owne</u>.
Now and then he is imployed at Funerals, which he performes
most pittifully. His unoyl'd colours fall off like other mourn-
ers: his <u>horse-gold</u> displaies the <u>integrity</u> of the <u>Artist</u>.[25]
If hee be so ambitious, as to fixe his lamentable Elegy on the
Hearse, his leane lines fall so flat, and cloze in such un-
joynted cadencies, as they ever redound to his shame. But in
these, as they are a spheare too high for his imployment, he

is rarely vers'd. My Lord Maiors day[26] is his Jubile, if any
such inferiour Artist be admitted to so serious a solemnity:
If not, Countrey presentments are his preferment; or else hee
bestowes his pencile on an aged peece of decayed Canvas in a
sooty Alehouse, where Mother Red cap must be set out in her
colours. Here hee and his barmy-Hostesse[27] draw both together,
but not in like nature; She in ale, hee in oyle. But her
commoditie goes better downe, which he meanes to have his full
share of, when his worke is done. If she aspire to the conceite
of a signe, and desire to have her birch-pole[28] pull'd downe,
hee will supply her with one; which hee performes so poorely,
as none that sees it but would take it for a Signe hee was
drunke when he made it. A long consultation is had, before they
can agree what Signe must be rear'd. A Meere-maide, sayes she,
for that will sing Catches to the Youths of the Parish. A Lyon,
sayes he, for that's the onely Signe that he can make. And
this he formes so artlesly, as it requires his expression:
This is a Lion. Which old Ellenor Rumming,[29] his Tap dame,
denies, saying, It should have been a Meere-maid. Now and then
hee turnes Rover,[30] and bestowes the height of his Art on
Archers stakes. Sundry Whimzies[31] hee ha's in his head, but
of all others there is none that puzzles him so much as this
one: Hee ha's a speciall handsome Master-peece (for so he
termes her) and is so jealous of her, as when any one inquires
for his picture, hee simply mistakes himselfe, and shewes them
Actaeon.[32] Gladly would he cure this inbred malady with the
secret receipt[33] of an Italian securitie,[34] could his Art

contrive it, or his <u>state</u> procure it. Well, so it is, that
hee who tooke the <u>draught</u> of others, and liv'd by it, must
now leave that Trade, for Death hath drawne him out to the
full body. His chiefe Master-Artists imprese was this: <u>No</u>
<u>day without a line</u>: but now the last line of his life is drawne. 5
If hee <u>dye well</u>, it is more than hee did all his life time.
His memory seldome survives him: being now the <u>Image of Death</u>,
as hee was before a <u>living picture</u>.

27. <u>A Pedler</u>

    Is a man of <u>Ware</u>. A wandring <u>Starre</u>;[1] One, whose chiefest 10
commerce is with Country Wenches. The materials of their
trucking are of his part, <u>Pinnes</u>, <u>Ribbons</u>, and <u>Laces</u>; of their<u>s</u>,
<u>Cony-skins</u>, <u>Lambe-skinnes</u>, and <u>Feathers</u>; for <u>Marrow-bones</u>, their
honest simplicity never knew the operation of them.[2] <u>What doe</u>
<u>yee lacke</u>, is his ordinary <u>Intergatory</u>; yet you may <u>lacke</u> many 15
things, ere he can supply you. Pepper doe ye want, and he will
<u>pepper</u>[3] it for you; He will sell you <u>clots</u>[4] for <u>Cloves</u>, course
<u>crummes</u> for <u>Currans</u>, <u>Orpine</u>[5] for <u>Saffron</u>, and compound your
<u>pepper</u> with his <u>Earth-pouder</u>, to gull you. It were a strange
disease, that his <u>fardell</u>[6] cannot cure; blessed bee his <u>Genius</u>! 20
hee ha's a receit to cure any one from <u>breaking</u>,[7] but himselfe:
and this is the least hee doubts, for his <u>Py-pouder Court</u>[8] is
his onely terror. He is no <u>scholer</u>, yet turning <u>Rope-maker</u>,
he drawes <u>strong lines</u>;[9] which draines more from <u>Cordener</u> than
<u>Philosopher</u>. It is a prety thing to observe how hee carries 25

his Trinkilo's[10] about him: which makes the Countrey Choughs[11] esteeme him a man of prize. A Countrey Rush-bearing, or Morrice Pastorall,[12] is his festivall: if ever hee aspire to plum-porridge, that is the day. Here the Guga-girles[13] gingle it with his neat nifles:[14] while hee sculkes under a Booth, and showes his wit never till then, in admiring their follies. He ha's an obscene veine of Ballatry, which makes the Wenches of the Greene laugh; and this purchaseth him, upon better acquaintance, a posset or a Sillibub.[15] Hee is ever removing his tents: and might bee complain'd of for nonresidence,[16] if his informer[17] could gaine ought by't. The Tinker of Turvie[18] cannot put him downe at long-staffe: Which hee could finde in his heart to employ for high-way receits, if his white liver would give him leave. Would you have a true survey of his family, and number them by the pole? you shall finde them subsist of three heads: Himselfe, his Truck,[19] and her Misset.[20] Where the last weares, commonly, the sleakest skinne. Hee might bee a good man by the Philosophers reason: for Every place is his country: and generally least trusted in his owne. His Atlanticke[21] shoulders are his supporters: if they faile, his revenues fall. His judgement consists principally in the choice of his ware, and place of their vent. Saint Martins Rings,[22] and counterfeit Bracelets are commodities of infinite consequence: these will passe for current at a May-pole, and purchase a favor from their May-Marian.[23] One would take him for some appendice of a Souldier, by his Lether, but you shall find as much valour in his Hamper. There is nothing so much disheartens him as the report of a Presse:[24] this makes him stirre his stumpes:[25] but

if that will not serve, he turnes Counterfeit Cripple; and as
one cut off by the stumps, he cants his maimes[26] most
methodically: and this practice hee most constantly retaines
till the coast be cleare. Sometimes he consorts with his
Bungs:[27] and these keepe Centinell neare his <u>Booth</u>, to take
notice of a fat prey; which purchase makes the silent Evening
in some blind Alley, or place of knowne receite, the divider
of their prize. He keeps a certaine Catalogue[28] of all the
principall Faires: where, though he have little to vend, he
can find some way or other to bring in a booty. He will not
sticke to pretend, for want of better supply, an extraordinary
skill in Physick: and so turnes most impudent dogmaticall
Quacksalver. What transnaturalized[29] Elixers will this
mercenarie Mountebanke produce to delude the vulgar: All which
hee findes experiments of usefull consequence, till the
whipstock[30] waine him from his practice. It were wonderfull
this generall Artist should not thrive, having so many irons
i'th fire. Yet he findes himselfe in nothing so constant as
in matter of <u>estate</u>[31] being for all his endeavour neither worse
nor better, but just as hee was at first, a direct beggar. Now,
should you aske him the reason: hee will tell you, one of his
calling cannot be <u>honest</u> and thrive too. If hee could have
faced and outfac'd truth, set a deceitfull glosse on his
adulterate wares, or dispencd with oaths to beget Custome,[32]
his <u>Pack</u> had beene a <u>storehouse</u> of rich commodities before
this time: but making conscience of his dealing, was his maine
undoing. Thus would hee make you credulously beleeve that he

were seaz'd of what he never had, nor shuld he live longer, would ever have. Well, something hee would gladly leave the young Hamperman, his hopefull heire, whom he furnisheth, to expresse his love, for want of better fortunes, with the improved example of his life. He shewes him in a Landskip the whole Modell of his Pedler-pilgrimage, with whom he may to his much benefit securely truck; and on whose simplicity hee may most usefully worke. He tells him some mysterious secrets, which he never durst till that houre discover,[33] lest they should have prevented him of a naturall death. Now hee is to leave the world, and to his successors griefe, to leave nothing unto him in all the world. His fathers empty hamper is his sole patrimony. Truth is he shewd great improvidence in the course of his life, not to leave one poore knot of blacke ribbon, to display his trade, and beget a few seeming mourners. But his comfort is, he dies on even board. His Executor (if any such minister bee requisite) may thanke God for his want of Credit, for it kept him out of debt. Well; now hee is to trace no more the mountaines nor vallies; this merry mate is now turn'd grave man. His funerall Obits are soone solemnized. Next day at the longest, his teare-feigning widow enters new commerce; and hopes to aspire to a joynture[34] e're shee dye. His sonne, as one retentive of his fathers memento's, traceth his pathes; lives in as honest name and fame as his Predecessor did: and that hee might resemble his father in fortune as well as fame, he dyes neither much indebted by reason of credit, nor leaves much owing him by those with whom he traded. And so for altogether have they joyntly shut up their Hamper.

28. A Piper

Is a very droane,¹ ever soaking and sucking from others
labours. In Wakes, and Rush-bearings he turnes flat rorer.
Yet the Youths without him can keep no true measure. His
head, pipe, and leg hold one consort. He cannot for his
hanging fit himselfe to any tune, but his active foote or   5
great toe will keepe time. Hee is never sober, but when hee
is either sleeping, or piping: for his repast partakes too
much of the pot, to keep him sober in his feeding. He is
generally more carefull how to get a coate for his Pipe than
his child. And a ribband hung in his Chamber drawes him into   10
an overweening humour and honour of so musicall a favour. Hee
might bee not altogether improperly charactred, An ill wind
that begins to blow upon Christmasse eve, and so continues very
loud and blustring all the twelve dayes: Or an airy Meteor
composed of flatuous matter, that then appeares and vanisheth   15
to the great peace of the whole family, the thirteenth day.
His Stentors voice² stretcheth it self to the expression of
a largesse upon receit of the least benevolence. Hee deserves
not his wench, that will not pay for her dance. He is a
dangerous instrument in the Common wealth; for drawing together   20
routs and riotous assemblies: yet so long as they dance after
his pipe, there can bee intended no great perillous project of
state.³ Since hee was enacted Rogue by Parliament,⁴ hee ha's

got hold of a shamelesse tunelesse Shalme[5] to bee his consort, that the statute might take lesse hold of his single quality. And to grace it the more, he ha's shrowded himself with the incorporate reverence of a pye-color'd livery.[6] Yet it is to be feared that the Snake must ere long, lose his slough;[7] for either his vailes faile him, or he falls from his vailes. A continued practice of his profession hath brought him to that perfection, as hee can pipe when hee cannot speake: so as, his Chanter becomes his interpreter, and performes the thankfull office of a true Servant, in speaking for his mute Master, who cannot speake for himselfe. Hee is oftner out of tune than his pipe; yet never plaies better voluntaries[8] than when he is drunke. In one respect, he may be compared to a downe-right Satyrist: he will not stick to play upon his best friends.[9] He infinitely preferres his art before all other mechanicks: yet all the meanes of his gettings is but from hand to mouth. The most dissorting[10] Companion for his humor, is the Tinker, for hee is a metall man, which the Piper is not: Besides, they are so unsociably affected to their liquor, as it is death to them to drinke to one another; yet the nooze of the law ofttimes reconciles them, when it injoynes them to hang both together. Hee is of an invincible strong breath, whereof hee leaves usually in the blast of his pipe such a vaporous and vicious steeme, as it would go neare to poyson any Creature but a Piper. Hee suites himselfe to the seasons of the yeere, wherein if his honest Neighbour partake of any benefit, hee expects his musicall share. And to winde him the

more in his love, without which hee cannot live, every distinct
time must bee accommodated to a severall tune. Hee ha's a
straine to inchant the sheepheard in his shearing;[11] an other
for the husbandman in his reaping; in all which hee ha's a
peculiar priviledge for gleaning. Sundry corners hee reserves
in his knapsack for these neighbourly bounties, which in short
time, by prescription,[12] become customarie to him, and all his
lineall successors of the same Science, after him. If his
bonny Blouze,[13] or dainty doxie, being commonly a collapsed[14]
Tinkers wife, or some high way commodity, taken up upon trust,
demand of him supply, after these numerous in-comes, hee bids
her goe pipe.[15] For his bed, hee leaves it the soonest, and
goes to it the latest. Hee is injoyned by his place, to rise
early, rore highly, and rouze the whole family. So as, his
pipe may be properly tearmed the instrumentall cause both of
their rising and his owne.[16] He is no constant dweller, and
yet he is no shifter. All he reedes, he puts into his pipe:
Which consisting of three notes, breaks out into a most
vociferous Syllogisme. He will be heard at Horse-races; where
it makes him infinitely proud, if the Horse will but vouchsafe
to lay his nose to his droane. This so transports him, as it
makes him think himself worthy to be recorded in those musicall
aires or annals of Orpheus and Arion,[17] who made beasts follow
them. Which hee doth dayly, for his Doxy dogs him. Being weary
of the Country, or shee rather weary of him, hee dives into some
Suburban or Citty-cellar, where hee rores like the Divell in a
vault. Heere hee deepely inhanceth his Cellar-rents, if hee had

grace to keepe them: but truth is, whatsoever hee draines from
the four corners of the Citty, goes in muddy taplash downe
Gutter-lane,[18] and so sinks down into Panier alley.[19] So he
get his morning draught, which ends about midday, at the
soonest, hee stands not much upon breakfast: Neither indeede
will his vailes finde supply both for thirst and hunger. This
sauce-fleam'd Porcupine, when his veines begin to warme, will
bee many times monstrously malapert, which purchaseth him a
beating with much patience. You may breake his head as good
cheape, as any mans in Europe. If his Prugge[21] aspire to so
much stock or so great trust, as to brew to sell; hee will bee
sure to drinke up all the gaines. Hee will not sticke to runne
on score with a score, so hee may have credit: but when they
come for their coine, hee solicits some longer time, and payes
them home with a tune: Tis merrie when malt-men meete.[22] But
they may pipe small e're they meete with their money.[23] By
this, his holy bush[24] is pulled downe, which proclaimes him
bankerupt: by which meanes, he may most politickly compound
upon indifferent tearms with his Malt-worms. Thus are his
fortunes no perpetuitie: An ill winde blasts them: being
commonly, lightly got amongst nimble heel'd fooles, and lewdly
spent amongst heavie headed knaves. His vocation is no peculiar
station, but a roving recreation. There is no man will more
sufficiently sit downe to eat, nor more cheerefully rise up to
play than himselfe. To keepe him company, and free him of that,
which his leaden conceit is seldome capable of, melancholy, he
wisheth no other associate than a Jackanapes,[25] or a Jolly

watermaukin:[26] wherein it is his highest straine of studie to
accommodate his Ape with a guarded Coate,[27] and so foole his
spectators out of their coine. He dies a sound man and merrily,
for hee dyes a Piper, but no good death, for hee hath played
away his time. Hee could finde in his heart to pipe longer, 5
but his winde failes him, which makes him play his last-goodnight.
His wealth may appear by his Inventorie which containes the over
worne remains of a Motley Livery, a decayed Pipe-bagge, and halfe
a shirt; all which, without his Neighbours charity, will scarce
amount to the purchase of a sheete. 10

1. *An Almanack-maker*

The seventeenth-century almanac combined astronomical data, prognostications based upon astrological computations, and practical information on almost any subject to create a highly popular genre--one that could be accommodated to any intellectual taste or social level. Although originating from the earth-centered Ptolemaic conception of the universe, the almanac flourished under the new Copernicanism. Thomas Bretnor, criticized in the plays of Jonson and Middleton, was one of the most enthusiastic of English Copernicans and also a popular almanac-maker. And in 1676 William Lilly, author of some of the most intricate astrological works, could still write a guide for astrologers in the era of the Royal Society. Although many scientists were sceptical of the practice of judicial astrology--the exact determination of the influence of the heavens over human affairs--natural astrology was conceded even by the formidable Bacon, who affirmed that "comets, out of question, have likewise power and effect over the gross and mass of things," and believed that one could predict violent upheavals in nature and the state.[1]

---

[1] "Of Vicissitude of Things," *Essays*, *Works*, ed. Spedding, Ellis, and Heath (London, 1857-1914), XII, 275; and *De augmentis scientiarum*, *Works*, II, 272-280.

Of more practical value than the casting of horoscopes to the large number of almanac readers--the low cost of almanacs enabled them to circulate more widely than family Bibles--was the mine of encyclopedic information that formed an essential part of each almanac. Here could be found the necessary data of everyday life: gardening and husbandry hints, recipes, names and locations of the principal fairs, tables of weights and measures, names of the well-traveled highways, chronological lists of important historical events, and even the beginnings of advertising. In a rapidly-expanding commercial society like seventeenth-century London, the all-purpose almanac was a natural result of an accompanying journalistic impulse. To the London artisan, professional, and laborer the almanac was a digest of popular science. It takes its place as an important influence among other intellectual forces that contributed to the Revolution. To the university-trained minority the almanac-maker was a vulgar quack and poetaster pandering to the public's low taste. But, as Christopher Hill says, "The sneers at almanac-makers of Greene, Ben Jonson, Middleton, and Sir Thomas Overbury, as well as Nashe, contrast with the co-operation of doctors, mathematicians, and Gresham professors."[2]

The Overburian character of "An Almanack-maker"--its authorship claimed by John Cocke in his dedicatory epistle to

[2] _Intellectual Origins of the English Revolution_ (Oxford, 1965), p. 50.

John Stephens's <u>Essayes</u> <u>and</u> <u>Characters</u> <u>Ironicall</u> <u>and</u> <u>Instructive</u> (1615)--maintains an aristocratic contempt for its subject and never gets beyond a rather dull catalog of some of the almanac-maker's practices. Brathwait's character, given below, although obviously dependent upon the earlier piece for many of its allusions to almanac-making, is more detached and objective in tone. It stresses the almanac-maker's poverty, thus creating an almost sympathetic character whose death is an ironic comment on a world in which another of like misfortune "will bee forthwith raked out of his ashes." In this first character Brathwait successfully achieved the goal outlined in the dedicatory epistle to <u>Whimzies</u>. The previous character-writers had "relished more of <u>Aphorisme</u> than <u>Character</u>." The "opinionate singularitie" of the author had ignored the subject of the character and acted as an outlet for the author's prejudices. Brathwait expanded his character, presented him in a variety of poses, and assumed the generally tolerant attitude of John Earle's <u>Micro-cosmographie</u> (1628).

1 <u>figure</u> or <u>cipher</u>. The almanac-maker simply changes the year on his new edition. There is also a pun on figures and ciphers as astrological signs that received special interpretations.

2 <u>familiars</u>: demons that could be called up by those with special powers. In Jonson's <u>The Alchemist</u>, Subtle the alchemist offers to sell to a lawyer's clerk familiars that will help him to win at gambling.

3 <u>Euclid</u>, <u>Ptolemie</u>, <u>Tiche-Brache</u>, etc. Euclid, the Greek mathematician and formulator of geometry, may seem out of place among astronomers. But cf. E. A. Burtt, <u>The Metaphysical Foundations of Modern Physical Science</u> (Garden City, New York, 1954), p. 44: ". . . throughout the ancient and medieval period to the time of Galileo, astronomy was considered a branch of mathematics, i.e., of geometry. It was the geometry of the heavens. Our current conception of mathematics as an ideal science, of geometry in particular as dealing with an ideal space, rather than the actual space in which the universe is set, was a notion quite unformulated before Hobbes. . . ." Ptolemy, the second-century Alexandrian, author of the <u>Almagest</u>, the chief astronomical source for centuries, created the cosmological system that was still followed in much early seventeenth-century thinking. The astrologer could find an apology for his pursuits in Ptolemy's

Tetrabiblas. Cf. Chaucer's invocation to the Ptolemaic system in his translation of Boethius' Consolation of Philosophy, Book I, Metrum 5: "O thow makere of the wheel that bereth the sterres, which that art festyned to thi perdurable chayer, and turnest the hevene with a ravysschygne sweigh, and constreynest the sterres to suffren thi lawe. . . ." Tycho Brahe (1546-1601), the Danish astronomer, "was the first competent mind in modern astronomy to feel ardently the passion for exact empirical facts" (Burtt, p.61). His observations of the new star, related in De Nove Stella in 1572, were important scientific contributions.

[4] many have spoke of Robin Hood. . . . Cf. John Lyly, Euphues and His England: "For there it more delighteth them to talke of Robin hood, then to shoot in his bowe. . . ." The Complete Works of John Lyly, ed. R. Warwick Bond (Oxford, 1902), II, 200.

[5] scrapes acquaintance: insinuates himself into the gentleman's acquaintance. Cf. 1 Return from Parnassus, The Three Parnassus Plays (1598-1601), ed. J. B. Leishman (London, 1949), 11.523-524: ". . . when the knaves begin to be ragged, then they scrape acquaintance to be trusted. . . ."

[6] Euphumemismus: probably Brathwait's invention; literally most fortunate."

[7] Parismus: the hero of an extremely popular chivalric romance, Parismus The Renoumed Prince of Bohemia (1598), by Emanuel Forde.

8 **Boni ominis captatio**: "a reaching after good omens."

9 **Apogaeum's . . . Epicycles.** The "apogaeum" or apogee is that point of the heavens where the sun, moon, or any planet is farthest from the center of the earth, as a "perigaeum" or perigee is the point where a planet or the like is at its nearest distance from the earth. The "hypogaeum" is the fourth of the twelve astrological houses or parts of the heavens considered with reference to the earth. See n. 11 below. An astrolabe was a mathematical instrument used for determining the position of the sun and for taking altitudes. "Cycle" is used here as a planetary orbit in the heavens, rather than as a measurement of time. "Epicycles," Cf. Chaucer, *Boece*, Book IV, Prosa 6: ". . . cerklis that tornen aboute a same centre or aboute a poynt, thilke cerkle that is innerest or most withinne joyneth to the symplesse of the myddle, and is, . . . a centre or a poynt to that othere cerklis that tornen abouten hym. . . ."

10 **Mazzaroth, Arcturus, . . . Job**: mentioned in Job xxxviii as constellations. Mazzaroth was usually used by the almanac-makers to refer to the twelve constellations, or signs of the zodiac. Cf. Edward Pond, quoted in *The Owles Almanacke* (1618), ed. Don Cameron Allen (Baltimore, 1943), p.15: "Within the compasse of the Zodiaque, are twelve Constellations of Starres, mentioned in the booke of Job, 38.32. by the name of **Mazzaroth**: called of us the twelve Signes."

[11] principall Angles . . . owne. The heavens were divided into twelve parts, called houses or mansions, each part having a special meaning or significance. Cf. Donne's use of the association of house with "rents," in his elegy "The Bracelet," *The Elegies and The Songs and Sonnets of John Donne*, ed. Helen Gardner (Oxford, 1965), p.3:

> Or let me creepe to some dread Conjurer,
> Which with fantastique schemes fulfills much paper,
> Which hath divided Heaven in tenements,
> And with whores, theeves and murtherers stuft his rents
> So full, that though he passes them all in sin,
> He leaves himself no room to enter in.

[12] Forty shillings: the standard payment for pamphlets and almanacs. The Overburian character mentions the same amount for the year 1615. In a period when real wages were extremely low, the almanac-maker seems to have been in especially dire straits.

[13] impression: a printing of additional copies from an already-composed setting of type, indicating an author "no lesse constant in his Method than matter."

[14] vailes: additional earnings.

[15] Art for stolen goods . . . figure. An essential function of astrologers and almanacs was the casting of figures, or horoscopes, stating the appropriate time and conditions for recovering lost or stolen property--called horary astrology. As the above quotation from Donne suggests, the astrologer paid particular attention to the twelve houses, which, when

related to the seven planets, gave information about special occupations. Thieves were influenced by the position of the moon. Cf. Samuel Butler, <u>Hudibras</u> (1664), II.iii.347-356:

> Draw <u>Figures</u>, <u>Schemes</u>, and <u>Horoscopes</u>,
> Of <u>Newgate</u>, <u>Bridewell</u>, <u>Brokers Shops</u>.
> Of <u>Thieves ascendent in the Cart</u>,
> And find <u>out all by rules of Art</u>.
> Which way a Serving-man that's run
> With Cloaths or Money away, is gone:
> Who pick'd a <u>Fob</u>, at <u>Holding-forth</u>,
> And where a <u>Watch</u>, for half the worth,
> May be redeem'd; or Stolen Plate
> Restor'd, at Conscionable rate.

16 <u>kennell</u>: gutter. The analogy is made with the scavenger, or city street-cleaner.

17 <u>additament</u>: addition.

18 <u>melldew'd</u>: mildewed or blasted.

19 <u>Planet-strucke</u>. He looked as if he were struck dead by a planet. A stroke or fatal seizure whose cause could not be diagnosed was attributed to the influence of a planet. Don Cameron Allen, alluding to the extent that astrological language became popular currency, says in <u>The Star-Crossed Renaissance</u>, p.156, that "the expression 'planet struck' becomes the pardoning phrase for a gaucherie or moment of mental aberration. . . ."

20 <u>Charles waine</u>: the constellation Ursa Major; also called "The Plough."

21 __Cardinals__ __hat__, or __Sarazens__ __head__. These are names of two taverns. Cf. Brathwait, __Barnabae__ __Itinerarium__ (1638), ed. J. Haslewood, rev. W. C. Hazlitt (London, 1876), where the following appears among a catalog of tavern signs: "Yea my merry mates and I too / Off to th' __Cardinals__ __Hat__ fly to." Cf. also __Confused__ __Characters__ __of__ __Coneeited__ __Coxcombs__ (1661), ed. James O. Halliwell (London, 1860), p.74: "I wonder he sels not his head to some ale wife, it would make an excellent Sarazen signe, if he could but spare it."

22 __keeps__ __a__ __terrible__ __quarter__: stays fixed in one position.

23 __Jacobs__ __Staffe__: an instrument for measuring height and position.

24 __Jacobs__ __well__: Christ rested at Jacob's well on his way to Galilee. Cf. John iv.3-12.

25 __Erra__ __pater__. Pseudonymous author of __Prognostication__ __for__ __Ever__ (1536), first of the non-scientific prognostications and one of the most popular astrological works for more than a century. It contained a discussion of the four complexions, a list of the kings of England, a table for determining cumulative savings, the day of the week that New Year's Day falls, and much other information. The name became a prestigious one for other authors of almanacs to use.

26 __Cabals__: secrets.

27 conveying the New River . . . London. The monopolist Sir
Hugh Myddelton formed the New River to augment the water
supply of a growing London in 1609-1613. See J. W. Gough,
Sir Hugh Myddelton: Entrepeneur and Engineer (Oxford, 1964).

28 Scruple . . . your Body. The almanac-maker could venture
into other fields than just casting of horoscopes. Erra
Pater, and many others, had a detailed illustrated anatomy
of a man's body with zodiacal signs pertaining to the essential body organs. This was accompanied by prognostications
governing those parts. An empyric, or quack doctor, used
such information as part of his treatment. A scruple is a
small measurement of weight used by an apothecary.

29 Chrisis. The critical stage of a disease was supposedly
influenced by a particular conjunction of planets.

30 best season for Phlebotomie. Many almanacs gave information
regarding the proper astronomical conditions for successful
blood-letting.

31 inspiration: infused with divine force.

32 experimentall rules: those rules proved valid through
experience.

33 strange and unbaptized language . . . cut either way. Like
the Delphian oracle whose ambiguous pronouncements could be
variously interpreted, the skilled almanac-maker was careful
not to make his prognostications too specific, thus rendering

himself open to accusations of fraud and failure. Many prognostications were therefore quite general and obvious. Some of them are mocked in The Owles Almanacke (1618), ed. Don Cameron Allen (Baltimore, 1943).

34 **mizling**: lightly-falling.

35 **threed-bare Chronologie**. Lists of kings and the years of their reign, together with the dates of events in English history, were found in many almanacs.

36 **imps**: a falconry term, meaning to graft new feathers into the wing and so improve the flight of the bird. Here the word is used derogatorily to refer to the almanac-maker's filling out of his almanac with extraneous matter.

37 **still**: always.

38 **Perspectives**. A perspective was a device or figure that could produce unusual visual effects. In Jonson's The Alchemist (1610), the tricky servant, Face, refers to it as one of the alchemist's special pieces of equipment for prognostication. Cf. III. iv. 87-91:

> Hee'll shew a perspective, where on one side
> You shall behold the faces, and the persons
> Of all sufficient yong heires, in town,
> Whose bonds are currant for commoditie;
> On th' other side, the marchants formes. . . .

39 **Blanke Almanack**. Some almanacs contained blank, ruled pages for taking notes or for writing down observations on astronomical data as a means of comparison with the prognostications of the author. Brathwait's almanac-maker

hopes to become popular enough so that his readers will be interested in checking his predictions.

40 <u>Classicke Author</u>: author of a Latin work.

41 <u>Clymactericall yeare</u>. Cf. Sir Thomas Browne, <u>Pseudodoxia Epidemica</u>, <u>The Works of Sir Thomas Browne</u>, ed. Geoffrey Keynes (London, 1964), II, 307:

> And so perhaps hath it happened unto the numbers 7 and 9, which multiplied into themselves do make up Sixty three, commonly esteemed the great Climacterical of our lives. For the daies of men are usually cast up by Septenaries, and every seventh year conceived to carry some altering character with it, either in the temper of body, mind, or both. But among all other, three are most remarkable, that is, 7 times 7 or fourty nine, 9 times 9 or eighty one, and 7 times 9 or the year of Sixty three; which is conceived to carry with it the most considerable fatality; and consisting of both the other numbers was apprehended to comprise the vertue of either: is therefore expected and entertained with fear, and esteemed a favour of fate to pass it over. Which notwithstanding many suspect to be but a Panick terrour, and men to fear they justly know not what: and to speak indifferently, I find no satisfaction, nor any sufficiency in the received grounds to establish a rational fear.

42 <u>perpetuall Almanack</u>: an almanac, like Erra Pater's, that was not limited to any particular year and could thus be used for many years. This ironic use of the almanac-maker's trade language gives the character a successful blending of caricature and social comment. Brathwait omits from his character the kind of heavy moralizing typical of an anti-astrological work like John Chamber's <u>A Treatise Against Judicial Astrologie</u> (1601). The serio-comic tone of the character can be misread as condemnation. Brathwait's playfulness is called "a scathing description" by E. F.

Bosanquet in his <u>English Printed Almanacks and Prognostications: A Bibliographical History to the Year 1600</u> (London, 1917). Many works of the period satirize the almanacs. There are characters: Overbury's, Butler's, and "The Character of a Quack Astrologer" (1673) ; and plays: Tomkis's <u>Albumazar</u> (1615), Middleton's <u>No Wit, No Help Like a Woman's</u> (1613), and Beaumont and Fletcher's <u>The Woman Hater</u> (1606). Specific almanac-makers were also attacked: Thomas Bretnor was ridiculed by Jonson in <u>The Devil Is an Ass</u>; and Samuel Butler satirized William Lilly in <u>Hudibras</u>. See Don Cameron Allen's discussion, "Elizabethan and Jacobean Satires on the Almanack and Prognostication," in <u>The Star-Crossed Renaissance</u>, pp. 190-246. He omits Brathwait's character in his discussion.

2. A Ballad-monger

[1] <u>Sussex</u> <u>Dragon</u>. The sudden appearance of "a strange monster out of Germany" (John Earle's character of "A Pot Poet") and similar prodigies of nature were favorite topics of ballads. Brathwait refers to an occurrence reported in 1614: "True and Wonderfull. A Discourse relating a strange and monstrous Serpent (or Dragon) lately discovered, and yet living, to the great Annoyance and divers Slaughters both of Men and cattell, by his strong and violent Poyson: In Sussex, Two Miles from Horsam, in a Woode called St. Leonard's Forest, and Thirty Miles from London, this present Month of August, 1614."

[2] <u>Shoelane</u> <u>man</u>. Shoe Lane was apparently a center for the design of woodcuts that adorned ballads, and for painted signs. Sugden, <u>A</u> <u>Topographical</u> <u>Dictionary</u>, quotes from Nabbes, <u>A</u> <u>Presentation</u> <u>for</u> <u>Prince</u> <u>Charles</u> (1638): "Instead of Shoelane hangings, may the walls of my house be painted with chalk."

[3] <u>one tune</u> . . . <u>any ditty</u>. Popular tunes made the rounds in many ballads. Nightingale, the ballad-maker in <u>Bartholomew Fair</u> (1614), sings to the tune of "Paggington's Pound" (III.v).

⁴ Quod licuit chartis, non licet ire mihi. Brathwait misquotes from Ovid's Amores, III.viii.6 : Quo licuit libris, non licet ire mihi, "Where my books could go, I may not go myself."

⁵ more holding vailes . . . voyce. The singer received greater remuneration than the composer of the ballad.

⁶ Virginians : Indians.

⁷ Polyhymnia : Muse of the sacred lyric.

⁸ Stentor . . . Batillus. The singer, with a stentorian voice, provides the ballad-maker with a timely subject. Bathyllus was mentioned in Donatus' life of Virgil as an inferior poet.

⁹ Garland of good will. The Garland of Good Will is a poetical miscellany ascribed to Thomas Deloney and containing poems by Breton, Ralegh, Shakespeare and others. It appears in the Stationer's Register for 1593, but the first edition of 1631 gives it topical value for Brathwait. The miscellany is printed in The Works of Thomas Deloney, ed. F. O. Mann (Oxford, 1912), pp.195-280.

¹⁰ botches and old ends: pieces of doggerel verse.

¹¹ Trinkilo. This is possibly a reference to Trinculo, the drunken sailor in The Tempest. But in Brathwait's A Strappado for the Divell (1615), ed. J. W. Ebsworth (Boston, Lincoln-shire, 1878), p. 114, there is probably an allusion to "Tom Trinkalo," a comic character in the popular Cambridge play, John Tomkis's Albumazar (1615). Cf. John Milton, Apology for Smectymnuus (1642), Columbia Milton, III, 300: " . . . when

in the Colleges so many of the young Divines, and those in
next aptitude to Divinity, have bin seene so oft upon the
Stage writhing and unboning their Clergie limmes to all the
antick and dishonest gestures of Trinculo's, Buffons, and
Bawds. . . ."

12 must suffer the Presse. Mopsa, in The Winter's Tale,
IV.iii. 262-263 justifies the ballad-maker's efforts: "I
love a ballad in print, a'life; for then we are sure they
are true."

13 Quarterne: a quarter of a hundred copies. Cf. O. E. D.:
"1584 Star Chamb. Decree (1863) Any Stationer that shall
bye a quarterne at ones or more; which quartern is XXV
bokes, in which case the byer hath alwaie a quarterne boke
given him freely, that is to saie, one boke for everie XXV
that he byeth."

14 Holborne. Holborn Hill was a well-traveled road, especially
known for being along the route to the gallows at Tyburn.

15 Janizarie of Costermongers. The Janizaries were the private
guards of the Turkish Sultan. Cf. Thomas Kyd, The Tragedie
of Soliman and Perseda, I.v.10-12: "Call home my hardie,
dauntlesse Janisaries, / And from the other skirts of
Christendome / Call home my Bassowes and my men of war. . . ."
Brathwait is, of course, burlesquing the motley assemblage of
onlookers. Costermongers were purveyors of fruits and
vegetables, literally sellers of costards, or apples.

16 <u>Nipps</u>, <u>Ints</u>, <u>Bungs</u> and <u>Prinado's</u>. Here and elsewhere Brathwait likes to display his knowledge of underworld cant. Cf. his <u>The Honest Ghost</u> (1658; written about 1632): "Flankt were my troups with bolts, bands, punks, and panders,/Pimps, nips and ints, Prinados." "Nips" are pickpockets. "Ints" are also probably some kind of trickster, but the meaning is obscure, since Brathwait is, according to <u>O</u>. <u>E</u>. <u>D</u>. citations, the sole source of the word. It may be a shortening of "intakers," or receivers of stolen goods. "Bungs" are cutpurses. The meaning of "Prinado's" is also obscure; <u>O.E.D</u>. states that it might be a corruption of Spanish preñada, "pregnant woman," hence a cant term for some kind of female trickster.

17 <u>holds in fee</u>. In <u>Bartholomew Fair</u>, II.iv.42-45, the cutpurse Ezekiel Edgworth outlines to Nightingale, the ballad-singer, the nature of their business arrangement: "And i' your singing, you must use your hawks eye nimbly, and flye the purse to a marke still, where 'tis worne, and o' which side; that you may gi' me the signe with your beake, or hang your head that way i' the tune."

18 <u>prevent</u>: anticipate.

19 <u>Panyer</u>: pannier, or basket for holding fish.

20 <u>cashier'd</u>: banished.

21 <u>Gyant in a pageant</u>. Cf. George Whetstone, <u>2 Promos and Cassandra</u> (1578), I.v., in <u>Six Old Plays</u>, ed. John Nichols (London, 1779), p.65:

> <u>Phallax</u>. With what strange showes doo they their Pageaunt grace?
> <u>Bedell</u>. They have <u>Hercules</u> of monsters conquerying, Huge great <u>Giants</u> in a forest fighting With <u>Lyons</u>, <u>Beares</u>, <u>Wolves</u>, <u>Apes</u>, <u>Foxes</u>, and <u>Grayes</u>. . . .

Cf. also Marston, <u>The Dutch Courtezan</u>, III.i: "And yet all will scarce make me so high as one of the Gyants stilts that stalkes before my Lord Maiors pageant."

22 <u>nectar-infused</u>: inspired.

23 <u>cuppe . . . token-pledge</u>. Because of the shortage of genuine coins, some London shopkeepers issued their own tokens, which they redeemed for the stated amount. A "cup of six" is beer sold from a barrel of beer selling at six shillings the barrel.

24 <u>conceite</u>: idea, creation.

25 <u>Bragadeery round</u>. A popular dance tune used for several ballads, usually known as "Bragandary." Cf. "A Warning for Wives " (1629), by Martin Parker, in <u>A Pepysian Garland</u>, ed. Hyder Rollins (Cambridge, 1922), p.300. The tune is not known.

26 <u>Polyphon</u>: a lute-like stringed instrument with many strings.

27 <u>Counter-tenure</u>. A counter-tenor is higher in pitch than the tenor voice. It was a common singing voice in the Renaissance.

28 artfull straine through the nose, . . . purer brother-hood.
He will imitate the strident, nasal delivery of the Puritan
preacher in order to attract his attention. The delivery of
the Puritan sermon was a constant source of satirical barbs
during this period, and Brathwait was a strong Royalist.
For a discussion of the broad range of satirical allusions
to the Puritans in prose, verse, and the drama, see William
P. Holden, Anti-Puritan Satire: 1572-1642 (New Haven, 1954).
Cf. Samuel Butler, Hudibras (1663), I.iii.1157-60:

>   And by the sound and twang of Nose,
>   If all be sound within disclose,
>   Free from a crack or flaw of sinning,
>   As men try Pipkins by the ringing.

29 Suburbane wits. Most references to the suburbs or their
residents were derogatory, for they were reputed to be
centers of prostitution and licentiousness. Cf. Thomas
Nashe, Christ's Teares Over Jerusalem (1593), Works, ed.
R. B. McKerrow (London, 1904), II, 148: "London, what are
thy Suburbes but licensed Stewes?"

30 Pernassian: poet; from Mt. Parnassus, the home of the Muses.

31 Proctor: guardian.

32 casts his slough: sheds his old clothes.

33 against: in the direction of.

34 Bartholomew Fair. Among the many attractions of the fair,
apart from those Jonson incorporated in the comic vision
of his play, were booths for the sale and exchange of

second-hand clothing. The fair, begun in 1120 and held in
Smithfield every August 24, also provided Brathwait with
material for his character of "A Zealous Brother."

35 <u>endanger</u>: make likely.

36 <u>cast suite</u>: second-hand suit.

37 <u>shifter</u>: a pun occasioned by the dubious honesty of
ballad-makers. To "shift off" is to remove a garment; a
"shifter" is a cozener or trickster.

3. <u>A Corranto-coiner</u>

The coranto was a news letter, written in English for
English readers but generally published abroad--usually in
Amsterdam. Its form was a single broadsheet, differing from
the newsbook, which appeared as a small quarto volume. The
coranto can be considered a predecessor of the modern newspaper
except for one limitation: it contained no news of domestic
events, for strict censorship was in effect all during the life
of the genre--1620-1642. With the abolition of the Star Chamber,
censorship came to an end--and with it the coranto. Interest
naturally shifted from the foreign to the domestic scene.
England was flooded with a succession of "mercuries" and
"intelligencers," genuine precursors of today's newspaper.
Attention shifted from news of the Thirty Years War to the
partisan reports of Marchamont Nedham and John Cleveland. By

its nature, the coranto was an ephemeral thing. Of the
thousands that were published only a few hundred are extant.
As Brathwait's character illustrates, even then the newspaper
was a convenient material for lining pots and wrapping food.

As might be expected, the coranto received its share of
satirical abuse. In the drama, Jonson's *Staple of News* (1626)
is the most accomplished and detailed of these satiric thrusts.
In prose, Brathwait's character is a humorous and complete
discussion of the coranto, emphasizing the qualities of this
hastily-contrived invention that were most open to criticism:
its often doubtful veracity and its exaggeration of events.
This character is one of Brathwait's most effective pieces, a
skillful selection of relevant details presented in a whimsical
manner quite suited to the subject. Joseph Frank reprints
Brathwait's character on pp.276-277 of *The Beginnings of the
English Newspaper, 1620-1660* (Cambridge, Massachusetts, 1961).
He discusses corantos on pp.3-8.

[1] *Genius . . . intelligencer.* His own guardian spirit is the
source of his news, rather than an informant or foreign agent.
A frequent criticism of the coranto author was that he invented
his information.

[2] *Mint*: wordplay on its meaning as (1) printing and (2) coinage.

[3] *Tokens*: omens.

[4] *Ordinaries.* They were not only eating-houses but favorite
centers of gossip and gambling for London gallants.

5 <u>Table-booke</u>: notebook.

6 <u>still</u>: always.

7 <u>Notarie</u>: drew up legal documents for a fee.

8 <u>Paules . . . in Winter</u>. The middle aisle of St. Paul's Church was a fashionable meeting-place for London courtiers and professional men. Cf. Francis Osborn, <u>Historical Memoires on the Reigns of Queen Elizabeth and King James</u> (1658), pp.64-65; "It was then the fashion of those times, and did so continue till these, for the principall Gentry, Lords, Courtiers and men of all professions not merely Mechanick, to meet in <u>Pauls Church</u> by eleven, and walk in the middle Ile till twelve, and after dinner from three, to six, during which time some discoursed of Businesse, others of Newes." There are many allusions to it in contemporary works; e.g. Thomas Dekker's <u>The Gull's Hornbook</u> (1609), Chapter IV, "How a Gallant should behave himselfe in Powles-walkes."

9 <u>Moorfields in Sommer</u>. Moorfields was reclaimed land turned into pleasant walking paths and a park in 1606. Cf. John Stow, <u>Annales, Or, A Generall Chronicle of England</u> (1631), p.1021: " . . . the new and pleasant walkes on the North-side of the City, anciently called Morefields, which field (untill the third yeere of King James) was a most noysome and offensive place, being a generall laystall, a rotten morish ground, whereof it first took the name." See also Richard Johnson's <u>The Pleasant Walkes of Moore-fields</u> (1607).

[10] States: the United Provinces of the Netherlands. From 1622-1632 between 60-70% of news material in English news letters originated from the Netherlands and particularly Amsterdam, according to Folke Dahl, "Amsterdam--Cradle of English Newspapers," The Library, IV (1949), 166-178. Crim chan. Cf. Giles Fletcher, the Elder, The Russe Commonwealth (1591), The English Works of Giles Fletcher the Elder, ed. Lloyd E. Berry (Madison, Wisconsin, 1964), p.246: "The greatest and mightiest of them [the Tartar tribes] is the Chrim Tartar, (whom some call the Great Cham) that lieth South, and Southeastward from Russia, and doth most annoy the Countrie by often invasions, commonly once every yeare, sometimes entring very farre within the inland parts."

[11] parcells: phrases.
parcell-gilt: partly gilded. Many bowls and cups were gilded only on the inside. Brathwait puns on the ostentatious pedantry of the author.

[12] veteri Stylo, novo Stylo. This is a reference to the old and new styles of reckoning dates. Dating would naturally be a cause for concern to the coranto-coiner. In 1582 in most of Europe--but not Protestant England--the Gregorian calendar, or new style, was substituted for the Julian, or old style. This required advancing the calendar by 10 days in order to emend past calculations regarding the length of the year; hence, November 10 in England would be November 20 in Rome. In addition, England retained Lady Day, March 25,

as the first day of the new year, whereas most of Europe accepted January 1.

13 **Palisado's**: staked fences forming an enclosure for defense.
Counterscarfes: counterscarps, or protective ditches or walls.
Rampiers: ramparts.

14 **Exchange time**: the opening of the Royal Exchange, London's financial center.

15 **vent**: reveal.

16 **ayrie Chameleon**. Cf. Sir Thomas Browne, *Pseudodoxia Epidemica*, Works, II, 225: "Concerning the Chameleon there generally passeth an opinion that it liveth only upon air, and is sustained by no other aliment. . . ."

17 **receite of Newes**. He will swallow a mixture of spurious news stories as quickly as he would a prescription of medicine.

18 **frontlesse**: shameless.

19 **Intelligencers**: informants.

20 **Gazetta's**: news sheets.
Pasquils: satirical broadsides.

21 **Landskip**: landscape.

22 **currant money**: money in active circulation.

23 **they melt like Butter, . . . and so Burne**. The two most prominent printers of news letters were Nathaniel Butter

(c. 1583-1664) and Nicholas Bourne (c. 1586-1660). After September 1624 they had a monopoly on the coranto trade. Puns on Butter's name are found in several works; see Jonson's The Staple of News (1626), I.iv.13. For the story of their varied careers, see Leona Rostenberg, "Nathaniel Butter and Nicholas Bourne, First 'Masters of the Staple'," The Library, XII (1957), 23-33. The multitude of their news letters is listed in Folke Dahl, "Short-title Catalogue of English Corantos and Newsbooks, 1620-1642," The Library, XIX (1938), 48-98.

[24] staves-aker: a plant whose seeds were used as a pesticide.

[25] Wapping and Longlane. Wapping was a center for seaman's commodities near the London docks. Long Lane was known for its second-hand clothing brokers. Cf. John Stow, The Survay of London (1618), p.716: "This lane is now lately builded on both sides with tenements for Brokers, Tiplers, and such like. . . ."

[26] Broker. Cf. Donald Lupton, London and the Countrey Carbonadoed (1632), sig. E5^r: ". . . the Jayler and Broker are Birds of a feather, the one Imprisons the Body, the other the Cloaths, both make men pay deare for their lodging. . . ."

[27] Gallobelgicus: Mercurii Gallo Belgici, a Latin news letter published at Cologne and ready widely in Europe from 1598-1630. It was ornamented with a woodcut of Mercury on a globe. An English translation appeared in 1614. Cf. John Earle,

<u>Micro-cosmographie</u> (1628), ed. H. Osborne (London, n.d.), p.41: "He doubles the pains of Gallobelgicus, for his books go out once a quarter, and they are much in the same nature, brief notes and sums of affairs, and are out of request as soon." See Frank, <u>The Beginnings of the English Newspaper, 1620-1660</u>, p.2.

4. A Decoy

In the late sixteenth and the seventeenth centuries interest in the lives of underworld characters was widespread. Although a succession of laws enacted ever stronger repressive measures to curb the actions of thieves and vagabonds, the pamphleteers and dramatists were inexhaustibly fascinated by the habits and language of the rogue. Brathwait's "decoy" is more of a confidence man than an ordinary criminal. He affects the speech and manners of the gallant in order to ingratiate himself with others of that class. Indeed he has a variety of outfits and schemes to suit the person to be gulled. Inevitably he finds his way to prison, among "the rascall multitude, as Cabbage-carriers, Decoyes, Bum-bayliffes, disgraced Pursevants, Botchers, Chandlers, and a rabble of such stinkardly companions, with whom no man of any reasonable fashion, but would scorne to converse."[1]

With his projects and his doxies, the decoy is a character right out of the rogue pamphlets of Harman and Awdeley. In those minutely-discriminating catalogs of criminal types there is little room for developing interest in the rogue as an

---

[1] Geffray Mynshul, Essayes and Characters of a Prison and Prisoners (1618), sig. E3^v.

individual human being. Brathwait's character follows the subject in his varied activities, but its main purpose is to lead him to his deserved unhappy end. It is not one of his more successful characters, for the decoy is too abhorrent to the author to be treated with any forgivingly humorous irony.

[1] **What sconce . . . build?** To "build a sconce," literally "build a fort," with a pun on the meaning of sconce as a tankard of ale, is to run up a bill at an alehouse with the probable connotation of not paying the bill.

[2] **Ward where he lives . . . bid stand.** Although he has never held any petty political office in his neighborhood district, he can compel you to stop as if he were a constable. London was composed of twenty-six wards, each represented by an alderman.

[3] **civill:** serious and restrained.
demure: reserved.

[4] **He . . . pregnant-present conceite.** He will argue with you about any current, witty topic in order to impress you.

[5] **Asian knight:** perhaps "turn Turk," i.e. rant and rave in an ill-tempered manner. Brathwait might have had in mind the antagonist of the English folk-plays, the "Turkish Knight." See E. K. Chambers, *The English Folk-Play* (Oxford, 1933) p. 27.

[6] **pragmatically:** dogmatically.

7 high-road revenewes. He lacks enough money to prevent himself from being arrested as a vagrant if he tries to leave London. Travelers without funds were severely treated.

8 Smithfield: the site of Bartholomew Fair and a large marketplace for the sale and purchase of horses. Cf. Donald Lupton, London and the Countrey Carbonadoed . . . (1632), sig. D2^r: "You may have a faire prospect of this square Fellow, as you passe from the streights of Pie Corner; this place is wel stored with good harbours for Passengers to put into for flesh and drinke, and fish it is admirable. . . ."

9 Demilance: a lightly-armed horseman, here meant to apply to the horse.

10 undigested: confused.

11 Custome: patronage.

12 receite of Custome. The decoy appears as well-dressed as an heir collecting the rent or tax from his tenants.

13 Essex Calfe. Cf. Thomas Fuller, The Worthies of England (1672), ed. P. A. Nuttall (London, 1840), I, 497: "Essex may better pretend to the Name of Italy, producing Calves of the fattest, fairest, and finest flesh in England, (and consequently in all Europe,) and let the Butchers in Eastcheap be appealed unto as the most competent Judges therein. Sure it is a Cumberland-cow may be bought for the Price of an Essex-calfe, in the beginning of the year." Hence it is a particularly profitable investment for the merchants.

[14] _Led suites_: spare suits of clothing.

[15] _cunning Impostor_. One of the stock character types of comedy is the _alazon_, or imposter. Like the decoy, he lives by his wits, constantly schemes, yet fails in his attempts to secure mastery over his environment. Northrop Frye, in _The Anatomy of Criticism_ (Princeton, 1957), treats the _alazon_ as an example of a "blocking character." See also the discussion of F. M. Cornford, _The Origin of Attic Comedy_ (Garden City, New York, 1961).

[16] _one of Volpone's true-bred Cubbes_. Only one as skilled in trickery and deception as Volpone, the fox, in Ben Jonson's play, can uncover the decoy. Volpone, feigning illness, deceived his business acquaintances by promising them treasure from his estate after his death.

[17] _more Doxes than a Gipsie_. Cf. Thomas Harman, _A Caveat or Warning for Common Cursitors_ (1566), _The Elizabethan Underworld_ (London, 1930), ed. A. V. Judges, p.105: "These doxies be broken and spoiled of their maidenhead by the upright-men, and then they have their name of doxies, and not afore." The upright men were second in the Gypsie ranks.

[18] _Unguentum album_: a common medicinal ointment. Cf. Richard Brome, _The Northern Lasse_ (1632), III.ii.307-311: "But when shee had so done what did shee than do? Bestow'd a penyworth of _Unguentum Album_, and it made him whole presently. Good

Mistress Traynwell send to your Pothecary for some: 'twill make him weell e'ne now."

19 impostum'd: swollen.

20 foist: a deft pickpocket, considered to be among the elite of thieves, since he did not cut the purse, but gently removed it.

21 Bowl-alleyes. Cf. John Earle, Micro-cosmographie (1628), ed. H. Osborne (London, n.d.), p.67: "The best sport in it is the gamesters, and he enjoys it that looks on it and bets not."

22 Genius: tutelary spirit.

23 goes by weeping-crosse. He always fails at his deceptions. Several places in England were marked with crosses and used as devotional occasions by mourners and penitents. Robert Nares, in his Glossary; Or, Collection of Words, Phrases, Names, and Allusions . . . in Works of English Authors, mentions actual crosses at Oxford, Stafford, and Shrewsbury. Cf. Tilley, A Dictionary of the Proverbs in English in the Sixteenth and Seventeenth Centuries, W 248: "But when this May-game was done, an hundred thousand of them came home by weeping crosse."

24 Crummes of Comfort: an allusion to Michael Sparke's The Crums of Comfort with Godly Prayers (7th ed., 1628), a popular compilation of prayers, meditations, and Biblical passages. According to Louis B. Wright, Middle-Class Culture in Elizabethan England (Chapel Hill, 1935), p.263, Sparke's

book was so attuned to middle-class needs that copies of it were "read out of existence." Wright notes that only three copies are extant prior to 1640, the earliest being the 7th edition of 1628.

[25] **sorts**: accommodates.

[26] **nitty**: infested with nits.
nasty: filthy.

[27] **veils**: occasionally-received funds.

5. An Exchange-man

London had two exchanges--the Old and the New. Both are commonly alluded to during the late sixteenth and seventeenth centuries. The Old Exchange received the name of Royal Exchange as a result of Elizabeth's visit in 1571. Built by Sir Thomas Gresham in 1566, it soon became a fashionable gathering place for London ladies as well as for men, since it contained shops stocking a large variety of merchandise. Brathwait's character probably concerns the New Exchange, built on the south side of the Strand by the Earl of Salisbury in 1609. Stow's Annales, in the continuation written by Edmund Howes, tells of James's visit to the Exchange at its opening, whereby he named it "Britain's Burse." Soon the New became a formidable rival to the Old as a palace of fashion. A contemporary engraving pictures a long, low building with an upper gallery of rooms occupied by shops.

1 <u>peremptorie</u> . . . <u>lacke</u>? An interrogatory was a formal question presented to an accused person. The Exchange-man presses his question on the passer-by with insistency. "What do ye lacke?" was the common street cry of London shopmen.

2 <u>pay</u> <u>Scot</u> <u>and</u> <u>lot</u>: pay enough to settle the purchase.

3 <u>vent</u>: displayed.

4 <u>Bable</u>: trifle.

5 <u>Diapred</u>: elaborately colored.

6 <u>poakes</u>: large hat brims.

7 <u>long</u> <u>Peripatetick</u> <u>gallery</u>. The Exchange included an upper gallery with a long line of stalls and shops. Cf. Donald Lupton, <u>London</u> <u>and</u> <u>the</u> <u>Countrey</u> <u>Carbonadoed</u> (1632), sig. C5^r: "The Merchants should keepe their Wives from visiting the upper Roomes too often, least they tire their purses by attyring themselves."

8 <u>Salique</u> <u>traine</u>. According to French Salique law, women were barred from succession to the monarchy. It is used here as a condescending term for the women who seem eager to buy whatever they see.

9 <u>It</u> <u>is</u> <u>his</u> <u>onely</u> <u>drift</u> . . . <u>basenesse</u>. He pretends that he does not have the base spirit to overcharge them.

10 __vacation__: before the end of the current court sessions. Business was much slower when the law courts were in adjournment.

11 __Myrmidons__: the bellicose followers of Achilles, here used as a term of abuse for the group of gallants.

12 __tyre__: head-dress. Cf. __Antony and Cleopatra__, II.v.21-23: "Ere the ninth hour, I drunk him to his bed; / Then put my tires and mantles on him. . . ."

13 __lime-twiggs__. Lime was smeared on branches as a means of ensnaring birds.

14 __Didapper__: small diving duck.

15 __tricke to catch the Old one__: an allusion to Thomas Middleton's play, __A Trick to Catch the Old One__ (1605).

16 __project__. There is much contemporary abuse of the "projector" and his often dishonest financial schemes.

17 __curious__: elaborately decorated.

18 __Superfluity . . . needfull family__. Cf. Montaigne, "Of Cannibals": "They are yet in that happy estate, as they desire no more, than what their naturall necessities direct them: whatsoever is beyond it, is to them superfluous."

19 __Synodall__: meeting.

20 __Tyre-woman__: dressmaker.

21 __bray__: pound into powder.

22 __renew__: revenue.

23 __fashions__: a pun on its meaning as a horse disease. See n. 10 to 15. "A Post-master."

24 __Michaelmas tearme__ . . . __reparation__. In the fall term of the High Court of Justice, London teemed with litigious citizens--thus also prospective customers.

25 __The Birds are flowne__. Cf. Giovanni Torriano, __The Proverbial Phrases__, s.v. "Scena," p.183: "The English of an empty purse say, The Birds are flown." Tilley B364.

6. A _Forrester_

"A Forester," said John Manwood in _A Treatise of the Laws of the Forest_ (1592; quotations are from ed. of 1615), "is an officier of the forest of the king (or of another man) that is wonne to preserve the Vert and Venison of the same forest, and to attend upon the wild beasts within his Bailiwick, and to attach offenders there. . . ." For centuries the forests were exempt from the Common Law of the land, governed only by the forest laws that were instituted for the convenience of the kings' hunting. At the time of Brathwait's character, forest law was a controversial subject; the king was interested in asserting his forest rights, and the Parliament wished to see them curtailed so that it might gain the initiative over the king. Edward Coke wished to see the forest laws brought under the jurisdiction of common law. Brathwait's forester enjoys hunting rights within his purlieu, which, as note 6 indicates, is land that has been disafforested, but which still has forest law jurisdiction over its game.

[1] __Windfals.__ Cf. John Manwood, _A Treatise of the Lawes of the Forest_ (1615), sig. Cc4^v: ". . . a Forester of fee may prescribe to have all the wind-fal-wood . . . within the forest, or thorowout all his bailiwike. . . ."

[2] __an ill winde . . . profit.__ Cf. Jonson, _The Gypsies Metamorphosed_ (1621), l.779: "It's an ill winde blowes no man to proffit." Tilley W421.

[3] __Chace.__ Cf. Manwood, _A Treatise_ . . . , sig. C8^r: ". . . a Forest doth differ from Chase. . . . For a Chase hath no particular Lawes, that are proper to a Chase onely, for all offendors in a Chase are to bee punished by the Common Law, and not by the Forest law. . . . A Chase hath no such officers as a Forest hath, for a Chase hath neither Verdorors, Foresters, . . . but onely Keepers and Woodwards."

[4] __fixed on his front.__ Although he wears a powder horn by his side, he would not wish to see a horn--the sign for a cuckold--appear on his head.

[5] __Pale:__ boundary.

[6] __Purlew.__ Cf. Manwood, _A Treatise_ . . . , sig. T2^v: "__Purlieu__, or __Pourallee__ is a certaine Territorie of ground adjoyning unto the forest, meered and bounded with unmoveable markes, . . .

which Territorie of ground was also once forest, and
afterwards disafforested againe. . . ."

7 **impaled**: enclosed, kept from straying.

8 **tappised**: concealed.

9 **Swetnams brood**. This is an allusion to Joseph Swetnam, author of <u>The Araignment of Lewd, Idle, Froward, and unconstant women: Or the vanitie of them, choose you whether. With a Commendation of wise, vertuous and honest Women. Pleasant for married Men, profitable for young Men, and hurtfull to none</u> (1615). Swetnam was the center of a passionate controversy regarding the nature of woman. Wright, <u>Middle-Class Culture in Elizabethan England</u>, p.487, describes the pamphlet as follows: "The pamphlet . . . rails at sins of extravagance and pride, which ruin and bankrupt even thrifty husbands. Women 'degenerate from the use they were framed unto, by leading a proud, lazie, and idle life, to the great hinderance of their poore Husbands.'" Swetnam himself was attacked in a play titled <u>Swetnam, the Woman-hater, Arraigned by Women</u> (1620). The forester, then, may find that his catch will prove to be as inconstant as one of Swetnam's subjects.

10 **Acteons bird**. Acteon, the mythological hunter, witnessed Diana, the chaste goddess of the hunt, bathing. In anger, Diana changed him into a stag; he was later killed by his own hunting dogs. Brathwait uses the figure of Acteon in

several places in <u>Whimzies</u>; in all cases it is employed as a synonym for a horned beast, i.e. a cuckold. The myth of Acteon was very popular in the late sixteenth and early seventeenth centuries. DeWitt T. Starnes and Ernest William Talbert, <u>Classical</u> <u>Myth</u> <u>and</u> <u>Legend</u> <u>in</u> <u>Renaissance</u> <u>Dictionaries</u> (Chapel Hill, 1955), pp. 206-207, discuss several interpretations given to the myth, including a connection to the disgrace of Essex in 1599-1600, and as a symbol of warning to the overly curious.

[11] <u>Calysto's egge</u>. Callisto was an Arcadian huntress and attendant of Diana. Zeus became enamoured of her and had her metamorphosed into a she-bear; she was then killed by Diana.

[12] <u>Mothers Livery</u>. He wears the color of forest green, like Diana.

[13] <u>Liberty</u>: bounded property.

[14] <u>Semele</u> . . . <u>in</u> her <u>Juppiter</u>. Brathwait seems to imply that Zeus appeared to Semele in the form of a forester, but this does not agree with the versions of the myth. Semele, spurred on by the jealous Hera, asked Zeus to appear to her in all his real splendor, not in any changed form. When Zeus approached her, the divine flames emanating from the god consumed her. Semele's unborn child was saved by Zeus, who carried the child--later Dionysus--in his thigh. One version states that the child would have perished if a thick ivy vine had not wound around the palace columns, creating a green

protective blanket between the unborn child and the flames. Perhaps this is the green to which Brathwait alludes.

15 Habit . . . an Embleme. His green clothing has emblematic significance.

16 our Spirituall enemy . . . his prey. Brathwait's insertion of these conventionally moralistic statements has perhaps been overstressed by commentators on his work, who tend to ignore the genial humor of the characters.

17 Antipodes to us. He is opposite in his habits from us, just as are those who inhabit the opposite ends of the earth.

18 Latona's servants. Latona is the Roman equivalent of the Greek goddess Leto, mother of Apollo and Artemis by Zeus. Brathwait seems to use Latona as a synonym for her daughter Artemis, or Diana. Cf. Thomas Middleton and William Rowley, The Changeling, ed. N. W. Bawcutt (London, 1958), IV.iii. 158-160: "Down, down, down a-down a-down, and then with a horse-trick, / To kick Latona's forehead, and break her bowstring."

19 Linehound: follows the line of scent of its quarry.

20 Sophistry: cunning.

21 cut large thongs . . . leather. Cf. Chapman, All Fools (1605), IV.i.147-148: "O, puissant wag, what huge large thongs he cuts / Out of his friend Fortunio's stretching leather."

22 __murraine__: animal disease.

23 __discourse__: conversation.

24 __Wakes__. These were festive occasions, commemorating the opening of parish churches, and not the usual modern usage.

25 __Hobbinols__. Cf. E. K., gloss to the January eclogue of Spenser's __Shepherd's Calendar__ (1579): "Hobbinol is a feigned country name."

26 __no land but Leases__. Throughout this period tenants were very much at the mercy of landlords. Cf. Donald Lupton, __London and the Countrey Carbonadoed__ (1632), sig. H6^v: "There compasse ordinarily is three Prentishippes in length, one and twenty yeares. Once in halfe a yeare they must bee sure to prepare for payment." Cf. also sig. H8^{r-v}: "The Landlord, Bayly, and other Informers are so cunning, that the Tenants shall but live to keep Life and Soule together, if through Poverty and hard Rents they forfeit not their Leases. You may know where they live ordinarily, for Leases runne now with this clause usually in them, __they must not let or sell away their right to another__."

27 __give a gibbet__: supply a gallows.

28 __fouch__: hind quarters of a deer.

29 __Xerxes__: King of Persia from 486-465 B.C. Brathwait is probably confusing him with his ancestor, Cyrus, the founder of the Persian Empire, who ruled from ca. 558-529 B.C. Cf.

Pliny's The Historie of the World (1601), trans. Philemon Holland, I.vii.23: "King Cyrus was able to call every souldier that he had through his whole armie, by his owne name." The exploits of both rulers are described in Herodotus, The Persian Wars.

30 quirresters: choristers.

31 Snites: snipes.

32 ancient discarded Servingman . . . neglect. According to the Elizabethan Poor Laws, a distinction was made between the deserving poor and the "professional poor," those who were poor from no fault of their own and those who were morally irredeemable, such as beggars and vagabonds. Cf. the character of "A Hospitall-man."

33 Endymion. Endymion fell into an eternal sleep after being kissed by the goddess Selene.

34 compounding: coming to an agreement of money terms.

35 Defessus sum ambulando. "I am tired of walking." Herford and Simpson, Ben Jonson, IX, 444, refer to Witts Recreations Augmented (1641), P3, where the Latin saying is given as the motto for a walker of Paul's middle aisle.

7. A Gamester

[1] __Merchant-venturer.__ Cf. Samuel Butler, "A Gamester," __Characters and Passages from Note-Books__, ed. A. R. Waller (Cambridge, 1908), p.225: "Is a merchant adventurer that trades in the bottom of a dicebox."

[2] __hazard__: a pun on the meaning of the word as (1) chance, fortune and (2) a popular dice game.

[3] __competent__: substantial.

[4] __Collects__: short daily prayers.

[5] __over-braves__: treats with excessive bravado.

[6] __Oratorie__: chapel, place of prayer. A pun on "preyes" is probably also intended.

[7] __Long acre . . . Alienation office.__ A long-acre was literally a long, narrow strip of land containing an acre; it is used here figuratively as the gamester's inheritance that passes through the alienation office--where the transfer of property was effected.

[8] __prevent__: anticipate.

[9] __little familiars.__ Demons that could be magically invoked are here used to suggest the gamester's sharp practices.

10 at a dead lift: in an emergency. Cf. John Webster, The White Divel, V.vi.25-26: "Looke, these are better far at a dead lift, / Then all your jewell house." Cf. also Tilley L271.

11 cogging: cheating.

12 barre him by and maine: bar him completely. In the dice game of hazard, the player trying to "make his number" was shooting for the "main." The numbers he actually threw while attempting to achieve his "main" were called the "bys," except for those numbers that caused him to lose the right to throw again, e.g. the double one--"snake eyes."

13 translating: transforming.

14 Stoicall Stocke. Cf. Sir John Harington's A New Discourse of a Stale Subject, Called the Metamorphosis of Ajax (London, 1596), ed. Elizabeth Story Donno (New York, 1962), p.250: ". . . if a man felt no discontent in these, I would say he were a stock & not a Stoicke."

15 Tullus Hostilius . . . goe from him. Lactantius, a fourth century Christian apologist, made a determined effort to point out the error in pagan thought. Tullus Hostilius was the third legendary king of Rome. Brathwait cites Lactantius' major work, the Divine Institutes, Chapter XX: "Tullus Hostilius fashioned and worshipped Fear and Pallor. What shall I say respecting him, but that he was worthy of having his gods always at hand, as men commonly wish?"

¹⁶ like the silent Woman . . . stage. In Jonson's Epicoene; Or the Silent Woman (1609), the title character, in reality a disguised boy, pretends to be submissive and mute during part of the play. There are numerous allusions to the behavior expected from a spectator seated on the stage. Dekker, The Gull's Hornbook (1609), cites the advantage of this location to the gallant. Cf. also the Induction to John Marston's The Malcontent (1604):

> Tire-man. Sir, the Gentlemen will be angry if you sit heare.
> Sly. Why? we may sit upon the stage at the private house: thou doest not take me for a country gentleman, doest? doest thinke I feare hissing? Ile holde my life thou took'st me for one of the plaiers.

¹⁷ encurtain'd Musique sounds. John Cranford Adams, in The Globe Playhouse, Its Design and Equipment (New York, 1961), pp. 298-325, describes in detail the context of Brathwait's allusion. The musicians in the major playhouses were situated in a gallery at the top of the tiring-house--a third level right above the stage. Preventing the musicians from distracting the attention of the spectators was a thin, translucent curtain. This curtain usually remained closed during performances.

¹⁸ inordinate walkers: frequenters of ordinaries.

¹⁹ Philip of Macedon . . . both. Cf. Erasmus, Apophthegmes, trans. Nicolas Udall (1564), ed. R. Roberts (Boston, Lincs., 1877), pp. 187-188: "Two feloes being like flagicious, and neither barell better herring, accused either other, the kyng

Philippus in his own persone sitting in judgement upon theim. The cause all heard, he gave sentence and judgement, that one shoulde with all spede and celeritee avoide or flee the royalme or countree of Macedonia, and the other shoulde pursue after him."

[20] Margites: the hero of a poem attributed to Homer. He was known for his ignorance and incapacity even for digging or plowing.

[21] Culverhouse: pigeon-house.

[22] dammaske pummell: a highly-polished ornamental chair knob made of damasked steel, used by the gamester as a device to mirror his victim's cards.

[23] Plato's golden rule . . . dayes-taske. The source is an anecdote in Diogenes Laertius, Lives of Eminent Philosophers, trans. R. D. Hicks (New York, 1925), III.36-39: "A story is told that Plato once saw some one playing at dice and rebuked him. And, upon his protesting that he played for a trifle only, 'But the habit,' rejoined Plato, 'is not a trifle.'"

[24] Bum-card: marked card.

[25] penitentiarie: penitent.

[26] Malevolo: Malvolio in Twelfth Night.

8. An Hospitall-man

The hospital-man is an inmate of a parochial or private charitable institution. The Elizabethan Poor Laws were mainly concerned with ridding England of its parasitic poor, taking no consideration of the root causes of poverty and how to deal with them effectively. By ignoring the genuine plight of the poor, the government encouraged the London merchants and gentry to set up the machinery to care for the poor in their own way. Up to the Revolution the private endowment of religious charitable institutions was the major element in poor relief. Stow's Survey lists hundreds of names of people who gave to Protestant charities. In this period are founded the great charitable and educational houses like the Charterhouse and Christ's Hospital. Brathwait's character is a poignant yet humorous account of one of the more fortunate poor, a man scraping around for a few of life's pleasures while he also affects the expected somber demeanor of the aged penitent.

[1] decayed Gentleman, a maimed Souldier, or a discarded Servingman: the three large classes of deserving poor, to be distinguished, in the eyes of Brathwait and his contemporaries, from the undeserving, or professional, poor. The latter would include peddlers and vagabonds. Cf. Donald Lupton, London and the Countrey Carbonadoed (1632), sig. E7^v: "It is a Reliefe for decaied Gentlemen, old Souldiers, and auncient Servingmen: tis to bee pittied, that such Religious, Charitable houses, increase not in number. . . ." Also pertinent to the hospitalman's indigence is W. K. Jordan, Philanthropy in England 1480-1660 (London, 1959), p.260: "For reasons not wholly clear, the momentum of giving for almshouses slackened significantly and steadily for three successive decades after 1620, to rise again most abruptly in the final decade of the era of the Puritan Revolution."

[2] Buttry hatch: the door to the buttery, where the liquor was stored.

[3] the hood that makes the Monke: originally an old Latin proverb, Cucullus non facit monachum. The Latin is cited in Twelfth Night, I.v.62. See Tilley H586 for other usages.

[4] Circumcellions: vagabond monks of the Middle Ages.

5 __Lambs-wooll__: a drink made from hot ale, roasted apples, sugar, and spices.

6 __Catarrhs__: colds.

7 __Limbecks of fluxes__: distillations of fluids.

8 __There is none . . . longer__. Cf. Thomas Adams, __Cosmopolite__ (1630): "No man is so old, but still he thinks he may live another yeare." Tilley Y13

9 __Commons__: food and quarters.

10 __Haxter__: swaggering bully.

11 __pricksong__: an accompanying melody or counterpoint to a simple melody, or plainsong.

12 __Clancular__: private.

13 __workes of Supererogation__: good deeds beyond what are considered necessary for salvation.

14 __It is but a Tabernacle . . . encloistred__. As long as his soul is still contained within his body, he is not free. A tabernacle is a temporary altar.

15 __upon his manumission . . . enfranchised__: technical feudal terms for describing the condition of a freed serf.

16 __Beadsman__: inmate of an almshouse.

9. A Jayler

[1] dissorting: incongruous.

[2] Meney: crew of prisoners.

[3] Almner. The almoner distributed alms in an official capacity.

[4] Night-walkers: thieves.

[5] Whipping-cheere: flogging. Cf. Robert Herrick, "Hell," Noble Numbers (1647): "Hell is the place where whipping-cheer abounds, / But no one Jailor there to wash the wounds."

[6] Iron age. This is a punning allusion to the iron age, last of the ages of man, according to classical thought. Thomas Heywood wrote five plays dramatizing the ages, which were of gold, silver, brass, and two ages of iron. Cf. George Chapman, trans. The Georgics of Hesiod (1618), ed. R. Hooper, (London, 1888), p.161:

> For that which next springs, in supply of this,
> Will all of Iron produce his families;
> Whose bloods shall be so banefully corrupt
> They shalt not let them sleep, but interrupt
> With toils and miseries all their rests and fares,
> The Gods such grave and soul-dissecting cares
> Shall steep their bosoms in.

[7] wards: guards.

8 <u>Jayler</u> <u>in</u> <u>the</u> <u>Acts</u>. The jailor asked for salvation after an earthquake broke Paul's chains, opening the doors to his cell and ending, if Paul so desired, the imprisonment imposed on him by Herod. See Acts xvi. 26-31.

9 <u>artificiall</u> <u>daies</u> <u>freedome</u>. Artificial day was composed of the hours from sunrise to sunset, in contrast to the natural day which was reckoned by the hours of the clock. Cf. Chaucer, Introd. to "The Man of Law's Tale," ll.1-3:

> Oure Hooste saugh wel that the brighte sonne
> The ark of his artificial day hath ronne
> The ferthe part. . . .

10 <u>Exhibition</u>: gift.

11 <u>reversions</u>: leftovers from a meal.

12 <u>amates</u>: disturbs.

13 <u>Sessions</u>: the quarterly terms of the London courts.

14 <u>hydropicke</u> <u>thirst</u>: unquenchable thirst as in a dropsical person.

15 <u>six</u> <u>shillings</u> <u>beare</u>: beer poured from a barrel costing six shillings; probably rather strong beer since this is a substantial price. Cf. n.29 to 12. "A Metall-man."

16 <u>male-tympanie</u>: a tympany, or swelling.

17 <u>If</u> . . . <u>Neck-verse</u>. A neck-verse was literally a verse to save one's neck. A literate person accused of a capital crime could save his life by reading a Latin verse, usually

the fifty-first Psalm. When Ben Jonson killed Gabriel Spencer, a fellow actor, in a brawl, he received benefit of clergy and was therefore punished by only having his thumb branded at Tyburn.

18 **If . . . expression.** If he bribes the jailer he can avoid being branded, but if he has no money he receives the "literall expression," i.e. the brand of the letter "F" for "Felon."

19 **Ordinaries funerall Sermon.** The Ordinary was the chaplain of Newgate prison who prepared condemned criminals for execution.

20 **New-gate bird.** The modern equivalent term is "jailbird."

21 **Crim Tartar.** The Tartar tribesman was known for his cruelty. See n. 10 to 3. "A Corranto-coiner."

22 **Cacus cave.** Cacus was a legendary three-headed thief who hid his booty in a cave. He was killed by Hercules. The jailer can benefit society by uncovering stolen property, but instead he seeks his own profit.

23 **him**: St. Paul.

10. A Keeper

¹ *If . . . recetter*. The alehouse keeper's house acts as a receiving station for stolen goods. A "rece**ipter**" was a receiver of stolen goods.

² *If . . . Livery*: punning on **livery** in its meanings as (1) a livery stable and (2) the official dress of a servant or member of a company.

³ *If . . . him*. Calling the keeper of a field a "night walker," since he watches over his preserve at night, occasions a pun on its other meaning as thief, with his "inmates" (fellow thieves-dogs) who "backbite" (deceive) him.

⁴ *Bellman*. The title page of Dekker's *The Belman of London* (1608) pictures the bellman on his nightly rounds as night-watchman and town crier, equipped with his pike and lantern and followed by his dog.

⁵ *If . . . him*. If there is no one around to witness it, the field keeper will share with a poacher, rather than reveal him.

⁶ *If . . . Colloguer*. The third day of a play was often a benefit performance for the dramatist. On a crowded third day, the doorkeeper will possibly intrigue to pocket the proceeds rather than turn them over to the author.

7 <u>But . . . Character</u>. An often-voiced theme was the passing
of true hospitality as exemplified by the country-house keeper,
whose gates, as in Carew's "To Saxham":

> . . . have been
> Made only to let strangers in;
> Untaught to shut, they doe not fear
> To stand wide open all the year. . . .

The genuine <u>otium</u> and generosity of the country gentleman are
praised in Jonson's and Herrick's country-house poems and in
Breton's <u>The Court and Country</u> (1618). Lupton's character
"Hospitality" expresses a similar sense of loss: "This true
noble hearted fellow is to be dignified and honor'd, wheresoever
he keeps house: It's thought that pride, puritans, coaches and
covetousnesse hath caused him to leave our Land. . . . He loved
three things, an open Cellar, a full Hall, and a sweating
Cooke. . . . wee can say that once such a charitable
Practitioner there was, but now hee's dead, to the griefe of
all England: And tis shroudly suspected that hee will never
rise againe in our Climate."

8 <u>Black Jack</u>: the large, black leather jug filled with beer
which the house-keeper makes available to all who are thirsty.

9 <u>Hee . . . score</u>. Knowing that Christian charity is his duty,
the gentleman keeps an accounting of the provisions he freely
dispenses to the poor.

10 <u>Competence</u>: an adequate but not excessive amount.

11 <u>The Court . . . it</u>. The court takes little notice of the country-
house keeper, but if he does achieve preferment, he does not

succumb to the intemperate habits of the courtier and the corrupt life at court.

12 <u>precise</u>: puritanical.

13 <u>If . . . Market</u>. In times of economic depression the gentleman purposely dispenses his stored provisions of grain and corn in order to prevent engrossers--speculators and hoarders who tried to inflate the price of these goods--from profiting at the expense of the poor.

14 <u>posie</u>: motto.

15 <u>partcloses</u>: portcullises, sliding gates or doors.

11. <u>A Launderer</u>

As Arnold Davenport pointed out in his edition of the poems of John Marston (Liverpool, 1961), the term "laundress" was used in three senses: as a washerwoman; as a woman of questionable reputation; and as a special term of reference for the housekeepers of rooms in the Inns of Court. Brathwait touches on all three associations of the term in his character of the social-climbing laundress who manages through her own shrewdness and diligence to achieve a certain degree of prosperity in her lifetime.

[1] __in the Sudds__: an expression meaning "in a depressed state" as well as its obvious literal meaning. The influence of the planet Saturn produced a melancholy complexion, hence a gloomy disposition.

[2] __Used shee Clipping . . . Statute__. Brathwait refers to the practice of clipping small particles of metal from coins, thus debasing them. Punishment for this crime was the clipping of the felon's ears. There is also a pun occasioned by the doubtul virtue ascribed to laundresses: "clipping" means embracing. Many other puns relating to the laundress's promiscuity are only thinly disguised throughout the character. Cf. below, "good bits," "Spirit to rise," "good turne," "recourse and familiar concourse," "put a Case."

[3] __Epicene . . . nature__. The title character of Jonson's __Epicoene__ was a boy disguised as a woman. Brathwait again alludes to the practice of wearing away particles of gold or silver from coinage. Cf. Lupton, __London and the Countrey Carbonadoed__, sigs. $C7^v-8^r$: "Some of the men are cunning __Landerers__ of plate and get much by washing that plate they handle, and it hath come from some of them, like a man from the __Brokers__ that hath casheer'd his cloake, a great deale the lighter."

⁴ no Shifter . . . Sharer. This probably means that were it not for the laundress, the trader-in of second-hand clothing would not be able to sell his old wares during the quarter sessions.

⁵ Collegiat Underbutlers. They helped to superintend the household of student residences.

⁶ Punie Clarkes in Innes of Chancery. Puny clerks were freshmen students, novices in the law schools. Inns of Chancery were residences for apprentices of law and were considered subordinate to the Inns of Court.

⁷ higher graduates: residents of the four Inns of Court.

⁸ Progresse time: official journeys of the court and its retinue to different parts of the realm.

⁹ Black-guard: servants in charge of the kitchen utensils during progresses.

¹⁰ sleevelesse arrands: wasted time; futile errands.

¹¹ assumpsits: verbal or unsealed contracts.

¹² Botcher: clothes-mender.

¹³ indent: come to an agreement with.

¹⁴ through-stitch. A thorough-stitch implies finishing something through to the end.

¹⁵ just particular . . . accrued. The implication is that the laundress is now acting in the capacity of madam, supervising

her under-laundresses and receiving a share of any income they obtain.

16 <u>stands up on her pantofles</u>: literally "stands upon her slippers," but connoting newly-acquired respectability and importance. Cf. Dekker and Webster, <u>Northward Ho</u> (1607): "Sometimes be merrie and stand upon thy pantoffles like a new elected scavenger." Tilley P43.

17 <u>Jugge</u>. "Jug" is a nickname for Joan, but has a lower social connotation.

18 <u>nose . . . flat</u>: the result of venereal disease or the mercury treatment which was frequently prescribed.

19 <u>agent and patient</u>: active participant and recipient. She collects both from her under-laundresses and their patrons.

20 <u>incorporate societie</u>: professional guild.

21 <u>Barbers-ball</u>: ball of soap.

22 <u>Comfits . . . Claret</u>. Comfits are sweetmeats, fruit preserved in sugar. Claret was considered an inexpensive wine.

12. A Metall-man

1 <u>beetle head</u> . . . <u>leaden heele</u>. A beetle is a heavy wooden-headed hammer. Thus, the metal-man is dull-witted and slow of foot.

2 <u>hollow-charnell</u>. His voice is as loud as if it were spoken in an empty tomb.

3 <u>Trunkhos'd</u>: wearing rather baggy breeches.

4 <u>ends</u> . . . <u>silver</u>: the street cry of the gold-end man, who gathered bits of gold and silver for resale.

5 <u>sublunarie</u> . . . <u>Mercurie sublimate unto them</u>. All the alchemist's helpers or associates are subordinate to him; he is poison to them. Metals that are sublunary, under the moon and thus subject to decay, are inferior. Sublimated mercury was a compound of mercury and arsenic used as a corrosive poison or ratsbane.

6 <u>longacres</u>: inheritances.

7 <u>Kelley</u>. Edward Kelley (1555-1595) was an ardent and notorious practitioner of the occult. In 1582 he became associated with the brilliant mathematician and occultist, John Dee. Together they traveled to the court of Rudolph II at Prague in order to

practice magic and alchemy with royal sponsorship. In 1595, having broken off with Dee and been expelled from Prague, he returned there, only to be imprisoned and then killed while trying to escape.

8 Sysiphus pocket. This implies that like Sisyphus who must continuously roll a huge stone up a mountain in Hades without any hope of reaching the summit, the metal-man will strive futilely to find the Philosopher's Stone, the substance which can transform the impure metal into the perfect proportion of elemental substances that exist in gold. Cf. Johnson's Alchemist, II.iii.208-210: "Sisiphus was damn'd / To roule the ceaselesse stone, onely, because / He would have made ours common." Herford and Simpson, X, 84, cite Jonson's reading in Delrio's Disquisitiones for the origin of Mammon's interpretation of the Greek myth. Brathwait's reliance on Jonson for supplying him with allusions and ideas is pronounced in several characters.

9 Aries: before the beginning of the new year, since Aries the Ram is the first sign of the zodiac.

10 Jason . . . fleece. Cf. Nashe, Nashe's Lenten Stuffe, Works, III, 221: "Cornelius Agrippa maketh mention of some Philosophers that held the skinne of the sheepe that bare the golden fleece, to be nothing but a booke of Alcumy written upon it. . . ."

11 crotchets: fantastic inventions.

12 <u>reparation</u> <u>of</u> <u>Pauls</u>. Cf. John Stow, <u>Annales</u>, <u>Or</u>, <u>A</u> <u>Generall</u> <u>Chronicle</u> <u>of</u> <u>England</u> (1631), p.1048: "King <u>James</u> . . . endeavoured to have repayred the decayed Cathedrall Church of S. <u>Paul</u> in London, being the most sumptuous Christian Monument in this part of the world . . . but being prevented by death, that holy worke rested for a season, and within short space after, it pleased God to possesse his sonne King <u>Charles</u> with a like Religious spirit and . . . by most profound advice ordayned most especiall Commission and Commissioners, for the speedy and ample repaire of that Church." When Laud became Archbishop in 1628, he initiated plans for the repairs, assigning the task to Inigo Jones. Although the first stone was placed in 1633, the Revolution prevented completion.

13 <u>Duke</u> <u>Humfreys</u> <u>knights</u>. The middle aisle of St. Paul's, the acknowledged center of social activity for London gallants and parasites, was erroneously named "Duke Humphrey's walk" because of a monument supposedly in honor of Humphrey, Duke of Gloucester, who was actually buried in St. Albans.

14 <u>Moorfields</u>. See note 9 to 3. "A Corranto-coiner."

15 <u>yellow-Hesperian</u> <u>Plants</u>. The elms must be turned into the golden apples of the gardens of the Hesperides, found on the Isles of the Blessed.

16 <u>Indies</u> <u>of</u> <u>this</u> <u>State</u>. His astrological calculations point to his eventual success. The Indies were fabled for their great wealth.

17 conceites: visionary notions of changing metal to gold.

18 Speculation: occult vision.

19 Elevate that tripode . . . Crucible. Sublimate that pipkin: Heat the contents of that small earthenware pot and then cool the vapor until it results in a solid again. Elixate your antimonie: Boil the antimony, or trisulphide. Intenerate your Chrysocoll: Soften the gold solder. John Bullokar, An English Expositor (1616), calls chrysocoll "a kinde of minerall found like Sand in the veines of some mettalles." Accelerate our Crucible: Speed up the chemical process in the crucible.

20 infused: poured in, diffused.

21 Democritus. The "laughing philosopher," whom Burton imitated in The Anatomy of Melancholy by using as a persona the name "Democritus Junior," was also used by Brathwait in his later political closet drama, Mercurius Britanicus (1641).

22 Paracelsian. Paracelsus (1493-1541), whose full name was Philippus Aureolus Theophrastus Paracelsus Bombast of Hohenheim, is a significant figure in the history of science. Believing that sulphur, mercury, and salt were the basic constituents of matter, he assumed that ill health was a result of an imbalance of these elements. His experimentation in chemistry led him, as it did other Renaissance empiricists, into alchemy and other aspects of the occult. He is usually placed in opposition to Galenic medicine of

applied laws based on Aristotelian natural philosophy.
Cf. Donne's Ignatius His Conclave (1611), sig. A8^V, where
Paracelsus, scorned as an innovator, is called to Lucifer's
throne as one of his select group of men who "gave an affront
to all antiquitie, and induced doubts, and anxieties, and
scruples, and . . . established opinions, directly contrary
to all established before." Not without his pride,
Paracelsus says: " . . . I broght all Methodicall Phisitians,
and the art it selfe into so much contempt, that that kind
of phisick is almost lost; This also was ever my principal
purpose, that no certaine new Art, nor fixed rules might be
established, but that al remedies might be dangerously drawne
from my uncertaine, ragged, and unperfect experiments. . ."
(sig. B3^{r-v}).

23 Amalthea . . . Amalga. Amalthea was the goat-nymph who
nursed Zeus upon his birth in Arcadia. In gratitude Zeus
took one of her horns and made it into the Cornucopia, or
horn of plenty, which yielded to its owner all the food he
might wish. An amalgama was a softened mixture of mercury
and another metal, usually gold or silver. Brathwait is
saying that the metal-man's efforts to find gold end in
the usual base mixture.

24 more Moone . . . in them. Gold was called Sol, and silver,
Luna, in the jargon of alchemy.

25 All these rubbes . . . byas. All these obstacles will not
turn him from his determined course. "Rubbes" in the game

of bowling were hindrances to the "bias," or curved course of the ball as it approached the pins.

26 delicious: luxurious.

27 Theogenes-like. Theagenes was the hero in Heliodorus' Aethiopica, translated by Thomas Underdown as the popular Ethiopian History (1569?). Theagenes, a Thessalian warrior, falls in love with Chariclea, a priestess of the Delphic oracle, while he is making a sacrifice and together they flee the land. Brathwait possibly refers to the smoke of the oracle and the speed with which the couple fell in love and escaped.

28 Philosopher: natural philosopher, or occult scientist.

29 cuppe of sixe: a cup of beer, from a barrel of beer costing six shillings. Cf. n15 to 9. "A Jayler."

30 aurum potabile. Literally "drinkable gold," this was, according to O. E. D., "a preparation of nitro-muriate of gold deoxydized by some volatile oil. . . ." It was reputed to have marvellous curative powers. Cf. George Ripley, The Compound of Alchymie (1471), in Elias Ashmole's Theatrum Chemicum Britannicum (1652), p.116:

> This naturall processe by helpe of craft thus consummate
> Dissolveth the Elixir spirituall in our unctuous Humiditie;
> Then in Balneo of Mary togeather let them be Circulat,
> Like new Hony or Oyle till they perfectly thicked be.
> Then will that Medicine heale all manner Infirmitie,
> And turne all Mettalls to Sonne & Moone most perfectly:
> Thus shall ye have both greate Elixir, and Aurum Potabile,
> By the grace and will of God, to whom be lawd eternally.

31 <u>Metall-men of Lothburie</u>. Cf. Stow, <u>The Survey of London</u>, p.498: "This street is possessed (for the most part) by Founders, that cast Candlestickes, Chafingdashes, Spice-mortars, and such like Copper or Laten works, and do afterward turne them with the foote, and not with the wheele, to make them smooth and bright, with turning and scratting (as some doe tearme it) making a loathsome noyse to the by-passers, that have not been used to the like; and therefore by them disdainedly called <u>Lothbury</u>."

13. **A Neuter**

¹ siege: anus.

² Hedgehog . . . Southward. Cf. Pliny's *The Historie of the World* (1601), trans. Philemon Holland, I.viii.37, on this characteristic of hedgehogs: "By stopping one or other of their holes, men know when the wind turneth, and is changed from North to South."

³ Urchin: hedgehog. Urchins were grouped with elves, witches, fairies, and other spirits as a kind of goblin in animal form. Cf. Milton, *A Mask* (1634), ll. 843-847:

>   . . . and oft at eeve
> Visits the herds along the twilight meadows,
> Helping all urchin blasts, and ill luck signs
> That the shrewd medling elf delights to make,
> Which she with pretious viold liquors heals.

Cf. also Brathwait's *A Survey of History: Or, A Nursery for Gentry* (1638), p.159: "Such Urchins, strict Criticisme may terme Temporizers; who are onely for complying with Time, seldome or never closing with Truth. . . ."

⁴ Gregory Nazienzen . . . Chameleon. Gregory of Nazianzus (c.325-389), contemporary of Julian the Apostate (c.331-363), wrote two lengthy tracts against him. Julian publicly renounced Christianity in early manhood, espousing an ascetic Hellenism. Gregory calls him a "chameleon" in *Contra*

Julianum I, Patrologiae Graecae, ed. J.-P. Migne (Paris, 1857), XXXV, 536.

5 **Laodicean.** See Rev. iii.15-16. The Laodiceans were "neither cold nor hot," hence not committed strongly to any matter of principle.

6 **Timists.** Cf. the Overburian character of "The Timist," or time-server, one who moulds himself to the prevailing temper of the time: "He hath no more of a conscience than fear, and his religion is not his but the prince's."

7 **Cringes:** servile bows.

8 **officiously:** dutifully.

9 **Pharisaicall:** hypocritical.

10 **Publican.** See Matt. xviii.17: ". . . if he neglect to hear the church, let him be unto thee as an heathen man and a publican." The publicans were Jewish tax collectors for the Romans, hence religious traitors.

11 **bravest:** most pretentious.

12 **fire-edge:** the edge of a weapon sharpened in a fire.

13 **Remora:** a fish that attaches itself to the bottom of ships and was supposedly able to stop them.

14 **betwixt Baal and Bethel:** between idolatry and devout worship.

15 **Puffin:** a sea bird with a rounded belly; hence, metaphorically a person swollen with pride.

16 <u>Recusants</u>: persons who refused to conform to the state regulations for church attendance; usually applied to those who professed sympathy for, or allegiance to, the Roman Catholic Church.

17 <u>Penall Statutes</u>: perhaps the Act against Popish Recusants of 1593 which restricted nonconformists to an area within five miles of their homes upon penalty of forfeiture of property.

18 <u>Martyrologies</u>: catalogs of martyrs and saints arranged according to their feast days in the calendar and followed by a short history of the saint. Each church had its own martyrology.

19 <u>practice of Pietie</u>: a glancing allusion to Lewis Bayly's extremely popular devotional handbook of that title. The book was so popular that all copies of the first two editions were read until they ceased to exist. The earliest copy extant is from the third edition of 1613. There were at least forty-three editions by 1640. See Wright, <u>Middle-Class Culture</u>, pp.259, 261.

20 <u>Polititian</u>. This word had a strong connotation of evil statecraft, since it was often connected with Machiavelli. Cf. Thomas Middleton's <u>A Game at Chess</u> (1624), V.iii.201-202: "Room for the mightiest Machiavel-politician / That e'er the devil hatch'd of a nun's egg!" For a discussion of this word and others that connoted a sinister intent as a result of

Machiavelli's influence in England, see Mario Praz's essay, "Machiavelli and the Elizabethans," in *The Flaming Heart* (Garden City, New York, 1958). See also Felix Raab, *The English Face of Machiavelli: A Changing Interpretation, 1500-1700* (Toronto, 1964).

[21] *treatie*: treatise.

14. An Ostler

[1] <u>Is . . . provender</u>. A bottleman is a dealer in bottles, or bundles, of hay or straw for provender. For the meaning of putting an edge on horses' teeth in order to save on provender, see n.11 below.

[2] <u>The masters . . . him</u>. Cf. Lyly, Euphues: The Anatomy of Wit (1578), Works, I, 245: "It is the eye of the maister that fatteth the horse, and the love of the woman, that maketh the man."

[3] <u>Litterature</u>: pun on litter, or straw.

[4] <u>Ostrie . . . Winchester</u>. His hostry must not experience what has happened to Winchester. Winchester was the depository of a standard of dry and liquid measure. Brathwait uses it metaphorically for an honest measure. Cf. Edward Sharpham, The Fleire (1607), ed. Hunold Nibbe (Louvain, 1912), II.i: " . . . if halfe will not serve your turne, take the whole, measure by your own yard, you shal have Winchester measure."

[5] <u>Withers</u>: the ridge where the shoulders meet the neck.

[6] <u>hoofe-bound</u>: having a dried or contracted hoof that could result in lameness if left neglected.

[7] <u>nappiest</u>: strongest.

8 <u>Oyle</u> <u>of</u> <u>Oates</u>. Gervase Markham, <u>Markhams</u> <u>Maister-Peece</u> (1615), sig.P3^r, describes this as a mixture of boiled milk, alum, and oats used for medicinal purposes.

9 <u>Beadle</u>: a parish constable, responsible for keeping order in church.

10 <u>Hypparchie</u>: literally "horse kingdom." Brathwait's usage is the only one recorded in <u>O</u>. <u>E</u>. <u>D</u>.

11 <u>Dentifrice</u> . . . <u>them</u>. A favorite trick of the ostler was to make the horses under his care lose their appetite, thus saving himself the expense of provender. One method, alluded to in <u>King</u> <u>Lear</u>, II.iv.126-127, was to grease the hay, thus making it unpalatable to the horse. Brathwait's reference to a "dentifrice" is the use of a candle, described by Dekker in <u>Lanthorne</u> <u>and</u> <u>Candle-light</u> (1608), Temple Classics Edition (London, 1904), p.270: " . . . hee first . . . tooke away, not onely all the Provander that was set before them, but also all the hay. . . . The poore Horses looked very rufully upon him for this, but hee rubbing their teeth only with the end of a <u>Candle</u> . . . tolde them, that for their Jadish trickes it was now time to weane them."

12 <u>verge</u>: jurisdiction or control.

13 <u>Stable-Lecture</u>. Lectures were delivered by free-lance clergy without benefices, who preached whenever and wherever they could obtain subsidizers. For their importance as a revolutionary force in this period see Christopher Hill,

"The Ratsbane of Lecturing," in <u>Society and Puritanism in Pre-Revolutionary England</u> (London, 1964).

[14] <u>officious</u>: dutiful.

[15] <u>resty</u>: lazy.

[16] <u>vailes</u>: wages and tips.

15. A Post-master

1 <u>Chequerman</u> . . . <u>him</u>. The postmaster's job was to convey the king's mail by posthorse from one stage or mail station to another. Various stages along the post-roads were established to supply riders with fresh horses. Brathwait here makes a strained analogy to the occupation of the chequer-man, employed in the exchequer to keep accounts. The postmaster receives his pay for carrying the mails beforehand; the chequer-man, dealing with large sums of money, will never overtake or surpass in pay what he handles as part of his duties--that is, his own post will not match what he pays out.

2 <u>price of his miles</u>. The charge per mile for carrying mail was regulated by the government. Travellers on official commission were charged $2\frac{1}{2}$ pence per mile; those on private business paid 3 pence. Although there was no official mail service for private correspondence, post horses were hired out for this purpose.

3 <u>artificiall day</u>: the hours of the day reckoned from sunrise to sunset. A pun is made on the postmaster's making--through the artifice of his occupation--night into day, since his work day could occur at night.

4 To save weight ... halter: another play on words, here based on the meanings of band as (1) the bands of a saddle: two metal pieces that hold the arched part of the saddle in place, and (2) the neck band or collar that was commonly worn in this time; and halter as (1) a rope placed around the horse's neck for leading it, and (2) a hangman's noose. A "sprig" is a youngster.

5 denere: denier, a small French coin valued at one-tenth of an English penny.

6 Portmantua: traveling case.

7 Lethe: the river of Hades that brought on forgetfulness of one's past life.

8 pampered Jade: a reminder of Marlowe's famous line, "Holla, ye pampered jades of Asia," from 2 Tamburlane, IV.iv.1.

9 foundered: lame. Cf. 2 H. IV, IV.iii.38-40: "I have speeded hither with the very extremest inch of possibility; I have foundered nine-score and odd posts. . . ."

10 budget: leather pouch.

11 Canterbury: a Canterbury pace or gallop such as pilgrims assumed on their way to Canterbury Cathedral.

12 spur-gall'd: irritated in the area where the spur hits the flesh; caused by overusing the spur.

13 Glanders ... Bogspavings. Cf. Gervase Markham, Markhams

Maister-Peece (1615): Glanders "is a running impostume ingendred either by cold, or by famine, or by long thirst, or by eating corrupt and musty meate. . ."(G3^v). Yellowes: "Jaundices, or Yellowes, have their beginnings from the evils of the liver. . ."(L3^v). Fashions: "The Farcy (of our ignorant Smiths called the Fashions) is of all outward sorrances the vilest, the most poysonous, infectious, and the most dangerous. . . . It is a kind of creeping ulcer, growing in knots, ever following alongst one veine or other. . ."(Ff4^r). Maladers: "Malander is a kind of dry hard scab, growing in the forme of lines or strakes overthwart the very bought or inward bent of the knee, and hath hard haires with stubborne rootes, like the rootes of a childes scabbed head. . ."(Aa3^v). Curbs: "A Curbe is a long swelling a little beneath the elbow of the hough, . . . which causeth the horse to halt after a little labour. . ." (Bb6^v-Bb7^r). Scratches "are long, scabby, dry chaps, . . . growing right up and downe, and overthwart on the hinder legges. . ."(Dd1^r). Staggers is "a dizzy madnesse of the braine, proceeding from corrupt, proceeding from corrupt blood, . . . which oppresse and make sicke the braine. . ." (Fl^v). Strangles is "a meane inflammation of the throate, proceeding from some cholerickes or bloody fluxion. . ." (T3^r). Ringbones: A ringbone "is a sorrance, which appeareth above upon the cronet of the hoofe, being a certaine hard gristell. . ."(Dd2^v). Windgalls: A windgall is "a little blebbe or bladder full of corrupt jelly, or like the white of an egge, growing on each side of the maister sinew of the leg. . ."(Cc3^r). <u>Navelgalls</u>: A navelgall occurs "when a horse at any time is bruised on the top of the chine of the back, behind the saddle, right against the navell. . ."(X5^r). <u>Bogspavings</u>: These are probably blood spavins, one of which is "a soft swelling, growing on both sides the hough, and seemes as though it went through the hough. . ."(Bb4^v).

14 <u>bootlesse</u>: profitless.

15 <u>quotidian feaver</u>: intermittently recurring fever.

16 <u>Hecticke</u>: wasting, consuming. A hectic fever was symptomatic of consumption and other wasting diseases.

17 <u>writ of ease</u>: certificate of discharge from employment.

16. A Questman

A "questman," or inquest man, was an elected official of a ward, the administrative units into which London was divided. Each ward--there were twenty-six--was required to hold sessions of hearings and adjudication called Wardmote Courts.[1] The aldermen of the ward were responsible for the upkeep of their local government's public services: maintaining the sanitation of streets by appointing scavengers, maintaining street signs, appointing watchmen to light the streets at night, checking up on taverns, and inspecting the ward for harlots and vagrants. To insure tighter control of the ward population, the ward was required to maintain a roll of all its residents, their addresses, trades, or professions. All abuses occurring in the ward were to be presented before the wardmote court. The inquest man assembled the necessary data and presented his findings to the court.

[1] See William Bohun, Privilegia Londini: Or, the Laws, Customs, and Priviledges of the City of London (London, 1702), pp. 355-363, for information pertaining to the administration of wards.

¹ New Troy. London was supposed to have been founded by Aeneas, descendant of Brutus, after his defeat by the Greeks. Accordingly it was also called Troynovant, as Brathwait humorously referred to it in Mercurius Britanicus: "In Troynovant . . . thou shalt see Coblers and Hucksters, that arise out of old Shoes and Panniers, beating the Pulpit and broaching new doctrines, as if they were Regii Professores, and held by the Rabble to be most profound Divinity. . . ." Quoted in Black, Richard Brathwait, An Account of His Life and Works (Philadelphia, 1928), p.76.

² Old-Rome. Brathwait is punning on the name quest-man and the Roman official, the quaestor, who had charge of the state treasury and public expenditures.

³ Common-place book. The commonplace book, meant to provide a copious supply of information and topics for future use, was usually arranged under different headings as a personal guide to its contents. The questman's register of parish names, of course, did not need to be so elaborate.

⁴ Election: word play on its meaning as God's predestination of eternal life for His chosen creatures.

⁵ Dew-lap: the pendulous skin on the throats of cows. Cf. The Tempest, III.iii.44-46: "Who would believe that there were mountaineers / Dew-lapp'd like bulls, whose throats had hanging at 'em / Wallets of flesh?"

6 <u>leaves not a token</u>: word play on the meanings of token as (1) coins and (2) the red spots that were symptoms of the plague. Called "God's tokens" in <u>Love's Labor's Lost</u>, V.ii.424, they were considered sure signs of death. Cf. Dekker, <u>Lanthorne and Candle-light</u> (1608), <u>Temple Classics</u> ed. (London, 1904), p.241: " . . . the dore of a poore Artificer (if his child had died but with one Token of death about him) was close ram'd up. . . ." See also Dekker's "Gods Tokens: or, A Rod for Run-awaies," in <u>The Plague Pamphlets of Thomas Dekker</u>, ed. F. P. Wilson (Oxford, 1925), pp.135-171.

7 <u>Presidents</u>: precedents.

8 <u>Revestrie day</u>: the day the vestry, or parish administrators, meets.

9 <u>Paracelsian</u>. See note no. 20 to 12. "A Metall-man."

10 <u>Dioscoridan</u>. Pedacious Dioscorides was a first- or second-century Greek physician and botanist who wrote a five-book treatise on <u>Materia Medica</u>, describing the articles used in medicine and their efficacy.

11 <u>Mountebanke Florentine</u>. Cf. Jonson's <u>Volpone</u>, II.ii, where Volpone disguises himself as "Scoto of Mantua" and declaims in inflated tones.

12 <u>bombast</u>: soft cotton fiber used for padding, in its original sense.

13 <u>silly</u>: stupid.

17. A Ruffian

[1] Is . . . Ruffe. A "roaring dame" or "roaring girl" is a coarse, slatternly woman whose habits take on the characteristics of men. See the sympathetic portrait of Moll Cutpurse in Middleton and Dekker's The Roaring Girl: Or Moll Cutpurse (1611). The ruffian, then, is a roaring dame without a ruff, the large starched collar worn during this period. Implied is the connotation of the word ruffian as a cant term for the devil. Dekker equates the two words in a brief list of underworld terms in Lanthorne and Candle-light, p.186. In 1 H. IV, II.iv, Prince Hall calls Falstaff "father ruffian." This is probably connected to the use of "ruffin" for the devil in the Chester Miracle plays (Cf. O.E.D., s.v. "Ruffin"). The association of "dam" with a word for the devil is probably an allusion to the expression "the devil and his dam" or "the devil's dam." Cf. the short character-like description of a ruffian in 2 Return from Parnassus, The Three Parnassus Plays (1598-1601), ed. J. B. Leishman (London, 1949), 11.269-274:

> Me thinks he is a Ruffian in his stile,
> Withouten bands or garters ornament.
> He quaffes a cup of Frenchmans Helicon,
> Then royster doyster in his oylie tearmes,
> Cutts, thrusts, and foines at whomsoever he meets,
> And strewes about Ram-ally meditations.

2 <u>white-liver'd</u>: a liver without blood in it--the sign of a coward.

3 <u>dangerous</u>: arrogant.

4 <u>Shallops</u>: small dinghies for use in shallow water; here used as a derogatory term.

5 <u>braves</u>: acts of bravado.

6 <u>mouchato's</u>: moustaches.

7 <u>bastinado'd</u>: beaten with a stick.

8 <u>experimentally know</u>: know from experience.

9 <u>May-games</u> . . . <u>Rush-bearings</u>. There are several references in Brathwait's works to these rural sports, a fact that can be partly attributed to his Westmoreland upbringing. Cf. <u>The English Gentleman</u> (1630), sig. Y3^v: "So in many places of this Kingdome, both Southward in their <u>Wakes</u>, and Northward in their <u>Summerings</u>, the very same <u>Recreations</u> are to this day continued."

10 <u>beneficiall</u>: kindly.

11 <u>Lord of the Mannour</u>: the landlord controlling the leases of copyhold tenants. Cf. John Cowell, <u>The Interpreter</u> (1607), s.v. "Lord": " . . . he that is owner of a maner, and by vertue thereof hath tenents holding of him in fee, and by copy of court rolle, and yet holdeth himselfe over of a superiour Lord." He could raise rents or terminate leases

almost arbitrarily when, as was very frequently the case, such tenures were traditional and formal records of them were lacking.

[12] **Drone . . . tune.** A drone is the bass pipe of a bagpipe, able to emit only one continuous sound.

[13] **out a square:** in a state of disorder.

[14] **frontlesly:** shamelessly.

[15] **Naprie groome:** servant in charge of the linens.

[16] **fardell:** miscellaneous bundle.

[17] **veile:** stoop.

[18] **restie:** indolent.

[19] **three-pennie Ordinarie.** Cf. Dekker, The Gull's Hornbook (1609), ed. R. B. McKerrow (London, 1904), p.46: "There is another ordinary, to which your London usurer, your stale bachelor, and your thrifty attorney do resort; the price threepence; the rooms as full of company as a jail; and indeed divided into several wards, like the beds of an hospital."

[20] **hungry Commons:** scant rations.

[21] **feare of Clubbes.** The cry of "Clubs!" indicated a disturbance that required the police. Cf. H. VIII, V.iv.53-56: "I missed the meteor once, and hit that woman, who cried out

'Clubs!' when I might see from far some forty truncheoners draw to her succour. . . ."

22 <u>Buff-jerkin</u>: military jacket made of leather.

23 <u>Haxters</u>: "roaring boys" or bullies.

24 <u>faire quarrel</u>: a glancing reference to Middleton and Rowley's comedy, <u>A Fair Quarrel</u> (1617).

25 <u>two-pennie roome</u>. Cf. Dekker, <u>Lanthorne and Candle-light</u>, p.198: ". . . pay thy two-pence to a <u>Player</u>, in his gallerie maist thou sitte by a Harlot." As a corrective to these unflattering references to the two-penny room, John Cranford Adams, <u>The Globe Playhouse, Its Design and Equipment</u> (New York, 1961), p.66, notes that it was "designed for theatregoers of average means, those for whose approval playwrights and actors put forth their best efforts." The respectable middle-class spectators avoided the poorest citizens who frequented the yard, and the gentlemen, who occupied the expensive rooms in the first and second galleries or sat on the stage.

26 <u>decayed Barmoodas</u>: a stale Bermuda cigar. The earliest usage recorded in <u>O.E.D.</u> is dated 1640. The catalog of the George Arents Tobacco Collection in the New York Public Library, II, no.257, notes that such tobacco did not necessarily come from Bermuda.

27 <u>Doxes</u>: doxies, or harlots.

28 <u>Lais</u> . . . <u>Laundry</u>. Lais was the name of two celebrated Greek courtesans. Laundresses, as charactered in 11. "A Launderer," were reputed to be of easy virtue.

29 <u>Tyndarian Tribe</u>: probably an allusion to Castor and Pollux, the twin sons of Leda by Tyndareus and Zeus, respectively. The twins, often referred to as the Tyndarides, were inseparable during their strenuous adventures.

30 <u>Long-lane:</u> center for second-hand clothing.

31 <u>Sword and Buckler</u>. The sword and buckler were crude weapons used by highwaymen and servingmen. "Ruffian's Hall" was part of Smithfield market set aside for matches with the sword and buckler. Brathwait's reference is either to a tavern or a clothing-broker's sign, probably the latter.

32 <u>tart-papers</u>: wrapping paper for baker's tarts. Clothes for resale were hung up on posts outside the broker's shop.

18. A Sayler

[1] __Amphibium__. Cf. Walton, _The Compleat Angler_, ed. A. W. Pollard (London, 1901), pp.40-41, on the nature of an otter: "__Piscator__: I pray, honest Huntsman, let me ask you a pleasant question: do you hunt a beast or a fish? __Huntsman__: . . . I have heard, the question hath been debated among many great clerks, and they seem to differ about it; yet most agree that her tail is fish: and if her body be fish too, then I may say that a fish will walk upon land. . . ."

[2] __meerestone__: stone used as a landmark.

[3] __Zabulon__: Zebulun, the tenth son of Jacob. Deut. xxxiii. 18-19 speaks of the wealth that his tribe will derive from the sea.

[4] __watchfull__ . . . __calme__. Cf. Holland's trans. of Pliny, I.x.23: "They maintaine a set watch all the night long, and have their sentinels. These stand upon one foot, and hold a little stone within the other, which by falling from it, if they should chance to sleepe, might awaken them. . . ." On the dormouse, a squirrel-like rodent, Pliny says: "They renue their age every yeare, by sleeping all winter: for they lie by it close,

snug all the while, and are not to bee seene. But come the Summer once, they bee young and fresh againe (I.viii.57)."

5 fish in troubled waters. Cf. Joseph Hall, Contemplations (1612-26), I,xviii: "Jeroboam had secretly troubled these waters, that he might fish more gainfully." Tilley F334.

6 Oare in every mans boate. Cf. Isaac Barrow, Sermon 24, The Theological Works, ed. A. Napier (London, 1859), II, 235: "He that will have a sickle in another's corn, or an oar in every man's boat, no wonder if his fingers be rapped." Tilley O5.

7 great vessel at Heidelberg. This is a reference to the huge wine barrel built in 1596 by Count Palatine Casimir. Thomas Coryate described it at length in his Crudities (1611). Cf. Abraham Cowley, Cutter of Coleman-Street (1663), II.v.: "We'l drink up a whole Vessel . . . so big, that the Tun of Heidelberg shall seem but a Barel of Pickled Oisters to 't."

8 Aries. The choleric complexion was associated with this sign; hence the irascibility of the sailor.

9 Phlegmatick: mixture of cold and moist qualities.

10 Sanguine: mixture of hot and moist qualities. The sanguine man was not held to be very bold in his behavior.

11 Ostridge-like . . . iron. Cf. Sir Thomas Browne, Pseudodoxia Epidemica, Works, II, 237: "That therefore an Ostrich will swallow and take down Iron, is easily to be granted: that

oftentimes it pass entire away, if we admit of ocular testimony not to be denied. . . . yet whether this be not effected by some way of corrosion, from sharp and dissolving humidities, rather than any proper digestion, chilifactive mutation, or alimental conversion, is with good reason doubted."

12 **Hanskins**: Hänschens, "little Jacks," diminutive of Hans; a familiar name for a group of sailors.

13 **Hydrarchy**: literally "sea dynasty." Brathwait's usage is the only recorded instance in O.E.D.

14 **Custome . . . passion**. Cf. George Pettie, *A Petite Palace of Pettie his Pleasure* (1576): "But use of no evil maketh us think it no abuse, sins oft assayed are thought to be no sin." Tilley C934.

19. A Traveller

[1] can never bee freeman. This follows from the opening pun on journeyman as a traveler and as an apprentice in its meanings. Regarding the importance of becoming a freeman, or master, David Ogg, England in the Reign of Charles II (Oxford, 1956), I, 95, says: "In order to enjoy full civic privileges, a man had to become free of a city company, which he might do in one of three ways: by birthright, if he were the son of a freeman; by service, that is by apprenticeship to a freeman; and by 'redemption,' or order of the court of aldermen."

[2] migrim: megrim, or fanciful whim.

[3] wandring Jew. The ceaseless and restless traveling of the Wandering Jew, doomed to roam the earth because he insulted Christ on his way to the cross, symbolizes the traveler. See George K. Anderson, "The Legend of the Wandering Jew," Books at Brown, XIX (1963), 143-159.

[4] impe: fill out. Se n.36 to 1. "An Almanack-maker."

[5] trencheth upon: touches upon; concerns.

[6] deblazons . . . Herald. He describes as if he were painting heraldic devices. "Deblazon" seems to be Brathwait's formation, since the only uses given in O.E.D. are his.

7 <u>with her imprese</u>: <u>ORBIS IN URBE</u>. <u>Imprese</u>, the plural of Italian <u>impresa</u>, are emblems, with an allegorical picture and accompanying motto, used as heraldic devices. <u>Urbi et Orbi</u>, "for the city and for the world," is a Papal blessing delivered on various occasions of the year.

8 <u>Timist</u>: time-server.

9 <u>made up in Wainescot</u>: rigid and impassive like wainscot, or oak paneling.

10 <u>cringe</u>: servile bow.

11 <u>Congie</u>: ordinary bow performed as a greeting.

12 <u>decrements</u>: losses.

13 <u>Bellona</u>: Roman goddess of war.
<u>Minerva</u>: Roman goddess of wisdom.

14 <u>Italian Canto</u>: madrigals, contrapuntal songs for several voices, sung in the vernacular.

15 <u>Crochets</u>: quarter notes in music, with a pun on its meaning as fantastic ideas.

16 <u>Budget</u>: wallet.

17 <u>vintage</u>: used abstractly to mean "season."

18 <u>Theatre of earth</u>. The <u>topos</u> of the <u>theatrum mundi</u> ("All the world's a stage. . . .") is touched on by Brathwait, but not developed. See the essay by Herbert Weisinger in <u>The Agony</u>

and the Triumph: Papers on the Use and Abuse of Myth (East Lansing, Michigan, 1964).

[19] factors: financial agents.

[20] vading: passing away, going. Used together with "fading," the word gives the context an elegiac recognition of the transience of life. Brathwait was attracted to the word, for he used it also in The English Gentlewoman and Barnabees Journal. Cf. also Marvell, "Clorinda and Damon": "Grass withers; and the Flow'rs too fade. / Seize the short Joyes then, ere they vade."

[21] indigested: disordered, chaotic.

[22] illaborate: unfinished, crude.

[23] Noli me tangere: "Touch me not," as Christ said to Mary Magdalen when he appeared to her after his resurrection. John xx.17.

20. An Undersheriffe

[1] Cf. Stow, *A Survey of London*, p.915: "Portgraves, since called sheriffes, and Judges of the Kings Court, and have there Under-Sheriffes, men, learned in the law, to sit in their Courts." The office of sheriff was highly charged with responsibility and financial risk, and the expense of maintaining a dignified and elegant public appearance contributed to making it a rather unappealing position. The undersheriff, on the other hand, was free from this restraint and able to profit liberally from his work. See Valérie Pearl, *London and the Outbreak of the Puritan Revolution: City Government and National Politics, 1625-43* (Oxford, 1961), pp.64-65.

[2] *Countenance*: position of importance.

[3] *pudder*: pother, or uproar.

[4] *repledges*: replevin, or restoration of seized property on the condition that the party involved will return it if the case is decided against him.

[5] *distresses*. Distress is the seizure of property as a means of forcing a person to pay his debts.

[6] *yealous*: fearful.

7 deaths head to an' Usurer. A death's head was a human skull
or ring with the image of a skull used as a memento mori.
The usurer would be terrified at the thought of his death
and the ensuing punishment for his sins. Cf. Richard Brome,
The Northern Lasse (1632), II.v. : "Shee broke me a tooth
once with a deaths Head-ring on her finger? It had like to
ha' cost mee my life! 't has been a true memento ever since."

8 Counter-gate. The Counters were debtors' prisons; hence it
would be dangerous to sharpen one's knife in full view of
desperate men. Cf. Merry Wives of Windsor, III.iii.84-87:
"Thou might'st as well say, I love to walk by the Counter-
gate; which is as hateful to me as the reek of a lime-kiln."

9 assay: endeavor.

10 Sheriffs turne: the sheriff's tourn, or circuit court,
that held summary sessions as it moved about the realm.

11 Buts: pistol butts.

12 distresse. The undersheriff benefits from the apprehension
of criminals no less than does the public, since the seized
property of offenders reverts to him.

13 Secretarie: confidant.

14 cry at the Crosse. Cf. R. Cotgrave, A Dictionarie of the
French and English Tongues (1611), s.v. "Sing": "Thou hast
not cried it at the cross, nor made all the world ring of
it; thou diddest not greatly publish, or brag of it."
Tilley C841.

15 **alter . . . them**. The pun on propriety as (1) ownership and (2) rightness indicates that the undersheriff probably has the payment for his services made out to another name, thus protecting himself.

16 **Authority . . . hand**. The undersheriff's office renders him immune to punishment; he is responsible only to himself.

17 **Subject of wrongs**: torts, or civil actions upon the trespass of rights.

18 **siens**: scions.

19 **dawbing**: servile flattery.

20 **Pismire**: ant.

21 **amerciaments**: arbitrary fines.

22 **hereditaments**: inherited property.

23 **Clerke of the Market**: an appointed official whose duties were to collect tolls and inspect the general business conditions at fairs and markets. Robert Burton held the office at Oxford.

24 **All Clerkes . . . wisest men**. Cf. Chaucer, "The Reeve's Tale," l.4054: "The gretteste clerkes been noght wisest men."

25 **interplea**: dilatory plea.

26 **demurre**: demurrer, or postponing action in the form of an objection or exception.

[27] __prevent__: anticipate.

[28] __Pioners__: diggers.

[29] __coupes__: coops up

[30] __competent__: adequate.

[31] __prolling__: conniving.

[32] __Quietus est__. "He is quit." This is a term used by the exchequer to indicate that a person is formally discharged of all his accounts with the government.

21. A Wine-soaker

[1] Is . . . Wheeles. "Engine" means "a witty one" or "brainy one" as well as its more obvious meaning. "To run on wheels" is to perform something incessantly or energetically. Brathwait's marginal note reads: "A Character upon a late occasion truely expressed." The fact that this character is based on an actual experience accounts for the sense of detailed narrative in the description. Brathwait was particularly fond of rendering drunken characters in his works. Barnabees Journall (1638) is the story of a drunken journey written in Latin verse with an accompanying English translation; The Laws of Drinking (1617) is an elaborate burlesque of German academic drinking etiquette.

[2] Braine-worme: disputant.

[3] pot-guns: mortars or short weapons with large bores giving the appearance of pots.

[4] Impressor . . . an Indenture. An impressor is literally one who makes an impression. An indenture is a zig-zag path frequently associated with drunkenness. Perhaps a pun is intended on the sense of impressor as one who impresses for the military or for service in the colonies; an indenture would then be some kind of contract or agreement to serve.

5 <u>Scavingers</u>: scavenger's, or street-cleaner's.

6 <u>if the Cellar doore be open</u>. Joan Parkes, <u>Travel in England in the Seventeenth Century</u> (Oxford, 1925), p.19, notes that the poorest of city residents lived in open-flapped cellars.

7 <u>Thrasonicall Thraskite</u>. Thraso was the stock braggart soldier in Terence's <u>Eunuchus</u>.

8 <u>frontineacke</u>: wine.

9 <u>val-dunke . . . rampant-drunke</u>. There is reference in <u>Barnabees Journal</u> to a prodigious drinker named Cornelius Vandunk, who is also the subject of "Cornelius Vandunk his Satyre" in <u>The Law of Drinking</u>. If this is a play of words on his name, it is quite obscure. <u>O.E.D.</u> also called its meaning obscure, since Brathwait's usage is the only one recorded. There is probably some pun intended on "rampant," a term used in heraldry, indicating a lion or bear with its forelegs raised and standing on its hind legs.

10 <u>Saint Anthonies fire</u>: erysipelas, a skin infection characterized by a serious inflammation and reddening.

11 <u>ignis fatuus</u>: the misleading light of burning marsh gases.

12 <u>cresset-flaming</u>: torch-like.

13 <u>Rug-gownes</u>: coarse gowns worn by watchmen.

14 <u>Hyppocrates twinnes</u>. In <u>De Civitate Dei</u>, V.2, St. Augustine cites from a lost work of Cicero, <u>De Fato</u>, the story that

Hippocrates assumed two brothers to be twins when both took sick together and their sickness passed through the same stages simultaneously. Cf. Lyly, <u>Euphues</u> <u>and</u> <u>His</u> <u>England</u>, <u>Works</u>, II, 77: "<u>Hippocrates</u> Twinnes, who were borne together, laughed together, wept together, and dyed together." Elsewhere in the same tale, <u>Works</u>, II, 5, Lyly has the twins as the subject of a painting, a representation so inaccurate that the painter was constrained to write the name of the twins above their head. Cf. also Chapman, <u>The</u> <u>Gentleman</u> <u>Usher</u>, <u>The</u> <u>Plays</u> <u>and</u> <u>Poems</u> <u>of</u> <u>George</u> <u>Chapman</u>, ed. T. M. Parrott (New York, 1914), IV.iii.17-21:

> And like the twins Hippocrates reports,
> If he fetch sighs, she draws her breath as short,
> If he lament, she melts herself in tears;
> If he be glad, she triumphs; if he stir,
> She moves his; in all things his sweet ape. . . .

15 <u>Supersedeas</u>: a writ that checks the course of legal proceedings; hence a form of self-protection.

16 <u>Amaryllis</u>: amorous nymph in the pastoral tradition. Cf. Milton's "Lycidas," ll.66-69:

> Were it not better don as others use,
> To sport with <u>Amaryllis</u> in the shade,
> Or with the tangles of <u>Neaera's</u> hair?

17 <u>Lazarello</u>: the hero of the Spanish picaresque tale <u>The</u> <u>Pleasaunt</u> <u>Historie</u> <u>of</u> <u>Lazarillo</u> <u>de</u> <u>Tormes</u>, trans. David Rouland (1586).

18 <u>Salamanders thirst</u>. Cf. Holland's trans. of Pliny, I.x.86: "He is so cold a complexion, that if hee doe but touch the fire, hee will quench it as presently, as if yce were put

into it." Since it cannot be consumed in fire, it must have a great thirst for the water that mixes with air to give it its complexion.

22. A Xantippean

1 **Scold in English**. Xantippe was the wife of Socrates. His forbearance of his wife's shrewishness is alluded to often in accounts of his life.

2 **Enclosure . . . charge**: pun on rails in its meanings as (1) scolds and (2) as fences for enclosing land that has been consolidated for grazing or cultivation.

3 **receite**: recipe.

4 **soveraigne**: efficacious.

5 **wormewood in bed**. Like absinthe, she is bitter and unpalatable.

6 **a good bit**: pun on "bit" as (1) a horse's mouthpiece and (2) sexual intercourse

7 **Indentures**: zigzag paths.

8 **Hoblin**: hobgoblin.

9 **affiance**: trust.

10 **caperclawed**: strongly abused.

11 **Cap a pe**: from head to foot.

12 <u>Non</u> <u>vox</u> . . . <u>certe</u>. The source is Virgil's <u>Aeneid</u>, I.328-329. Aeneas says this when he accosts Venus, who is disguised in the garb of a huntress, in order to ask her where he has recently been shipwrecked: ". . . your speech rings not of humankind. Goddess surely you are" (trans. C. Day Lewis). Cf. <u>The Tempest</u>, I.ii.424-425, when Ferdinand first becomes aware of Miranda: "Most sure the goddess / On whom these airs attend!"

13 <u>with naturall reading</u>: with reference to something in nature.

14 <u>If cudgelling</u> . . . <u>more dutifull</u>. Cf. Webster, <u>The White Divel</u>, V.i.183-185:

> Why do you kicke her? say,
> Do you thinke that she's like a walnut-tree?
> Must she be cudgel'd ere shee beare good fruite?

15 <u>Cucking-stoole</u>: a chair to which an obstreperous woman was fastened and then immersed in water as a public punishment.

16 <u>stoole of repentance</u>: a stool placed in Scottish churches for offenders against chastity. The earliest usage recorded in <u>O.E.D.</u> is for 1647.

17 <u>Jubile</u>: according to Biblical history, a year of emancipation occurring every fifty years. Cf. Brathwait's <u>The English Gentleman</u> (1630), sig. Aal[r]: "In the yeere of <u>Jubile</u> all captives were delivered, all slaves enfranchised, al debts discharged."

18 <u>by generall suffrage</u> . . . <u>espoused</u>. Brathwait seems to be conflating two different classical sources regarding the

Greek philosophers that circulated widely in the Renaissance. Diogenes Laertius tells of the golden tripod found by fishermen of Miletus and sent to the wise men, who argued as to who would get it. Submitting their dispute to the Delphic oracle, they were told to give it to "whosoever is most wise." Thales was the natural recipient; however, he gave it to another of the seven sages--perhaps Bias, as in Plutarch's version in the life of Solon--who gave it to another, and so on. Solon settled it by stating that the god was most wise and sent it back to Delphi. The other story concerns Socrates, who stated in The Apology that he was judged by the Delphic oracle to be the only wise man in Greece, because he was the only one to assert that he knew one thing--nothing--whereas the rest claimed to know what they did not know.

[19] currish opinion . . . stored. Plutarch, in his life of Antony, tells of the misanthrope Timon, who made a fig tree in his garden available for Athenians anxious to hang themselves. This anecdote seems to have shifted to an emphasis on misogyny. Erasmus relates a similar version in his Apophthegmata. Brathwait also referred to it in his courtesy book of 1630, The English Gentleman: ". . . so as going forth one day into his Orchard, and finding a woman hanging upon a wilde Fig-tree: O God (quoth he) that all trees brought forth such fruit!" (sig. Kk4^v) For an illuminating comparison of treatments of the Timon story in classical and Renaissance literature, see Willard Farnham, Shakespeare's Tragic Frontier: The World of His Final Tragedies (Univ. of Calif., 1950),

pp. 50-67. Farnham does not mention, however, the intrusion of a woman into Timon's garden.

20 Curst bee . . . hang on Bowes. The Latin is given in the margin: Esto procul nostris Timonia ficus ab hortus, / Foemina non ramis facta sed acta thoris.

23. A Yealous Neighbour

1 yealous. Jealous is used throughout to mean suspicious, rather than covetous.

2 Aries: the sign of the Ram, causing a choleric temperament.

3 Brancher: fledgling bird.

4 Acteon. He was turned into a stag by Diana and killed by his own hounds. The presence of horns brands him as a cuckold.

5 yellowes: jaundice.

6 The Bird Galgulus. Cf. Edward Phillips, The New World of Words: Or, Universal English Dictionary (6th ed., 1706): "Galgulus, a Bird, which if one see that has the Yellow Jaundice, the Person recovers and the Bird dies."

7 Giges. Gyges, before he became king of Lydia, found a ring accidentally while performing his duties as a shepherd. The ring was on the hand of a huge corpse which Gyges found on a hollow brazen horse. Playing with the ring, he suddenly became invisible when the hoop came to the inside of his

hand. When he turned the ring again to the outside, he became visible. The story is related in Plato's _Republic_, II.359-360.

8 _Hans **Carvile**_. The story of Hans Carvel is found in Rabelais, _Pantagruel_, III.xxviii. There are analogues in Poggio's _Facetiae_; the _Cent Nouvelles nouvelles_; Ariosto, Satire V; and in the anecdote "Of the iolous man," no. xviii of _Mery Tales and Quicke Answers_, in _Shakespeare Jest-Books_, ed. W. C. Hazlitt (London, 1864), I, 28. Hans Carvel, lapidary to the king of Melinda, married in his old age a bailiff's daughter. Soon he became suspicious of her cordiality to others. In order to convince her of the merits of fidelity, he read her legends, presented her with a MS in praise of fidelity, and gave her a sapphire necklace. One night he dreamed that the Devil gave him a ring which would protect him against cuckoldry so long as he wore it on his middle finger. Carvel awoke with his hand in his wife's genital organs, thinking that someone was trying to steal his ring. Cf. Middleton's _The Family of Love_ (1608), V.iii.418-421: ". . . and here, by my edict, be it proclaimed to all that are jealous, to wear their wives' rings still on their fingers, as best for their security, and the only charm against cuckoldry."

9 _conventicles_: the prohibited clandestine meetings of the Puritans.

10 _affects_: desires.

11 semi-brev'd: punctuated as with semibreve rests in music; i.e. long sighs, since a semibreve is a rest for the duration of a whole bar.

12 Lettice: lattice.

13 Aries, Taurus, or Capricorne. Aries the Ram, Taurus the Bull, and Capricorne the Goat are all horned beasts, hence portentous for the cuckold.

14 Supersedeas: legal obstacle.

15 Hang out . . . maids: the cry of the bellman.

16 diapason: consonance.

17 Gentleman-Usher. This frequent butt of jealous husbands in Jacobean and Caroline drama always walked before his lord or lady.

18 Prosperina: daughter of Zeus taken down to the underworld by Pluto.

19 articulate: come to terms.

20 Roach: massive rock.

24. A Zealous Brother

1 **Amsterdam print.** Many of the church reformers took residence in Amsterdam with the increasingly repressive policies that were being instituted under James I and Charles I. Sugden, *A Topographical Dictionary*, quotes from Cockayne's *Trapolin IV*: "He hath writ a paltry book against the bishops, printed it in Amsterdam in decimo sexto."

2 **Decimo Sexto:** 16mo, hence a very small size.

3 **Antipos:** one strongly opposed.

4 **Shrove-Tuesday.** Instead of observing the solemnity of the anniversary of Christ's crucifixion, he celebrates as if it were Mardi Gras. On Shrove Tuesday the apprentices traditionally celebrated by rioting, wrecking brothels and theatres. This, of course, would add to the zealous brother's pleasure.

5 **Blank Almanack:** an almanac with blank pages for recording personal information.

6 **Sister . . . piacular:** not necessarily his sister by birth. **Piacular** means requiring expiation, hence sinful.

8 **preferring that Act . . . Monuments.** The Poor Law of 1572 classified pipers as vagabonds. See n. 4 to 28. "A Piper." On John Foxe's *Acts and Monuments* (1563), William Haller,

Liberty and Reformation in the Puritan Revolution (New York, 1955), pp.47-48, says:

> It was much more than a Protestant martyrology. Foxe served both Protestant piety and English patriotism by presenting a view of universal history centering upon England and the English church. All history, he held, was occupied with the struggle of Christ and Antichrist for the souls of . . . Englishmen. . . . And English Protestants were taught by Foxe . . . that the true church since apostolic times had always been present in some guise in England. . . . Here for English Protestants was the explanation of everything that had happened to England since that time. Here for Puritans, any times after Laud's rise to power, was justification for their attacks upon prelacy.

9 Band . . . Superlative. Many of the Puritans wore a small, simple neck band rather than the elaborate ruff. There is also a pun on collar-choler.

10 Sirpe-cloath: surplice.

11 Monopoly . . . them. Although monopolies had been forbidden by Parliament in 1624, the granting of monopoly privileges was a fundamental part of Stuart economic policy. The engrossing of corn in order to sell dear and to speculate was another example of economic exploitation in the period.

12 Lilie . . . sacerdos. William Lily, or Lyly (1468-1523), was a humanist, grammarian, and grandfather of the dramatist. Brathwait refers to the widely-used "Lily's Latin Grammar," alluded to by Shakespeare, Jonson, and many others. The book comprises two parts, each separately titled--a Latin grammar in English called An Introduction of the Eyght Partes of

Speche; and a Latin version, not the same, called Institutio Compendiaria Totius Grammaticae. The earliest extant edition is from 1542. The book was more commonly known in the form that appeared at least as early as 1548--A Shorte Introduction of Grammar and Brevissima Institutio seu Ratio Grammatices. C. G. Allen, in an article in The Library, IX (1954), "The Sources of 'Lily's Latin Grammar': A Review of the Facts and Some Further Suggestions," concludes that both halves of the work were derivative, representing the efforts of Colet and Lily--perhaps others--in the English part; and of Lily, Linacre, Melanchton, Despauterius, and Erasmus in the Latin section. Allen calls it more appropriately "The Royal Grammar," a "command performance based on the best available talent." Brathwait's reference to a declination of sacerdos, "priest," is not supported by the text itself. In fact, the word appears only once--at the end of a list of nouns in Brevissima . . . , sig. Bl^v. Jonson quotes the word in this context in Tale of a Tub, III.vii.72.

13 Mother tongue: probably Hebrew. In the 17th century there was much discussion concerning what was the original language spoken by Adam in Eden; the most commonly-held view--held by various ardent Anglicans, some Roman Catholics, and some of those more Protestantly inclined--was that this language was Hebrew.

14 Apocryphall Pastor. In the Anglican position the Apocrypha and Pseudepigrapha were not regarded as having the authority

of the canonical books but were included in the King James
version as being useful and complementary, but certainly
not to be relied on. The more Protestant groups within the
Church of England, the few separatists, and the Scottish
Presbyterians followed Luther in denying any authority to
the Apocrypha.

15 convent him: call him to a conventicle.

16 Lammasse . . . tide. Lammas is about August 1, the time of
the harvest festival that occurs on this date. Michaelmas,
the feast of St. Michael, is on September 29. Candlemas is
celebrated on February 2, when candles are blessed in honor
of the purification of the Virgin Mary. Cf. Jonson, The
Alchemist, III.ii.42-44:

> Subtle. And, then the turning of this Lawyers pewter
> To plate, at Christ-masse —
> Ananias. Christ-tide, I pray you.

17 revestry: vestry, group of elders.

18 Deponent: one who gives testimony under oath.

19 Babies: puppets.
Jewtrumps: Jew's-harps.

20 Beast: Rev. xiii, the vision of John of Patmos: "And I stood
upon the sand of the sea, and saw a beast rise up out of the
sea, having seven heads and ten horns, . . . and upon his
heads the name of blasphemy."

21 irruminating. The pig does not ruminate, or chew its cud;
hence it is unclean according to Judaic law.

22 AMAN . . . DINA. Aman is Haman, the wicked king tricked by Mordecai. Amon, whose name means trustworthy and faithful, was King of Judah ca. 642-640 B. C. Diana is, of course, the Roman goddess of chastity, neatly contrasted here with Dinah, daughter of Leah and Jacob, who was raped.

23 Academicks: Plato's Academy.

24 Latin: wordplay on latten, brass or brass-like metal.

25 Vice-verger. A verger superintends a church building.

26 verge: authority.

27 late asthma . . . silence. The Declaration on Religion of 1629 attempted to suppress the Lecturers. They could not deliver afternoon sermons or discuss controversial topics; any departure from the Articles of Religion was forbidden. All ministers entering a new cure had to read the Declaration in church. See S. R. Gardiner, History of England from the Accession of James I to the Outbreak of the Civil War, 1603-1642 (London, 1863-82), VII, 20.

28 Familists. The Family of Love was an Anabaptist sect founded by David George of Delft, who announced himself as a messiah of Israel. In 1580 their books were ordered burned and their members imprisoned. Brathwait is using the term loosely, just as the label "Brownist" was often applied to any sect. The term "Familist" became a pejorative reference for sexual promiscuity. Middleton satirized the Family roundly in The Family of Love (1608).

29 __Versicles__: short sentences, usually from the Psalms, sung in an antiphonal manner.

30 __Conventuall__: pertaining to a conventicle.

31 __rid . . . bryers__: got him out of difficulties.

32 __Cornelius . . . honour__: a pun on the name Cornelius as (1) the first name of the Roman historian, Tacitus, which Brathwait also plays on in its Latin meaning as "silent" and (2) the "Cornelius tubs," the tubs which were used for the sweating cure of venereal diseases. Loss of hair was one of the results of the disease. The hypocritical zealous brother, then, has been silenced regarding good works since his own venality has been disclosed. As William P. Holden points out in __Anti-Puritan Satire 1572-1642__ (New Haven, 1954), p.56: "The intensely religious manner, the devout talk, and the pious behavior of the Puritan must certainly have been an irritation; the charge of hypocrisy could arise in the course of a diligent search for faults, since the Puritan could scarcely be in all respects perfect, and the demands of satire could enlarge minor lapses to crimes. At any rate, the precisian as a hypocrite comes to be almost central to the satire."

33 __Bells . . . death__. Many of the Puritans were against church bells for their papist associations and their lack of utility.

25. An Apparator

When Chaucer created his scathing descriptions of the apparitor, or summoner, in the Prologue and Friar's Tale, he was following an already established literary tradition.[1] In the late fourteenth century the apparitor was fixed in the popular mind as an example of ecclesiastical corruption and exploitation. The main function of the apparitor was the serving of citations for the consistory court, calling offenders of the church canons to appear before the church authorities. In the early seventeenth century the ecclesiastical courts still had jurisdiction over many aspects of personal conduct.[2] The Canons of 1604 codified the practices already in existence and reasserted the power of the church to enforce discipline among the people and their ministers. As the lowest member of the ecclesiastical hierarchy, although a lay official, the apparitor was a likely object of criticism for church abuses--his offenses were most flagrant.

[1] See Louis A. Haselmayer, "The Apparitor and Chaucer's Summoner," Speculum, XII (1937), 43-57.

[2] See Christopher Hill's discussion of the ecclesiastical courts, called the "bawdy courts," in Society and Puritanism in Pre-Revolutionary England (London, 1964), pp.298-343.

The actual duties of an apparitor were more varied than just the serving of citations.[3] As messenger for the church courts, he also delivered orders of excommunication and even certified that penance was properly performed. He was also the official bookseller of the diocese, providing ministers with copies of the Homilies, Thirty-nine Articles, and church canons. One service of the apparitor mentioned in Brathwait's character below, is his appearance before the church court as a proxy for litigants who could not, or who feared to, attend themselves.

Probably the most unpopular of the apparitor's duties was his function as church policeman. In the diocese of York, for example, the apparitors provided the courts with a multitude of cases.[4] The Canons of 1604 gave the apparitor a long list of offenses to ferret out: "'. . . adultery, whoredom, incest, drunkenness, swearing, ribaldry, usury' and any other 'uncleanness and wickedness of life,' schism, interference with church services or rude and disorderly behaviour in church, defending popish and erroneous doctrine, not communicating at Easter, hindering the execution of the Canons of 1604."[5] His fees for his labors were fixed by the church authorities. When serving

---

[3] This discussion of the apparitor's duties is derived from F. Douglas Price's article, "Elizabethan Apparitors in the Diocese of Gloucester," The Church Quarterly Review, CXXXIV (1941), 37-55.

[4] Ronald A. Marchant, The Puritans and the Courts in the Diocese of York 1560-1642 (Aberdeen, 1960), p.134.

[5] Hill, pp.301-302.

citations he was paid 1d. the mile, 2d. if for excommunication. Whitgift permitted them 4d. for the detection of an abuse and 16d. for every sentence; if the apparitor were not paid, he could sue the debtor and have him excommunicated.

As the middle-man between the church and the populace, the apparitor was indeed in a tempting position for making advantage. For the right price he could pretend to have served an offender his citation; or he could arrange to see the litigant's case through the courts without the offender himself having to appear. The apparitor could also be bribed to keep the case out of court in the first place. There are few records of punishment being meted out to wayward apparitors.[6] The fact that there appear to be more complaints over the apparitors' venal acts than actual removals from office indicates that they served a useful function for the established authorities. Occasionally the apparitors were simply carrying out orders from their corrupt superiors.[7] In any event, the fees that apparitors received were not extravagant, often probably just enough for subsistence.

In addition to Brathwait's character, there is one of an apparitor in Lupton's London and the Countrey Carbonadoed, the Overburian characters, and a character of a Commissary in Lenton's Characterismi.

---

[6] Price, "Elizabethan Apparitors in the Diocese of Gloucester." The apparitors were brought up on charges of embezzlement, incontinence, and recusancy, as well as for incompetence.

[7] F. Douglas Price, "An Elizabethan Church Official—Thomas Powell, Chancellor of Gloucester Diocese," The Church Quarterly Review, CXXVIII (1939), 108. Powell, a man guilty of incredibly flagrant corruption, used his apparitor, Draper, as a middle-man for extorting money from parishioners.

¹ <u>white sheet</u>: worn by penitents as part of receiving absolution. Apparitors attested to the successful performance of absolution and reported as such to the church courts.

² <u>pragmatically</u>: dogmatically.

³ <u>partiall-guilt</u>: partly-gilded. He considers it a part of his occupation to benefit himself while he secures absolution for his clients.

⁴ <u>Ephemerides</u>: astronomical almanacs. Cf. Thomas Lodge, <u>Wits Miserie</u> (1596), sig. C2^{r-v}: "This Divel prefers an Ephimerides before a Bible . . . he will not eat his dinner before he hath lookt in his Almanake."

⁵ <u>head-peece</u>: brain.

⁶ <u>blow up</u>: inform on.

⁷ <u>Suburbane Traders</u>: prostitutes.

⁸ <u>trucks</u>: has illicit dealings with, of a financial and sexual nature.

⁹ <u>reformation of this malady</u>. The apparitors inspected rural parishes for evidence of heretical or seditious preaching and for failure to abide by the fixed church services. Cf. Donald Lupton, <u>London and the Countrey Carbonadoed</u> (1632), sig. K3^r: "The Curate must reade Prayers on <u>Wednesdayes</u> and

and <u>Fridayes formaliter, sub paena</u> of a further Charge: they are sworne to their Office before admitted, but being admitted, oftentimes they dispense with the Oath. . . ." "They" refers to the apparators. The worst thing for the apparitor's business, according to Brathwait, is actual reformation of the abuses he investigates.

10 <u>Chappell of ease</u>: a chapel built for those who live too far from the parish church; hence for one's own convenience.

11 <u>Choake</u>: silencing of witnesses.

12 <u>President</u>: precedent.

13 <u>choakt</u> . . . <u>Civilian latine</u>: Latin terms used in law. The apparitor had to have a smattering of Latin--at least be able to read it, if not understand it. When he presented an offender with a citation from the courts, in actual practice he showed him the Latin seal and then handed him the <u>notitiam</u>, or "English note," which gave a summary of the charges. Brathwait is also probably punning on another signification of the name apparitor, since R. Cotgrave, <u>A Dictionarie of the French and English Tongues</u> (1611), gives it as another name for a hangman.

26. A Painter

¹ Table: word play on the board or flat surface on which a picture was painted.

² Cat of Mount: wildcat.

³ Westminster. The courts of Common Law and of Chancery were held in Westminster Hall.

⁴ Hee . . . exquisite. If he can paint you exactly, he will not miss one hair of your head.

⁵ excrement: growth.

⁶ curious: skillfully executed.

⁷ yet . . . temper. This is probably an allusion to the tempera paint, called "distemper," used by painters. The pigments are combined with a sticky substance like egg yolks mixed with water, and applied to a surface like plaster or chalk.

⁸ Tweakes: whores.

⁹ loose roabes. He paints the whores in the incongruous apparel of old women. Cf. Brathwait's A Strappado for the Divell, ed. J. W. Ebsworth (Boston, Lincolnshire, 1878), pp.40-41: "A civill matron . . . / In Grave attire. . . ./ Her outward rayment in a loose-gowne made."

10 Poakes: hat brims.

11 His judgement . . . Physnomy. His judgement about how to render his subject is not determined by the person's actual physical appearance or by the painter's feelings about the person, but by what he is able to infer about the subject's character from her face; hence, he then knows how to please her by flattering her actual appearance. Physiognomy was the practice of reading character and making prognostications on the basis of facial characteristics.

12 Pomatum: cosmetic pomade.

13 Saint Antonies fire: erysipelas.

14 Zeuxes. Pliny, Natural History, II.xxxv.10, tells the story of Zeuxes' ability to paint clusters of grapes so life-like that birds began to peck at them.

15 Hobson the Carrier. Thomas Hobson (1544?-1631), the famed coachman of Cambridge, had recently died. His insistence that customers hire horses that were scheduled to be ridden and no others, accounts for the proverbial "Hobson's choice." Milton wrote two poems on Hobson's death; a third has been ascribed to him by William R. Parker in the Columbia Milton, XVIII, 590-592, and is in Shawcross's ed. (New York, 1963).

16 Nine Worthies. As cited in Caxton's preface to Malory's Morte d'Arthur, they were three pagan heroes: Hector, Alexander, and Julius Caesar; three Jewish: Joshua, David, and Judas Maccabeus; and three Christians: Arthur, Charlemagne, and Godfrey of Boulogne.

17 <u>Caparisons</u>: ornamental trappings for a horse.

18 <u>prescription</u> . . . <u>exception</u>. No disapproval of his lack of skill can be made by an observer of his work, since the painter has been doing it this way for so long.

19 <u>three Graces</u>: the three mythological spirits of beauty and charm, Aglaia, Thalia, and Euphrosyne.

20 <u>freedome</u> . . . <u>Company</u>. Punning on "poetical license" as if it means membership in a professional guild or company of poets, Brathwait states that the painter has not qualified for membership and therefore cannot partake of the "freedoms" or privileges of a company. See n.1 to 19. "A Traveller."

21 <u>Painters libertie</u>. Following from the note above, "liberty" means privilege or special right.

22 <u>his</u> . . . <u>Pen</u>. His brush must submit to their pen.

23 <u>Proteans</u>. He gives the ancient heroes any appearance he wishes. Proteus the sea god could assume different shapes at will.

24 <u>Chronicle stories</u>. Lupton, <u>London and the Countrey Carbonadoed</u>, names some of the painter's subjects in a character of "Ale-houses": "In these houses you shall see the History of <u>Judeth, Susanna, Daniel</u> in the Lyons Den, or <u>Dives and Lazarus</u> painted upon the Wall."

25 <u>his</u> . . . <u>Artist</u>. The gold paint remains undamaged. "Integrity" means here "in its original condition" as well as "true to moral principles."

26 <u>Lord Maiors day</u>. On November 9, the Lord Mayor led his retinue of Aldermen and city officials to Westminster to receive official court recognition of his election. At different times, both Dekker and Middleton were responsible for overseeing the Lord Mayor's Day pageants that were part of the procession.

27 <u>barmy-Hostesse</u>. The tap dame is covered with barm, or ale froth.

28 <u>birch-pole</u>: tavern sign. See n.15 to 28. "A Piper."

29 <u>Ellenor Rumming</u>: the bawdy tap dame of Skelton's "The Tunning of Elinour Rumming."

30 <u>Rover</u>: a pun on its meanings as (1) wanderer or perhaps the folk-play character, Captain Rover, and (2) an archery term for a target set at an unfixed but usually distant point.

31 <u>Whimzies</u>: fantastic ideas.

32 <u>Actaeon</u>. He shows himself to be a cuckold.

33 <u>receipt</u>: recipe.

34 <u>Italian securitie</u>: charlatan's nostrum.

27. A Pedler

[1] <u>wandring Starre</u>. The planets were called wandering stars because of their course through the heavens.

[2] <u>Marrow-bones</u> . . . <u>them</u>. This seems to refer to the bones that were used to distend the huge farthingales, or petticoats, worn by fashionable women of the period. A pun on the meaning of marrow-bones as "knees" is also possibly intended. In both contexts the country girls show their simplicity and innocence.

[3] <u>pepper</u>: pound into fine pieces.

[4] <u>clots</u>: hardened lumps of earth.

[5] <u>Orpine</u>: a yellow mineral used as a pigment.

[6] <u>fardell</u>: bundle of goods.

[7] <u>breaking</u>: breaking wind, with a pun on "fardell."

[8] <u>Py-pouder Court</u>. The court of Pie Powders was a court specially set up to handle disputes at fairs and markets. The vivid name derives from the French <u>pied poudreux</u>, "dusty foot." The character of the peddler as a "wandring Starre," trudging over highways with his peddler's hamper, renders visual the origin of the term. Cf. the pompous character of

Justice Overdo in Jonson's <u>Bartholomew Fair</u> (1614), II.i.41-43: "Many are the yeerley enormities of this <u>Fayre</u>, in whose courts of <u>Pye-pouldres</u> I have had the honour during the three dayes sometimes to sit as Judge."

⁹ <u>strong lines</u>. Brathwait's pun arising from the peddler's tightly-drawn pack is a slight reference to the critical term he applied in his preface to <u>Whimzies</u> to other character works. Strong lines, Brathwait affirmed, "smelled too much of the Lampe and opinionate singularitie." For an excellent discussion of this concentrated, argumentative, and conceited style, see Helen Gardner's introduction to <u>The Metaphysical Poets</u> (London, 1957).

¹⁰ <u>Trinkilo's</u>. <u>O.E.D.</u> suggests that Brathwait means "trinkets" and is playfully giving it an Italian- or Spanish-sounding ending. Brathwait is possibly alluding, however, to the comic antics of the peddler, rather than to his wares. See the reference to "Trinkilo" in n. 11 of 2. "A Ballad-monger."

¹¹ <u>Countrey Choughs</u>: chatterers. Choughs are jackdaws.

¹² <u>Morrice Pastorall</u>: Morris dance.

¹³ <u>Guga-girles</u>. The girls are playing with gewgaws, or Jew's harps, making jingling sounds.

¹⁴ <u>nifles</u>: trifles.

¹⁵ <u>posset or a Sillibub</u>: drinks made of hot, spiced milk, curdled with liquor and sweetened.

16 nonresidence. Peddlers, according to the stipulations of the influential Poor Laws, beginning with the one of 1572 (14 Elizabeth, Chapter 5), were classified as vagabonds. They were, therefore, considered to be undeserving of charitable treatment and were thus restricted to their home parish as their legal residence. All vagabonds apprehended outside their home district were whipped and sent back home. Repeated offenders had their ears cut off. For a detailed discussion of the Poor Law legislation and its social implications see W. K. Jordan, Philanthropy in England, 1480-1660 (London, 1959), pp.77-108.

17 informer. The informer made his living by keeping a sharp eye out for abuses of the penal statutes. Extortion was not entirely shunned as a technique by the informer, as references in a character of this type by Francis Lenton indicate: "An Informer, Is a spye or knave errant, that peepes into the breaches of penall Statutes, not for love to the Commonwealth, as his own lucre, amongst which . . . th' assize of bread and beere are his greatest Revenues, for winking at small faults, and coozening the King and Subjects both at once. . . ." In addition to this character from Characterismi (1631), there is a description of an informer in John Stephens's Satyrical Essayes, and Others (1615).

18 Tinker of Turvie. A collection of six fabliaux originally entitled The Cobler of Canterburie (1590), The Tincker of Turvey (1630) uses the Chaucerian device of the journey as

a frame for the narrative. A tinker, cobbler, smith, scholar, and seaman amuse each other on a barge trip from Billingsgate to Gravesend. The tinker's tale is of a peddler who is cozened but who turns the tables on his cozeners. But there is no connection between the tale and this character. For the modernized text of this collection and other examples of contemporary fiction, see Short Fiction of the Seventeenth Century, ed. Charles C. Mish (New York, 1963).

19 Truck: bundle of goods.

20 Misset: messet, or pet dog.

21 Atlanticke: Atlas-like.

22 Saint Martins Rings: imitation gold rings named after St. Martin's le Grand, the London street where they were sold. Cf. Geffray Mynshul, Essayes and Characters of a Prison and Prisoners (1618), sig. D4^r: "They are like the rings and chaines bought at S. Martines, that weare faire for a little time, but shortly after will prove Alchimy, or rather pure copper."

23 May-marian: a character in the traditional Morris Dance, who was usually given an unfriendly description because of her low morals. Cf. Thomas Heywood, 1 The Iron Age, (London, 1874), III.i:

> . . . should I venter
> To damme my selfe for painting, fanne my face
> With a dyde Ostritch plume, plaster my wrinkles
> With some old Ladies Trowell, I might passe
> Perhaps for some maide-marrian.

24 <u>Presse</u>: impressment of men to serve in the military.

25 <u>stirre his stumpes</u>: get moving quickly.

26 <u>cants his maimes</u>: groans about his wounds. The Poor Laws mention among the undeserving poor to be treated harshly, beggars who counterfeit maimed soldiers.

27 <u>Bungs</u>: pickpockets.

28 <u>Catalogue</u>. Almanacs gave a list of the principal fairs.

29 <u>transnaturalized</u>: strange.

30 <u>whipstock</u>: whipping-post.

31 <u>estate</u>. His estate, meaning his possessions, remains constant, consisting only of his peddler's hamper. Also unchanging is his position in the traditional hierarchy of social classes—the estates of nobility, clergy, and commons.

32 <u>beget Custome</u>: draw customers.

33 <u>discover</u>: reveal.

34 <u>joynture</u>: the property or estate of a husband and wife held jointly in life, and as a provision for the wife after her husband's death.

28. A Piper

[1] <u>droane</u>: bass pipe of a bagpipe.

[2] <u>Stentors voice</u>. Stentor was the soldier in the <u>Iliad</u> with a powerful voice.

[3] <u>project of state</u>. The Declaration of Sports of James I in 1618 and Charles I in 1633 encouraged the pursuance of traditional recreations like church wakes and Sunday gatherings. If men were occupied with these jollities, they would have neither the time nor inclination for seditious discussion of religious issues or for attending afternoon sermons of Puritan preachers. Brathwait the Royalist would prefer to see his rural neighbors at play.

[4] <u>enacted Rogue by Parliament</u>. The Poor Law of 1572 named pipers, along with peddlers, tinkers, beggars, vagabonds, and players, as undesirable poor; henceforth they were to be prohibited from unrestricted travel and sent back to their home parish. For the harmful effects of this law and others on English music, see W. E. Woodfill, <u>Musicians in English Society from Elizabeth to Charles I</u>, <u>Princeton Studies in History</u>, IX (Princeton, 1953).

[5] <u>Shalme</u>: an oboe-type instrument with a low, stately sound.

6 <u>pye-color'd</u> <u>livery</u>: the variegated attire of a musician fortunate to receive official sponsorship, thus rendering himself immune to the statutes.

7 <u>slough</u>: skin; used figuratively for clothing.

8 <u>voluntaries</u>: spontaneously sung tunes of his choice.

9 <u>In . . . friends</u>. This is perhaps a veiled allusion to Hamlet, who in III.ii is "played on" by Rosencrantz and Guildenstern. Hamlet has the bluntness of speech and the melancholy temperament characteristic of the satirist's <u>persona</u>.

10 <u>dissorting</u>: incongruous.

11 <u>Hee . . . shearing</u>. Brathwait, in light of his many other passing references to contemporary dramas, is possibly referring to the sheep-shearing scene in <u>The Winter's Tale</u> and the character of Autolycus.

12 <u>by prescription:</u> by continued practice.

13 <u>Blouze</u>: beggar's whore.

14 <u>collapsed</u>: impoverished.

15 <u>some high way commodity . . . pipe</u>. This is an indirect allusion to the commodity swindle, a frequently-mentioned sharp practice of the time. A gentleman who needed to keep up appearances and who wished to continue leading a life in high style but was short on ready cash, could contract a

loan with a usurer. In order to avoid the penalties for usury, the loan was given in part cash and part commodities--generally useless goods like toys, hobbyhorses, or brown paper. Additional cash was obtained when the goods were sold back to the usurer--at a loss. The piper, of course, refuses to give his wife any of the goods he has acquired during the day.

16 <u>his pipe . . . owne</u>. An instrumental cause is a secondary or contributory cause; thus, the pipe is a contributory cause of his family's rising in the morning and of the piper's rising in the world. A marginal addition reads: "<u>His dreaming</u> Droane <u>plaies the grand imposter; his merry chanter a meere inchanter, causing people to skip in a ring, as if he had rais'd the divell in a circle</u>."

17 <u>Orpheus and Arion . . . them</u>. Orpheus could charm inanimate as well as animate objects with the music of his lyre. Arion, a Greek poet, was known for his ability at the cithara, a lyre-like instrument. He was saved from drowning by dolphins he had charmed with his music.

18 <u>Gutter-lane</u>: a street in London running north from Cheapside to Gresham St.

19 <u>Panier alley</u>. Cf. Stow, <u>The Survay of London</u>, p.656: " . . . is another passage out of <u>Pater Noster Row</u>, and is called of such a signe, <u>Panyer</u> Alley, which commeth out into the North over against <u>Saint Martins lane</u>."

20 sauce-fleam'd: saucefleme, a swelling of the face accompanied by pimples and inflammation. Chaucer's summoner in the Prologue, 11.624-625, "hadde a fyr-reed cherubynnes face, / For saucefleem he was, with eyen narwe."

21 Prugge: possibly "prog," or food--today's equivalent would be "grub." Brathwait seems to mean liquid refreshment, but this meaning is not indicated by O.E.D. The earliest usage for "prog" as food is given to Fuller in 1655.

22 Tis merrie . . . meete: a ballad. See The Roxburghe Ballads, ed. W. Chappell and J. W. Ebsworth (London, 1871-99), I, 59. Samuel Rowlands parodied the title in his poem 'Tis Merry When Gossips Meet (1602).

23 pipe small: pun on small as (1) in a low tone and (2) "small beer," diluted or inferior beer.

24 holy bush: the sign of a tavern. Cf. Lupton, London and the Countrey Carbonadoed, sig. L8^r: "If these houses have a Boxe-Bush, or an old Post, it is enough to show their Profeshion. But if they bee graced with a Signe compleat, it's a signe of good custome."

25 Jackanapes: monkey.

26 watermaukin: possibly a water dog.

27 guarded Coate: trimmed or laced coat of a servingman.

List of Textual Changes

Page Line	
150.28	Almanack; / Almanack.;
161.17	gentile, estimation / gentile estimation A
164.11	shoppes / shoops Errata gives 'shoppe'
168.25	quirresters / guiresters A
170.23	swifter / smifter
171.19	Envie, / Envie
179.9	liberty, / liberty;
190.15	shall, / shall
199.6	Dentifrice / Deutifrice
200.13	of / off
205.16	yet / yet,
206.15	tongue / tougue
206.21	sconce, / sconce
210.9	wenches, / wenches
213.5	you / you,
213.18	argues / argues,
218.19	freight A / fright
218.22	relations / reations
219.20	Countrey / Couztrey
222.5	than / thun
223.3	familiarly /familiarly,
224.15	lieu / lien

228.2	long-neckt / long neckt
228.15	this A / his
232.2-3	successive / sucoessive
232.18	no / uo
232.22	<u>Dea</u> / <u>Lea</u>
234.17	speechlesse / speechlesse,
234.18	long): / long:)
235.5	hugge, / hugge
236.18	feeles / feeles,
247.9	clandestine / clandestnie
247.11	least / laest
258.18	Tinker, / Tinker
258.19	liquor, / liquor

List of Works Consulted

Abstract of Some Late Characters. London, 1643.

Adams, John Cranford. *The Globe Playhouse, Its Design and Equipment.* 2nd ed. New York, 1961.

Adams, Thomas. *Diseases of the Soule: A Discourse Divine, Morall, and Physicall.* London, 1616.

_____. *Mystical Bedlam, Or the World of Mad-Men.* London, 1615.

Aldington, Richard, ed. *A Book of "Characters."* London, 1924.

Allen, C. G. "The Sources of 'Lily's Latin Grammar': A Review of the Facts and Some Further Suggestions," *The Library*, IX (1954), 85-100.

Allen, Don Cameron. *The Star-Crossed Renaissance: The Quarrel about Astrology and Its Influence in England.* Durham, North Carolina, 1941.

Anatomy of the Separatists. London, 1642.

Anderson, Paul Bunyan. "Anonymous Critic of Milton: Richard Leigh? Or Samuel Butler?" *Studies in Philology*, XLIV (1947), 504-518.

Ashmole, Elias. *Theatrum Chemicum Britannicum.* London, 1652.

Auerbach, Erich. *Mimesis: The Representation of Reality in Western Literature*, trans. Willard Trask. Garden City, New York, 1957.

Augustine, Saint. *The City of God Against the Pagans*, trans. William M. Green and others. 7 vols. London, 1957-65.

Babb, Lawrence. "The Background of 'Il Penseroso'," *Studies in Philology*, XXXVII (1940), 257-273.

Bacon, Francis. *The Works of Francis Bacon*, ed. James Spedding, R. L. Ellis, and D. D. Heath. 14 vols. London, 1857-74.

Baker, Ernest A. *The History of the English Novel.* 10 vols. London, 1924-39.

Baldwin, E. C. "Ben Jonson's Indebtedness to the Greek Character-Sketch," Modern Language Notes, XVI (1901), 385-396.

_____. "The 'Character' in Restoration Comedy," PMLA, XXX (1915), 64-78.

_____. "The Relation of the English 'Character' to Its Greek Prototype," PMLA, XVIII (1903), 412-423.

_____. "Relation of the 17th-Century Character to the Periodical Essay," PMLA, XIX (1904), 75-114.

Bauer, Josephine. "Some Verse Fragments and Prose Characters by Samuel Butler Not Included in the Complete Works," Modern Philology, XLV (1948), 160-168.

Black, Matthew W. Richard Brathwait, An Account of His Life and Works. Philadelphia, 1928.

Bohun, William. Privilegia Londini: or, the Laws, Customs, and Priviledges of the City of London. London, 1702.

Bosanquet, Eustace F. English Printed Almanacks and Prognostications: A Bibliographical History to the Year 1600. London, 1917.

_____. "English Seventeenth-Century Almanacks," The Library, X (1930), 361-397.

Boyce, Benjamin. "History and Fiction in Panthalia: Or The Royal Romance," Journal of English and Germanic Philology, LVII (1958), 477-491.

_____. The Polemic Character 1640-1661. Lincoln, Nebraska, 1955.

_____. The Theophrastan Character in England to 1642. Cambridge, Massachusetts, 1947.

Brathwait, Richard. Barnabae Itinerarium: or, Barnabee's Journal, ed. W. Carew Hazlitt. London, 1876.

_____. The English Gentleman. London, 1630.

_____. A Strappado for the Divell, ed. J. W. Ebsworth. Boston, Lincolnshire, 1878.

_____. A Survey of History: Or, A Nursery for Gentry. London, 1638.

_____. Whimzies: Or, A New Cast of Characters. London, 1631.

_____. Whimzies: Or, A New Cast of Characters, ed. James O. Halliwell. London, 1859.

Breton, Nicholas. *Characters upon Essaies Morall and Divine*. London, 1615.

_____. *Fantasticks: Serving for a Perpetuall Prognostication*. London, 1626.

_____. *The Good and the Badde, or Descriptions of the Worthies and Unworthies of this Age*. London, 1616.

Brooke, Tucker. "The Renaissance (1500-1660)," *A Literary History of England*, ed. Albert C. Baugh. New York, 1948.

Brown, Huntington. *Rabelais in English Literature*. Cambridge, Massachusetts, 1933.

Browne, Sir Thomas. *The Works of Sir Thomas Browne*, ed. Geoffrey Keynes. 2nd ed. 6 vols. London, 1964.

Buckminster, Thomas. *An Almanack and Prognostication for the Year 1598*, introd. E. F. Bosanquet. Shakespeare Association Facsimiles, No. 8. London, 1935.

Bullokar, John. *An English Expositor: Teaching the Interpretation of the hardest words used in our Language*. London, 1616.

Burtt, Edwin Arthur. *The Metaphysical Foundations of Modern Physical Science*. Garden City, New York, 1954.

Bush, Douglas. *English Literature in the Earlier Seventeenth Century 1600-1660*. 2nd ed. Oxford, 1962.

Butler, Samuel. *Characters and Passages from Note-Books*, ed. A. R. Waller. Cambridge, 1908.

_____. *Hudibras*, Part I. London, 1663.

_____. *Hudibras*, Part II. London, 1664.

_____. *Samuel Butler: Miscellaneous Poetry and Prose*, ed. René Lamar. Cambridge, 1928.

Camden, Carroll, Jr. "Elizabethan Almanacs and Prognostications," *The Library*, XII (1931), 83-108; 194-207.

Campbell, Oscar J. *Comicall Satyre and Shakespeare's Troilus and Cressida*. San Marino, California, 1938.

Chambers, E. K. *The English Folk-Play*. Oxford, 1933.

Chapman, George. *The Plays and Poems of George Chapman*, ed. Thomas Marc Parrott. 2 vols. New York, 1914.

Character of a Bigotted Prince. London, 1691.

Character of a Jacobite. London, 1690.

Character of the Parliament, commonly called the Rump. London, 1660.

Character of A Popish Successour. London, 1681.

Character of a Presbyter, or Sr. John Anatomized. London, 1660.

Character of A Rebellion. London, 1681.

Character of a Turbulent, Pragmatical Priest. London, 1678.

Character of a Williamite. London, 1690.

Chaucer, Geoffrey. *The Works of Geoffrey Chaucer*, ed. F. N. Robinson. 2nd ed. Cambridge, Massachusetts, 1957.

Clarendon, Edward, Earl of. *The Life of Edward Earl of Clarendon, Lord High Chancellor of England and Chancellor of the University of Oxford: In which is included a Continuation of His History of the Grand Rebellion*. 3 vols. Oxford, 1827.

Clausen, William G. "The Beginnings of English Character-Writing," *Philological Quarterly*, XXV (1946), 32-45.

Cleveland, John. *Cleaveland Revived*. London, 1660.

_____. *Clievelandi Vindiciae*. London, 1677.

_____. *The Poems of John Cleveland*, ed. John M. Berdan. New York, 1903.

Confused Characters of Conceited Coxcombs, ed. James O. Halliwell London, 1860.

Cotgrave, Randle. *A Dictionarie of the French and English Tongues*. London, 1611.

Cowell, John. *The Interpreter: Or Booke Containing the Signification of Words*. Cambridge, 1607.

Cowley, Abraham. *Essays, Plays and Sundry Verses*, ed. A. R. Waller. Cambridge, 1906.

Crane, William G. *Wit and Rhetoric in the Renaissance: The Formal Basis of Elizabethan Prose Style*. New York, 1937.

Croll, Morris W. "The Baroque Style in Prose," *Studies in Philology, A Miscellany in Honor of Frederick Klaeber*, ed. Kemp Malone and Martin B. Ruud. Minneapolis, 1929.

Curtius, Ernst Robert. *European Literature and the Latin Middle Ages*, trans. Willard Trask. New York, 1953.

Dahl, Folke. "Amsterdam--Cradle of English Newspapers," *The Library*, IV (1949), 166-178.

―――――. "Short-Title Catalogue of English Corantos and Newsbooks, 1620-1642," *The Library*, XIX (1938), 44-98.

DeArmond, Anna Janney. "Some Aspects of Character-Writing in the Period of the Restoration," *Delaware Notes*, Sixteenth Series (1943), 55-89.

Dekker, Thomas. *The Gull's Hornbook*, ed. Ronald B. McKerrow. London, 1904.

―――――. *The Guls Hornbook and The Belman of London*. Temple Classics Edition. London, 1904.

Deloney, Thomas. *The Works of Thomas Deloney*, ed. Francis O. Mann. Oxford, 1912.

Doney, Paul H. "The Life and Works of Richard Flecknoe," Unpublished Harvard University dissertation, 1928.

Donne, John. *The Elegies and The Songs and Sonnets of John Donne*, ed. Helen Gardner. Oxford, 1965.

―――――. *Ignatius His Conclave Or His Inthronisation in a Late Election in Hell*, introd. Charles M. Coffin. Facsimile Text Society Publication No. 53. New York, 1941.

―――――. *The Poems of John Donne*, ed. Herbert J. C. Grierson. 2 vols. Oxford, 1912.

Dunham, William H. and Stanley Pargellis, eds. *Complaint and Reform in England 1436-1714*. New York, 1938.

Earle, John. *Microcosmography, or A Piece of the World Discovered in Essays and Characters*, ed. Harold Osborne. London, n.d.

Elliott, Robert C. *The Power of Satire: Magic, Ritual, Art*. Princeton, 1960.

Ellis, Clement. *The Gentile Sinner, Or, England's Brave Gentleman*. London, 1664.

Erasmus, Desiderius. *The Apophthegmes of Erasmus*, trans. Nicolas Udall. Boston, Lincolnshire, 1877.

Erra Pater. *Prognostication for Ever*. London, 1536.

Exact Description of a Roundhead. London, 1642.

Felltham, Owen. *A Brief Character of the Low Countries Under the States*. London, 1652.

Fisch, Harold. *Jerusalem and Albion: The Hebraic Factor in Seventeenth-Century Literature*, New York, 1964.

Flecknoe, Richard. *A Collection of the Choicest Epigrams and Characters of Richard Flecknoe*. London, 1673.

_____. *Enigmaticall Characters, All Taken to the Life, from severall Persons, Humours, and Dispositions*. London, 1658.

_____. *Richard Flecknoe's Aenigmatical Characters*. London, 1665.

Fletcher, Giles, the Elder. *The English Works of Giles Fletcher, the Elder*, ed. Lloyd E. Berry. Madison, Wisconsin, 1964.

Frank, Joseph. *The Beginnings of the English Newspaper, 1620-1660*. Cambridge, Massachusetts, 1961.

Fried, Harvey. "A Critical Edition of Brome's *The Northern Lasse*." Unpublished New York University dissertation, 1958.

Frye, Northrop. *Anatomy of Criticism*. Princeton, 1957.

Fuller, Thomas. *The Holy State and the Profane State*, ed. Maximilian G. Walten. 2 vols. New York, 1938.

_____. *The Worthies of England*, ed. P. A. Nuttall. 3 vols. London, 1840.

Gally, Henry. *A Critical Essay on Characteristic-Writings from his translation of The Moral Characters of Theophrastus (1725)*. Augustan Reprint Society, Publication Number 33. Los Angeles, 1952.

Gardiner, Samuel R. *History of England from the Accession of James I to the Outbreak of the Civil War 1603-1642*. 10 vols. London, 1863-82.

Gibson, Dan, Jr. "Samuel Butler," *Seventeenth Century Studies*, ed. Robert Shafer. Princeton, 1933.

Gordon, G. S. "Theophrastus and His Imitators," *English Literature and the Classics*. Oxford, 1912.

Graves, Robert. *The Greek Myths*. 2 vols. London, 1955.

S. Gregorius Nazianzenus. *Patrologiae Graecae Tomus XXXV, Patrologiae Cursus Completus*, ed. J. P. Migne, Paris, 1857.

Gough, J. W. *Sir Hugh Myddelton: Entrepeneur and Engineer*. Oxford, 1964.

Greenough, Chester Noyes. *A Bibliography of the Theophrastan Character in English with Several Portrait Characters, Prepared for Publication by J. Milton French*. Cambridge, Massachusetts, 1947.

_____. *Collected Studies by Chester Noyes Greenough, With an Introduction by Wilbur Cortez Abbott*. Boston, 1940.

Hall, Joseph. *The Collected Poems of Joseph Hall, Bishop of Exeter and Norwich*, ed. Arnold Davenport. Liverpool, 1949.

_____. *Heaven Upon Earth and Characters of Vertues and Vices*, ed. Rudolf Kirk. New Brunswick, New Jersey, 1947.

Haller, William. *Liberty and Reformation in the Puritan Revolution*. New York, 1955.

Halliwell, James O. *A Dictionary of Archaic and Provincial Words, Obsolete Phrases, Proverbs, and Ancient Customs from the Fourteenth Century*. London, 1881.

Harbage, Alfred. *Cavalier Drama*. New York, 1936.

Harington, Sir John. *Sir John Harington's A New Discourse of a Stale Subject, Called the Metamorphosis of Ajax (London, 1596)*, ed. Elizabeth Story Donno. New York, 1962.

The Harleian Miscellany, ed. William Oldys and Thomas Park. 10 vols. London, 1808-13.

Haselmayer, Louis A. "The Apparitor and Chaucer's Summoner," *Speculum*, XII (1937), 43-57.

Haydn, Hiram. *The Counter-Renaissance*. New York, 1950.

Head, Richard. *Proteus Redivivus*. London, 1675.

_____ and Francis Kirkman. *The English Rogue Described in the Life of Meriton Latroon, A Witty Extravagant*. New York, 1928.

Herbert, George. *The Works of George Herbert*, ed. F. E. Hutchinson. Oxford, 1945.

Herrick, Robert. *The Poetical Works of Robert Herrick*, ed. L. C. Martin. Oxford, 1956.

Hesiod. *The Georgics of Hesiod*, trans. George Chapman, ed. Richard Hooper. London, 1888.

Heywood, Thomas. The Dramatic Works of Thomas Heywood. 6 vols. London, 1874.

Hill, Christopher. The Century of Revolution 1603-1714. London, 1961.

———. Intellectual Origins of the English Revolution. Oxford, 1965.

———. Society and Puritanism in Pre-Revolutionary England. London, 1964.

Hogs Character of a Projector. London, 1642.

Holden, William P. Anti-Puritan Satire: 1572-1642. New Haven, 1954.

Houghton, Walter E. The Formation of Thomas Fuller's Holy and Profane State. Cambridge, Massachusetts, 1938.

Howell, Wilbur S. Logic and Rhetoric in England, 1500-1700. Princeton, 1956.

Independency Stript and Whipt. London, 1648.

Johnson, Francis R. Astronomical Thought in Renaissance England. Baltimore, 1937.

Johnson, Ralph. The Scholars Guide from the Accidence to the University. London, 1665.

Jonson, Ben. The Alchemist, ed. Charles Montgomery Hathaway, Jr. Yale Studies in English, XVII. New York, 1903.

———. Ben Jonson, ed. C. H. Herford and Percy and Evelyn Simpson. 11 vols. Oxford, 1925-52.

———. The Complete Poetry of Ben Jonson, ed. William B. Hunter, Jr. New York, 1963.

Jordan, Wilbur K. Philanthropy in England, 1480-1660. London, 1959.

Judges, A. V., ed. The Elizabethan Underworld. London, 1930.

Kernan, Alvin C. The Cankered Muse: Satire of the English Renaissance. New Haven, 1959.

Kimmey, John L. "John Cleveland and the Satiric Couplet in the Restoration," Philological Quarterly, XXXVII (1958), 410-423.

Knights, L. C. Drama and Society in the Age of Jonson. London, 1937.

Kocher, Paul. *Science and Religion in Elizabethan England*. San Marino, California, 1953.

Kyd, Thomas. *The Works of Thomas Kyd*, ed. F. S. Boas. London, 1901.

Lactantius. *The Divine Institutes, Ante-Nicene Fathers*, ed. Alexander Roberts and James Donaldson. Volume VII. New York, 1925.

Laertius, Diogenes. *Lives of the Eminent Philosophers*, trans. R. D. Hicks. 2 vols. New York, 1925.

Langer, Susanne K. *Philosophy in a New Key, A Study in the Symbolism of Reason, Rite, and Art*. New York, 1948.

Leishman, J. B., ed. *The Three Parnassus Plays (1598-1601)*. London, 1949.

Lenton, Francis. *Characterismi: Or, Lentons Leasures*. London, 1631.

Levin, Harry. "John Cleveland and the Conceit," *Criterion*, XIV (1934), 40-53.

Lewis, C. S. *English Literature in the Sixteenth Century, excluding Drama*. Oxford, 1954.

Lievsay, John L. "Braggadochio: Spenser's Legacy to the Character-Writers," *Modern Language Quarterly*, II (1941), 475-485.

Lily, William. *A Shorte Introduction of Grammar*, introd. Vincent J. Flynn. Scholars' Facsimiles and Reprints. New York, 1945.

The Lively Character of the Malignant Partie. London, 1642.

Lloyd, David. *Memoires of the Lives, Actions, Sufferings and Deaths of Those Noble, Reverend, and Excellent Personages, That Suffered By Death, Sequestration, Decimation, or otherwise, for the Protestant Religion, And the great Principle thereof, Allegiance To the Soveraigne, In our late Intestine Wars, From the Year 1637, to the Year 1660. and from thence continued to 1666. With the Life and Martyrdom of King Charles I*. London, 1668.

Lodge, Thomas. *Wits Miseries*. London, 1596.

Lucifers Lacky, or the Devils New Creature. Being the true Character of a dissembling Brownist. London, 1641.

Lupton, Donald. *London and the Countrey Carbonadoed and Quartred into severall Characters*. London, 1632.

Lyly, John. *The Complete Works of John Lyly*, ed. R. Warwick Bond. 3 vols. Oxford, 1902.

M., W. *The Man in the Moone, Telling Strange Fortunes, Or The English Fortune Teller*, ed. James O. Halliwell. London, 1849.

MacDonald, W. L. *The Beginnings of the English Essay.* Toronto, 1914.

Mack, Maynard. "The Muse of Satire," *Yale Review*, XLI (1951-52), 80-92.

Manwood, John. *A Treatise of the Lawes of the Forest.* London, 1615.

Marchant, Ronald A. *The Puritans and the Church Courts in the Diocese of York 1560-1642.* Aberdeen, 1960.

Markham, Gervase. *Markhams Maister-Peece.* London, 1615.

Marston, John. *The Plays of Marston*, ed. H. Harvey Wood. 3 vols. London, 1934.

_____. *The Poems of John Marston*, ed. Arnold Davenport. Liverpool, 1961.

Martz, Louis L. *The Poetry of Meditation: A Study in English Religious Literature.* Rev. ed. New Haven, 1962.

Marvell, Andrew. *Poems and Letters*, ed. H. M. Margoliouth. 2 vols. Oxford, 1952.

Maycock, A. L. "Little Gidding Discovery," *Times Literary Supplement*, January 27, 1966.

McLuhan, Marshall. *The Gutenberg Galaxy.* Toronto, 1962.

Middleton, Thomas. *The Works of Thomas Middleton*, ed. A. H. Bullen. 8 vols. London, 1885.

_____. and William Rowley. *The Changeling*, ed. N. W. Bawcutt. London, 1958.

Milton, John. *The Works of John Milton*, ed. Frank A. Patterson and others. 18 vols. New York, 1931-38.

_____. *The Complete English Poetry of John Milton*, ed. John T. Shawcross. New York, 1963.

Mintz, Samuel I. *The Hunting of Leviathan.* Cambridge, 1962.

Mohl, Ruth. *The Three Estates in Medieval and Renaissance Literature.* New York, 1933.

Montaigne, Michel de. *The Essayes of Michael Lord of Montaigne*, trans. John Florio. 3 vols. Everyman's Library. New York, n.d.

Morley, Henry, ed. *Character Writings of the Seventeenth Century*. London, 1891.

Murphy, Gwendolen. *A Bibliography of English Character-Books, 1608-1700*. Oxford, 1925.

_____, ed. *A Cabinet of Characters*. Oxford, 1925.

Mynshul, Geffray. *Essayes and Characters of a Prison and Prisoners*. London, 1618.

Nares, Robert. *A Glossary; Or, Collection of Words, Phrases, Names, and Allusions to Customs, Proverbs, etc. . . . in Works of English Authors, Particularly Shakespeare and His Contemporaries*, ed. J. O. Halliwell and T. Wright. 2 vols. London, 1872.

Nashe, Thomas. *The Works of Thomas Nashe*, ed. Ronald B. McKerrow. 5 vols. Rev. F. P. Wilson. London, 1958.

Nedham, Marchamont. *True Character of a Rigid Presbyter*. London, 1661.

Nevo, Ruth. *The Dial of Virtue: A Study of Poems on Affairs of State in the 17th Century*. Princeton, 1963.

Ogg, David. *England in the Reign of Charles II*. 2 vols. 2nd ed. Oxford, 1956.

Old Book Collectors Miscellany, ed. Charles Hindley. 3 vols. London, 1872-73.

Ong, Walter J., S. J. "Oral Residue in Tudor Prose Style," *PMLA*, LXXX (1965), 145-154.

Osborn, Francis. *Historical Memoires on the Reigns of Queen Elizabeth and King James*. London, 1658.

Overbury, Sir Thomas. *The Overburian Characters*, ed. W. J. Paylor. Oxford, 1936.

Ovid. *Heroides and Amores*, trans. Grant Showerman. New York, 1921.

The Owles Almanacke, ed. Don Cameron Allen. Baltimore, 1943.

Owst, G. R. *Literature and Pulpit in Medieval England*. Cambridge, 1933.

P., J. *Tyrants and Protectors Set forth In their Colours*. London, 1654.

Parkes, Joan. *Travel in England in the Seventeenth Century*. Oxford, 1925.

Partridge, Eric. *A Dictionary of Slang and Unconventional English*. 4th ed. London, 1951.

Patch, Howard R. "Characters in Medieval Literature," *Modern Language Notes*, XL (1925), 1-14.

Paylor, William J. "The Editions of the 'Overburian' Characters," *The Library*, XVII (1937), 340-348.

_____. "Thomas Dekker and the 'Overburian' Characters," *Modern Language Review*, XXXI (1936), 155-160.

Pearl, Valerie. *London and the Outbreak of the Puritan Revolution: City Government and National Politics, 1625-43*. Oxford, 1961.

Phillips, Edward. *The New World of Words: Or, Universal English Dictionary*. 6th ed. London, 1706.

Phoenix Britannicus, ed. J. Morgan. Volume I. London, 1732.

Pliny, the Elder. *The Historie of the World. Commonly Called, The Naturall Historie of C. Plinius Secundus*, trans. Philemon Holland. London, 1601

Plutarch. *Plutarch's Lives*, trans. Bernadotte Perrin. 11 vols. New York, 1914.

Praz, Mario. *The Flaming Heart: Essays on Crashaw, Machiavelli, and Other Studies in the Relations between Italian and English Literature from Chaucer to T. S. Eliot*. Garden City, New York, 1958.

Price, F. Douglas. "Elizabethan Apparitors in the Diocese of Gloucester," *The Church Quarterly Review*, CXXXIV (1941), 37-55.

_____. "An Elizabethan Church Official--Thomas Powell, Chancellor of Gloucester Diocese," *The Church Quarterly Review*, CXXVIII (1939), 94-112.

Puritane Set forth in his Lively Colours. London, 1642.

Quintana, Ricardo. "Samuel Butler: A Restoration Figure in a Modern Light," *ELH*, XVIII (1951), 7-31.

Rabelais, Francois. *Oeuvres de Rabelais, Edition Variorum*, ed. Esmangart and Eloi Johanneau. 9 vols. Paris, 1823.

Randolph, Mary Claire. "The Medical Concept in English Satiric Theory," *Studies in Philology*, XXXVIII (1941), 125-157.

_____. "The Structural Design of Formal Verse Satire," *Philological Quarterly*, XXI (1942), 368-384.

The Reformado, Precisely Charactered by a Transformed Churchwarden, at a Vestry. London, 1643.

Richards, Edward Ames. *Hudibras in the Burlesque Tradition*. New York, 1937.

Robinson, Howard. *The British Post Office, a History*. Princeton, 1948.

Rollins, Hyder, ed. *A Pepysian Garland: Black-Letter Broadside Ballads of the Years 1595-1639, Chiefly from the Collection of Samuel Pepys*. Cambridge, 1922.

Rostenberg, Leona. "Nathaniel Butter and Nicholas Bourne, First 'Masters of the Staple'," *The Library*, XII (1957), 23-33.

Saint Hillaries teares. London, 1642.

Saltonstall, Wye. *Picturae Loquentes, Reprinted from the Editions of 1631 and 1635*, ed. C. H. Wilkinson. Oxford, 1946.

Samuels, Irene. "A Theophrastan Character in Milton," *Notes and Queries*, V, no. 12 (December, 1958), 528-530.

Savile, George, First Marquess of Halifax. *The Complete Works of George Savile, First Marquess of Halifax*, ed. Walter Raleigh. Oxford, 1912.

Shakespeare Jest-Books, ed. W. Carew Hazlitt. 3 vols. London, 1864.

Shakespeare, William. *The Complete Works of Shakespeare*, ed. W. J. Craig. Oxford, 1936.

Shakespeare's England, ed. Sir Sidney Lee and C. T. Onions. 2 vols. Oxford, 1916.

Sharpham, Edward. *The Fleire*, ed. Hunold Nibbe. *Materialien zur Kunde des älteren Englischen Dramas*. Louvain, 1912.

Short, Compendious, and True Description of a Roundhead. London, 1642.

Short Fiction of the Seventeenth Century, ed. Charles C. Mish. New York, 1963.

Singer, Charles. *A Short History of Science to the Nineteenth Century*. London, 1941.

Six Old Plays, ed. John Nichols. London, 1779.

Smith, David Nichol, ed. *Characters from the Histories and Memoirs of the Seventeenth Century*. Oxford, 1918.

Somers Tracts, ed. Sir Walter Scott. 13 vols. London, 1809-15.

Spenser, Edmund. The Poetical Works of Edmund Spenser, ed. J. C. Smith and E. De Selincourt. Oxford, 1912.

Stauffer, Donald A. English Biography Before 1700. Cambridge, Massachusetts, 1930.

Stephens, John. Essayes and Characters Ironicall and Instructive. London, 1615.

——. Satyrical Essayes Characters and Others. London, 1615.

Stow, John. Annales, Or, A Generall Chronicle of England. Begun by John Stow: Continued and Augmented with matters Forraigne and Domestique, Ancient and Moderne unto the end of this present yeare, 1631, by Edmund Howes. London, 1631.

——. The Survey of London: Containing, The Originall, Antiquitie, Encrease, and more Moderne Estate of the sayd Famous Citie, cont. by Anthony Munday. London, 1618.

A Strange Metamorphosis of Man, Transformed into a Wildernesse, ed. Don Cameron Allen. Baltimore, 1949.

Stuart Tracts 1603-1693, ed. C. H. Firth. London, 1903.

Sugden, Edward H. A Topographical Dictionary to the Works of Shakespeare and His Fellow Dramatists. Manchester, 1925.

Sypher, Wylie. Four Stages of Renaissance Style: Transformation in Art and Literature 1400-1700. Garden City, New York, 1955.

Thompson, E. N. S. Literary Bypaths of the Renaissance. New Haven, 1924.

——. The Seventeenth-Century English Essay. Iowa City, 1926.

Tilley, Morris P. A Dictionary of the Proverbs in English in the Sixteenth and Seventeenth Centuries. Ann Arbor, 1950.

Tomkis, Thomas, Albumazar: A Comedy, ed. Hugh G. Dick. University of California Publications in English, XIII. University of California, 1944.

Traill, H. D. and J. S. Mann, eds. Social England. 6 vols. London, 1902-04.

The True Character of an Untrue Bishop. London, 1641.

True Presbyterian Without Disguise. London, 1661.

Virgil. *The Aeneid*, trans. C. Day Lewis. Garden City, New York, 1953.

Webster, John. *The Complete Works of John Webster*, ed. F. L. Lucas. 4 vols. New York, 1937.

Whitlock, Richard. *Zootomia, or, Observations on the Present Manners of the English*. London, 1654.

Williamson, George. *The Senecan Amble: A Study in Prose Form from Bacon to Collier*. Chicago, 1951.

Willis, Leota Snyder. *Francis Lenton, Queen's Poet*. Philadelphia, 1931.

Wilson, F. P. *Elizabethan and Jacobean*. Oxford, 1945.

_____. *Seventeenth-Century Prose*. University of California, 1960.

_____. "Some English Mock-Prognostications," *The Library*, XIX (1938), 6-43.

Wilson, Thomas, *The Arte of Rhetorique*, ed. George Herbert Mair. Oxford. 1909.

Withington, Eleanor. "The Canon of John Cleveland's Poetry," *Bulletin of the New York Public Library*, LXVII (1963), 307-327; 377-394.

Wright, Louis B. *Middle-Class Culture in Elizabethan England*. Chapel Hill, 1935.

For Product Safety Concerns and Information please contact our EU
representative GPSR@taylorandfrancis.com
Taylor & Francis Verlag GmbH, Kaufingerstraße 24, 80331 München, Germany